# The
# MOTO GUZZI
## Story

**Third Edition**

## Other great books from Veloce:

### Enthusiast's Restoration Manual Series
Beginner's Guide to Classic Motorcycle Restoration, The (Burns)
Classic Large Frame Vespa Scooters, How to Restore (Paxton)
Ducati Bevel Twins 1971 to 1986 (Falloon)
How to Restore Classic Off-road Motorcycles (Burns)
How to restore Honda CX500 & CX650 – YOUR step-by-step colour illustrated guide to complete restoration (Burns)
How to restore Honda Fours – YOUR step-by-step colour illustrated guide to complete restoration (Burns)
Triumph Trident T150/T160 & BSA Rocket III, How to Restore (Rooke)
Yamaha FS1-E, How to Restore (Watts)

### Essential Buyer's Guide Series
BMW Boxer Twins (Henshaw)
BMW E30 3 Series 1981 to 1994 (Hosier)
BMW GS (Henshaw)
BSA 350, 441 & 500 Singles (Henshaw)
BSA 500 & 650 Twins (Henshaw)
BSA Bantam (Henshaw)
Choosing, Using & Maintaining Your Electric Bicycle (Henshaw)
Ducati Bevel Twins (Falloon)
Ducati Desmodue Twins (Falloon)
Ducati Desmoquattro Twins – 851, 888, 916, 996, 998, ST4 1988 to 2004 (Falloon)
Hinckley Triumph triples & fours 750, 900, 955, 1000, 1050, 1200 – 1991-2009 (Henshaw)
Honda CBR FireBlade (Henshaw)
Honda CBR600 Hurricane (Henshaw)
Honda SOHC Fours 1969-1984 (Henshaw)
Kawasaki Z1 & Z900 (Orritt)
Moto Guzzi 2-valve big twins (Falloon)
Norton Commando (Henshaw)
Royal Enfield Bullet (Henshaw)
Triumph 350 & 500 Twins (Henshaw)
Triumph Bonneville (Henshaw)
Triumph Thunderbird, Trophy & Tiger (Henshaw)
Velocette 350 & 500 Singles 1946 to 1970 (Henshaw)
Vespa Scooters – Classic 2-stroke models 1960-2008 (Paxton)

### Biographies
Chris Carter at Large – Stories from a lifetime in motorcycle racing (Carter & Skelton)
Edward Turner – The Man Behind the Motorcycles (Clew)
Jim Redman – 6 Times World Motorcycle Champion: The Autobiography (Redman)
Mike The Bike – Again (Macauley)
'Sox' – Gary Hocking – the forgotten World Motorcycle Champion (Hughes)

### General
BMW Boxer Twins 1970-1995 Bible, The (Falloon)
BMW Cafe Racers (Cloesen)
BMW Custom Motorcycles – Choppers, Cruisers, Bobbers, Trikes & Quads (Cloesen)
British 250cc Racing Motorcycles (Pereira)
British Café Racers (Cloesen)
British Custom Motorcycles – The Brit Chop – choppers, cruisers, bobbers & trikes (Cloesen)
BSA Bantam Bible, The (Henshaw)
BSA Motorcycles – the final evolution (Jones)
Ducati 750 Bible, The (Falloon)
Ducati 750 SS 'round-case' 1974, The Book of the (Falloon)
Ducati 860, 900 and Mille Bible, The (Falloon)
Ducati Monster Bible (New Updated & Revised Edition), The (Falloon)
Ducati Story, The - 6th Edition (Falloon)
Ducati 916 (updated edition) (Falloon)
Funky Mopeds (Skelton)
How your motorcycle works (Henshaw)
Italian Cafe Racers (Cloesen)
Italian Custom Motorcycles (Cloesen)
Japanese Custom Motorcycles – The Nippon Chop – Chopper, Cruiser, Bobber, Trikes and Quads (Cloesen)
Kawasaki Triples Bible, The (Walker)
Kawasaki Z1 Story, The (Sheehan)
Moto Guzzi Sport & Le Mans Bible, The (Falloon)
The Moto Guzzi Story - 3rd Edition (Falloon)
Motorcycle Apprentice (Cakebread)
Motorcycle GP Racing in the 1960s (Pereira)
Motorcycle Road & Racing Chassis Designs (Noakes)
Motorcycling in the '50s (Clew)
MV Agusta Fours, The book of the classic (Falloon)
Norton Commando Bible – All models 1968 to 1978 (Henshaw)
Scooters & Microcars, The A-Z of Popular (Dan)
Scooter Lifestyle (Grainger)
Scooter Mania! – Recollections of the Isle of Man International Scooter Rally (Jackson)
Trikes, the little book of (Quellin)
Triumph Bonneville Bible (59-83) (Henshaw)
Triumph Bonneville!, Save the – The inside story of the Meriden Workers' Co-op (Rosamond)
Triumph Motorcycles & the Meriden Factory (Hancox)
Triumph Speed Twin & Thunderbird Bible (Woolridge)
Triumph Tiger Cub Bible (Estall)
Triumph Trophy Bible (Woolridge)
TT Talking – The TT's most exciting era – As seen by Manx Radio TT's lead commentator 2004-2012 (Lambert)
Velocette Motorcycles – MSS to Thruxton – Third Edition (Burris)
Vespa – The Story of a Cult Classic in Pictures (Uhlig)
Vincent Motorcycles: The Untold Story since 1946 (Guyony & Parker)

# www.veloce.co.uk

First published in 2005 by Haynes Publishing Group, reprinted July 2008. This reprint by Veloce Publishing Limited published in May 2018.
Veloce Publishing Limited, Veloce House, Parkway Farm Business Park, Middle Farm Way, Poundbury, Dorchester DT1 3AR, England. Tel +44 (0)1305 260068 / Fax 01305 250479
e-mail info@veloce.co.uk / web www.veloce.co.uk or www.velocebooks.com.
ISBN: 978-1-787111-32-5 UPC: 6-36847-01132-1.
All photographs are from the author's collection except where stated.

# The MOTO GUZZI Story

**Third Edition**

IAN FALLOON

## VELOCE PUBLISHING

THE PUBLISHER OF FINE AUTOMOTIVE BOOKS

# CONTENTS

New for 2008 was the Stelvio,
a dual-purpose motorcycle
powered by an 1151cc four
valve V-twin engine.
Moto Guzzi

# INTRODUCTION AND ACKNOWLEDGEMENTS

The story of Moto Guzzi is one of a fiercely proud and individual company. In the world of motorcycling, there is no other marque that has been brave enough to be original, and to follow that with incredible racing success. From the outset, Carlo Guzzi, and his underrated brother Giuseppe, eschewed conventionality. Their designs were so advanced that they had extraordinarily long production runs. Along with the large number of small capacity motorcycles produced after World War II, and specialised racing machines, it was the horizontal four-stroke single-cylinder engine, with the large external flywheel, that epitomised Moto Guzzi until the mid 1960s. From the late 1960s, the transversely mounted 90° V-twin engine became the company's symbol.

That these two engine designs have featured so strongly in the company's history, says much about Moto Guzzi. It is a company steeped in tradition and innately conservative, and its location at Mandello del Lario has isolated it from any temptation to be a dedicated follower of fashion. During the 1980s and 1990s, production levels were modest and the range consisted of only a few models. That changed in 2000 when Aprilia acquired Moto Guzzi, and a program of technological development and investment in production was implemented. This continued when Piaggio bought Aprilia at the end of 2004. Moto Guzzi has since built on its heritage as one of Italy's leading motorcycle manufacturers. One of the things that Moto Guzzi is determined to retain is its individuality, and all enthusiasts will be thankful that Guzzi won't become just another motorcycle manufacturer, producing bland products.

My own interest in Moto Guzzi spans a 45-year period, which began after riding and owning a V7 Sport. So memorable was that motorcycle that it led me to other 750 Sports and various Le Mans models. In recent times, while Moto Guzzi still produces sporting models, they have moved towards the touring and cruiser market. This third edition focuses on the shift of emphasis.

This book is arranged by categorising each type of motorcycle as chronologically as possible. With such a plethora of individual models, and some having extraordinary production runs, a pure chronological assessment is not really practical. I have tried to organise the book in such a way that it is easy for the reader to find information. Technical data is often inconsistent between factory bulletins and publicity brochures, so where there has been conflict, I have opted for the official data rather than publicity material. Emphasis has also been placed on racing and civilian production models, with particular attention towards technical details, so as to provide a useful source of reference. Other books cover prototypes, record breaking specials, and military vehicles in greater depth. While these are all mentioned, their coverage has been limited in order to concentrate on areas that have not previously been thoroughly documented.

Writing such a detailed history would not have been possible without the contribution of many enthusiasts around the world, particularly Teo Lamers, who shared his amazing collection of motorcycles and documentation. I was fortunate to interview both Umberto Todero and Giulio Carcano before they died, which provided a valuable insight into racing and development. Former Moto Guzzi factory rider, Ken Kavanagh, proved an invaluable source of information on the important racing era of the mid 1950s. Those at Moto Guzzi and Aprilia who have helped over the years include: Eleonora Scali, Serafino Valsecchi, Gabriella Stropeni, Daniele Torresan, and most recently Anuja Weeranarayana (Piaggio Marketing Communications Manager, Asia Pacific 2 Wheeler). Finally, none of this would have been possible without the continued support of my wife, Miriam, and wonderful boys, Ben and Tim.

**Ian Falloon**

Undoubtedly one of the most spectacular settings
for a motorcycle factory anywhere. With Mt Grigna
looming above, Mandello del Lario on the shores
of Lake Como, near Lecco, has been the home of
Moto Guzzi since 1921.

# 1 EARLY DAYS

Although Carlo Guzzi had long dreamed of building his own motorcycle, it was not until the First World War, as a 29-year-old mechanic in the Italian Air Force, that his dream could become a reality. In the air force he found two equally passionate motorcycling enthusiasts, and many long nights were spent discussing his ideas. So enthusiastic were these three for this motorcycle that they decided, after the end of the war, to get together and produce it. Guzzi's two companions were the young pilots Giorgio Parodi and Giovanni Ravelli, and they formed an alliance that would eventually see the formation of one of Italy's greatest motorcycle manufacturers.

While many young men dream and talk of doing such things, the Guzzi, Parodi and Ravelli combination differed in that all three could bring with them the necessary and complementary skills. It was not only this that set the new venture apart from the many fledgling enterprises that emerged at the end of the war, as both Guzzi and Parodi were geniuses in their respective fields. Unfortunately, Ravelli was never given the chance to establish his credentials as the rider spearheading the new motorcycle on the racetrack: tragically he was killed in a flying accident shortly after the end of the war. The indications were that he would have been successful. A native of Brescia, Giovanni Ravelli had several notable racing results on a Triumph in the years leading up to the outbreak of war. In Ravelli's honour the Italian Air Force eagle was used on the Moto Guzzi nameplate, and this continues to the present day.

Carlo Guzzi was born in Milan on 4 June 1889, where he studied and gained a Diploma di Copo Tecnico. He came from a strong engineering family, his father at one time owning an engineering consultancy. Prior to the war he worked for the motor company Isotta Franchini, but it was the influence of a Mandello blacksmith that led him to motorcycles. The Guzzi family spent much time in a small fishing village on the shores of Lake Como just north of Lecco, Mandello-Tonzanico. Later, the name was to change to Mandello del Lario, and here, Carlo Guzzi and the local blacksmith, Giorgio Ripamonti, would dismantle motorcycles and analyse their faults. Carlo was a fanatical motorcyclist, and his first plans for a motorcycle date well before the war. When Carlo's

would also be Carlo Guzzi's clear engineering ideals that would shape the course of the company. These ideals were often outside that of mainstream, although they were brilliant in their conception and execution, and were also generally very advanced for their day.

# THE 'G.P.'

Carlo Guzzi's first horizontal four-stroke 500cc single-cylinder engine was cast in aluminium, the engine in unit with the three-speed gearbox. Along with a helical gear primary drive and considerably oversquare engine dimensions of 88 x 82mm bore and stroke, the engine deviated markedly from that considered normal for the period. Laying the engine horizontal in the frame not only aided engine cooling, but also enabled a low-slung chassis to be built around it. The geared primary drive meant that the engine rotated in the reverse direction, another unusual feature at that time. To smooth out vibration and to allow for a more compact crankcase unit there was a 280mm external flywheel, which also became a Guzzi trademark. The lubrication system was exceptionally advanced, with an oil pump driven from the camshaft supplying oil to an external tank mounted in the air stream. Another Guzzi characteristic that would appear for many decades was the multi-plate metal-to-metal clutch lubricated by oil mist. The clutch was located in the large primary gear that drove the gearbox, only a small amount of oil getting to the clutch from the primary gear chamber. Clever design also saw the drive chain receive lubrication.

Aeronautical engineering practice was evident in the cylinder head design that used four parallel overhead valves operated by an overhead camshaft driven by a shaft and bevel-gears. These valves were closed by exposed hairpin valve springs. Twin spark plugs and a dual ignition were used to ignite the mixture through a Bosch magneto. Compression was a modest 3.5:1, and with 12 horsepower the first Moto Guzzi was capable of 100km/h (62mph). It may not sound fast today, but this was a good speed for 1920.

The chassis was designed in co-operation with Carlo's older brother, Giuseppe. Like Carlo, Giuseppe was also a highly innovative engineer but, as he was so reserved, has never received much of the credit due for his input. The tubular frame was quite unusual for the period, in that it had twin front downtubes. The rear

mother moved to Mandello during the war, Mandello del Lario became the family home.

Giorgio Parodi was born in Venice in 1897 to a wealthy Genoan family of ship owners, and it was he that had guaranteed the financial backing for the venture. He approached his father, Emanuele Parodi, and in a letter of 3 January 1919 Emanuele granted approval for 1,500 to 2,000 lire to be used to fund the prototype. This letter is still on display at the Moto Guzzi museum at Mandello del Lario, and was pivotal in enabling Carlo Guzzi to proceed with his plans. Furthermore, Emanuele took more than a passing interest in the project and promised more funds if he approved of the project.

It was not until 1920 that the prototype began to take shape and it closely followed the concept that Carlo Guzzi had envisaged before the war. He wanted to eliminate hand-pumped lubrication systems and exposed primary drive chains. Unlike many motorcycles of the time, the engine was pivotal to the design and featured many characteristics that would distinguish Moto Guzzis for the next 50 years. It

BELOW The 'G.P.' still survives, on display in the Moto Guzzi museum at Mandello.

BOTTOM The engine of the Normale featured an unusual arrangement of side inlet and overhead exhaust valves.

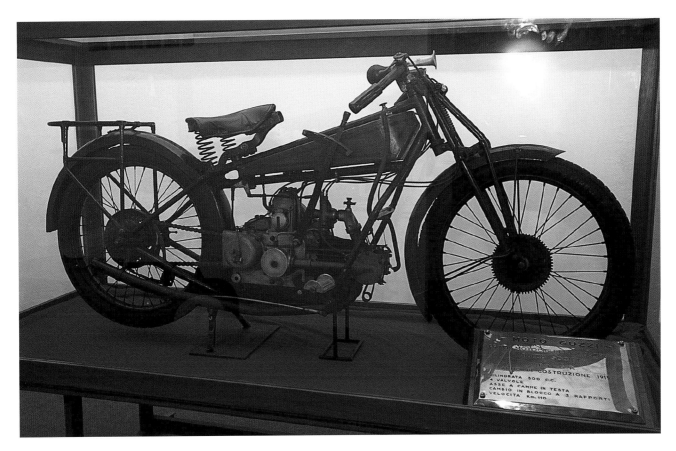

bolted triangle was unsprung with girder forks and dual springs at the front. Only the rear wheel had a brake, the front wheel carrying a gear to drive the speedometer. This prototype was called the 'G.P.', or Guzzi-Parodi, but was soon changed to Moto Guzzi as Giorgio Parodi had not wanted the initials confused with his own.

## THE NORMALE

The prototype G.P. was soon followed by a production version, the Normale. While the G.P. had been an expression of Carlo Guzzi's engineering purism, the Normale of early 1921, incorporated several modifications for economic necessity. Announced in *Motociclismo* on 15 December 1920, the first change was to the four-valve cylinder head and bevel-gear driven overhead camshaft. These were replaced by an unusual arrangement of two opposed valves. A side 45mm inlet closed by a coil spring, and an overhead 42mm exhaust valve was operated by a pushrod and rocker and closed by a hairpin spring.

The use of hairpin valve springs was very rare at that time but would become virtually universal on racing engines many years later. The location of the exhaust overhead with the inlet on the side was also the reverse of what was usual at that time. It was Guzzi's idea to place the valve most prone to overheating directly in

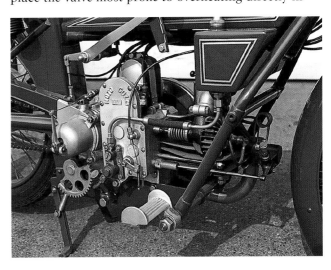

the airflow. As expected, valve timing was very moderate with the inlet opening 3° before top dead centre, closing 45° after bottom dead centre, the exhaust opening 50° before bottom dead centre, and closing 10° after top dead centre. Side inlet valves were not known for their good breathing characteristics, and thus with a 4:1 compression ratio and an Amac 15 PSY 1-inch carburettor, the power produced by the Normale was less than the G.P. at 8 horsepower at 3,200rpm.

The rest of the engine followed the format established by the prototype. Bore and stroke were identical, but the vertically split unit-construction aluminium crankcase (with cast-iron cylinder and head) featured many differences to the G.P. The Normale also had a more basic total loss oil system using a hand-operated pump to supply oil to the crankcase.

The frame too followed the example set by the prototype, but it was one-piece, the rear triangle braced by a piece of sheet metal. A similar girder fork was used with dual springs and no damping. Wheels were the usual 26 x 2¼in used at that time, shod with

Dunlop 26 x 3in beaded edge tyres. There was still only a rear brake and a single Brooks seat. Weighing in at only 130kg (278lb), the Normale had a top speed of 85km/h (53mph). For 1920, the Normale was an unusual motorcycle. Not only were many of its features unique, but it also looked strangely utilitarian with its olive green paint highlighted by gold pin-striping.

With the appearance of the Normale, Emanuele Parodi had sufficient confidence in the design to establish the Società Anomina Moto Guzzi in Genoa, with himself as president, on 15 March 1921. In addition to Carlo Guzzi and Giorgio Parodi, two other engineers were also involved, Carlo's brother Giuseppe, and Giorgio's cousin Angelo. Even though the company was named after Carlo Guzzi, the elder Parodi was astute enough to retain all the shares in the company. Carlo was paid a royalty for each machine produced, but never had any financial interest in the company. Although the total production of 1921 was a modest 17 motorcycles, it was the beginning for one of the greatest Italian motorcycle marques, and also one of the longest lived.

The company was established in a 30 square-metre building at Mandello del Lario (still part of the Moto Guzzi complex), with 17 workers. The location, away from any immediate large cities, has always meant that Moto Guzzi draws its workforce from the local area. Thus several generations of the same families have worked at Moto Guzzi and even today, the average worker's life with the company is 35 years. This continuity and sense of community involvement has meant that Moto Guzzi is a unique company within the world of motorcycling. It has probably also contributed to Moto Guzzi's individuality.

Soon after the formation of the company, local parliamentarian Aldo Finzi tested one of the new motorcycles. Finzi was a prominent sportsman and motorcycle enthusiast and was so impressed with the bike that he endeavoured to convince Carlo Guzzi to go racing. Carlo was not particularly enthusiastic about racing, but Finzi finally exerted enough political pressure that Parodi and Guzzi had no option but to agree. They would provide Finzi with a bike for the Raid-Nord Sud, a road race from Milan to Naples and the premier event on the Italian racing calendar. Prior to that a racing Moto Guzzi was entered in the first Circuito del Lario on 28 May 1921. Valentini Gatti was to ride an official G.P. but he did not race.

Thus the first participation by Moto Guzzi in racing was the Raid Nord-Sud, Aldo Finzi and Mario Cavedini riding production Normales with modified lighting, leaving Milan in the late evening of 17 September 1921. After 22 hours, Cavedini arrived in Naples, in 20th place, and four hours behind the winning Indian 1000 of Nazzaro Biagio. Finzi finished 22nd after crashing near Modena and continuing without lights. It had been an encouraging result for a new design and Aldo Finzi's brother Gino, immediately took one of the Normales down to Sicily for the Targa Florio Motociclista a week later. On 25 September 1921 he gave Guzzi their first victory with a win in the 500cc class on the classic Madonie circuit.

The following year, 1922, saw a consolidation, both in production and racing. The Normale continued in modest production, and the racing bikes, rather than being specific competition designs were still modified Normales. Guzzi entered nine events and won two, both with Cavedini. The Circuito del Piave in May, and the third Ravelli Cup in July. However, the more important events, the Nations Grand Prix held at the new Monza Autodrome, the Raid Nord-Sud, and the

Circuito del Lario, continued to elude them. Guzzi improved on their 1921 result in the Raid Nord-Sud with Carlo Marazzani finishing eighth overall, but their most significant result of the year was Valentino Gatti's second place in the prestigious Circuito del Lario on a lightly modified Normale.

The Circuito del Lario was held around Lake Como and was considered the Italian TT. With Guzzis filling fifth, 11th, 12th, and 14th places it was enough to give them the team trophy. The company was ecstatic and advertised this racing success in *Motociclismo* only four days after the race. This encouraging result on their home ground, convinced Guzzi to design a real racer, and eventually a more sporting production motorcycle. These would appear in 1923. In the meantime, a few improvements flowed through to the Normale, notably an automatic lubrication system. A scavenge pump was fitted in the crankcase, and the dual ignition became an option. There were also larger cooling fins on the cylinder head and cylinder. An increase in the compression ratio to 4.7:1 saw the power increase to 8.5 horsepower at 3,400rpm.

# THE C2V

While the basic format of the Moto Guzzi 500cc single-cylinder motorcycle was retained, it was primarily by fitting a new cylinder head that Carlo Guzzi expected to make the bike a competitive racer. Two 45mm overhead valves were inclined at a very

narrow 7°20', operated by exposed pushrods, and
closed by exposed hairpin valve springs. With an
increase in compression to 5.25:1, and a 1-inch Amac
racing carburettor, power was increased to 17
horsepower at 4,200rpm, enough to propel the Corsa 2
valvole (C2V) to around 120km/h (74mph).

Dual ignition was an option and later, the
carburettor became a 25mm Dell'Orto. Along with this
revised engine the C2V received a new frame, with a
tubular rear section and a longer, 1,410mm (55½in)
wheelbase to add to the straight line stability. Colours
also changed to bright red for the first series of C2V,
the first time that colour was used on Guzzis. In 1924,
when the C4V was introduced, the C2V reverted to the
green paintwork and sharing its frame with the Sport.
Production continued until 1927 when it was deleted,
being offered again in 1928. The C2V was replaced by
the 2VT in 1930.

The C2V was an immediate improvement on the
earlier Normale-based racers, and its first success was
an economy contest organised by *Motociclismo*. Carlo
Guzzi's brother-in-law Valentino Gatti achieved 74.955
kilometres on one litre of fuel at 51.545km/h
(32.93mph). In April 1923, a team was entered in the
Giro d'Italia. This 2,470km (1,535 miles) road race
was a classic and important annual event and was won
by Guido Mentasti at an average speed of 51km/h
(32mph). Another noteworthy victory was in the
Circuito del Lario, won by Gatti at an average speed of
61km/h (37.8mph). However, even the 2CV was being
outpaced by the end of 1923 by more specific racing
designs, and there would be a new engine, the C4V, for
the following season.

## THE SPORT

In the meantime, the Normale was discontinued in
favour of the Sport, a combination of a more powerful
Normale engine and a frame and running gear similar
to the C2V but without reinforcing. These were to be
the only production Guzzis from 1923 until 1928 and
came with a variety of options, specifically a side-car
attachment, front brake, and Bosch lighting system.
With a compression ratio of 4:5:1, power was up to 13
horsepower at 3,800rpm but increasing this was always
limited by the side inlet and overhead exhaust cylinder
head design. However moderate the power may have
been, it was still enough to propel the 130kg (287lb)

Sport to a maximum speed of 100km/h (62mph).
From 1923 until 1927 the Sport was painted green
like the Normale, but for 1928 it was red. The green
2CV also featured the non-reinforced frame of the
Sport.

## THE C4V

Much more effort was spent on developing racing
bikes during this period, and 1924 saw the C4V and
a return to the four-valve cylinder head pioneered by
the G.P. The earlier C2V also remained available as a
catalogued racer. Providing privateers with these
factory racers was a shrewd marketing move,
contributing to the increased public awareness of
Moto Guzzi as a successful racing motorcycle; this
was an approach that would serve the company well
in the future.

With its four-valve cylinder head and bevel-gear
driven overhead camshaft, the C4V was a much more
serious Grand Prix racer than earlier racing Guzzis,
despite retaining the hand-change three-speed
gearbox and unsprung frame. As before, the bore and
stroke were 88 x 82mm, but the two 37mm and two
34mm exhaust valves were inclined at a wider,
58°40'. Valve timing for a racing engine was very
moderate with the inlet opening 9° before top dead
centre, closing 61° after bottom dead centre. The
exhaust valve opened 60° before bottom dead centre
and closed 20° after top dead centre. The four-valve
layout allowed for a central 18mm spark plug. With a
racing Amac 28.5mm carburettor and a 6:1
compression ratio, the C4V initially produced 22
horsepower at 5,500rpm. There was a new frame
with a shorter, 1,380mm (54½in) wheelbase, a rim
brake on the front and 27 x 2.75in tyres.
Performance of the 130kg (287lb) C4V was
considerably improved over the C2V, with a top
speed of approximately 140km/h (87mph).

This increase in performance immediately
translated into victories on the racetrack. For the
1924 season the Ghersi brothers, Pietro and Mario,
joined Gatti and Mentasti in the Guzzi team. The
debut of the C4V took place on 9 June 1924 at
Cremona for speed trials. Guido Mentasti set a lap
record of 125.265km/h (78mph) and a speed of
135.142km/h (84mph) for a timed 10kkm (6.2 miles),
a new 500cc class record.

The first race for the C4V was on 29 June at the Circuito del Lario. Here, Pietro Ghersi won at an average speed of 67.631km/h (42mph), with Mentasti second and brother Mario fourth. Other victories for the C4V followed at Lugano, Tortona and La Spezia, but the most significant win was in the first Championship of Europe, held at Monza on 7 September. In a field consisting of the works Sunbeam, Norton, Sarolea, and twin cylinder Peugeot, Mentasti won at an average speed of 130.647km/h (81mph). Shortly before the race, Mentasti had most of the gearbox removed, also dismantling the hand gearchange. Running with primary gears only, he soundly beat ace rider Tazio Nuvolari on a Norton TT over the 400km (250 miles) race to establish Guzzi as a serious force in 500cc racing. Emphasising Guzzi's superiority, local track expert Erminio Visioli finished second, and Pietro Ghersi, fourth. These C4Vs were almost standard bikes, except for strengthening of the rear frame triangle, a shortened rear mudguard, no seat springs and the oil tank being located on top of the fuel tank.

When Pietro Ghersi rode a C4V to victory at the German Grand Prix at Avus on 21 September Guzzi was no longer an obscure Italian motorcycle manufacturer. From the original idea in 1919, by 1925 Carlo Guzzi's individual and unusual design had been well and truly vindicated. Shortly after these victories the C4V was added to the regular catalogue as a production racer and was available until 1926.

During 1925 there were still officially entered factory bikes and the C4V managed 32 victories. On 29 September Guzzi made its first attempt on world speed records with the C4V. At Monza, Siro Casali, Ghersi, and Prini, broke 37 world records, including 500 miles (800km) at an average speed of 129.629km/h (80mph). Modifications to the C4V for this attempt included an André steering damper and Excelsoir front fork friction dampers. As a Grand Prix racer however, the C4V was beginning to be outclassed, so for 1926 Carlo Guzzi decided to create a completely new 250, purely for competition. While it looked like a scaled-down C4V, this new engine was so advanced that it would form the basis of successful 250cc racing Guzzis for 30 years.

# THE TT250

By 1926, the success of the racing programme was beginning to pay dividends. There were now 350 employees at Mandello producing around 3,000 motorcycles a year. With the classic Guzzi layout of a horizontal engine, tubular double-cradle frame and three-speed unit gearbox now well established, the 250 would also follow this pattern. Carlo Guzzi's intention was to compete in the Isle of Man TT, and on 1 May 1926 he made the new 250 available to *Motociclismo* for testing.

The lines closely followed that of the C4V but the engine now had square dimensions, 68 x 68mm bore and stroke, and a bevel-gear driven single overhead camshaft operating two valves. These had an included angle of 58°, a very narrow angle for that time, and this undoubtedly contributed to the very high specific power output of 60hp per litre. This was an extraordinary figure for normally aspirated engines at that time, and was only matched by the Delage and Bugatti Grand Prix cars. With an 8:1 compression ratio, the 15

horsepower was produced at 6,000rpm. This increase in rpm was enabled through the use of roller big-end bearings instead of plain bushes, and these were soon adopted on the 500cc C4V. Weighing in at only 105kg (231½lb), the TT250 was capable of around 118km/h (73.3mph).

In June, a 250 and 500 were taken to the Isle of Man for Pietro Ghersi to ride in the Lightweight and Senior TTs. On the TT250, now with a Binks hand throttle and André steering damper, Ghersi astonished the partisan crowd by finishing second behind C. W. (Paddy) Johnston's Cotton and setting the fastest lap at 63.12mph (101.6km/h). Unfortunately, Ghersi was disqualified for changing an unspecified spark plug (to a FERT instead of KLG) during the race but it had been an impressive racing debut in the most prestigious race in Europe. He retired during the Senior TT.

Although the Isle of Man had been a disappointing event, 1926 was a very successful year for Guzzi in competition, with 42 victories. A month after the TT, at the Circuito del Lario, Ugo Prini rode to victory in

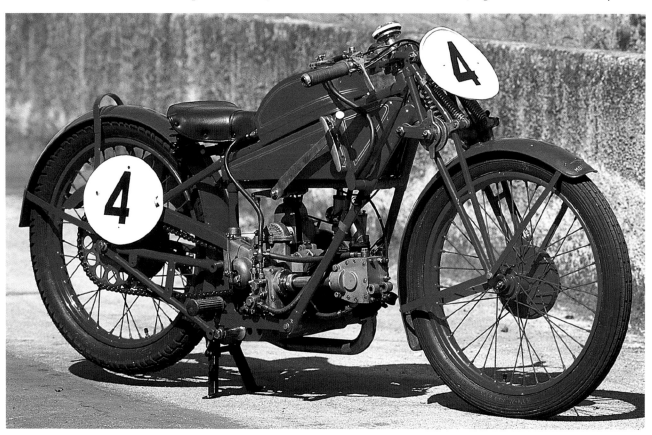

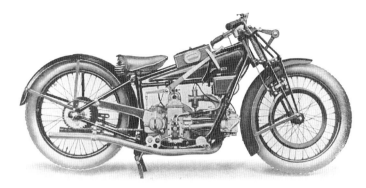

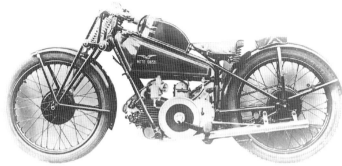

the 250 Class, although Pietro Ghersi was defeated by the Sunbeam of Achille Varzi in the 500 class. The most important event of the year in Italy was the Nations Grand Prix held at Monza in September. Here again, the 250 was triumphant, with Prini and Ghersi joint winners. The TT250 was then marketed as a catalogue racer.

# THE 4VTT

In 1927, production of the 250cc and 500cc racers increased alongside that of the 500cc Sport street bike, and for that year the 500cc C4V catalogue racer became the 4VTT. Essentially based on the 1926 factory four-valve Circuito del Lario 500 racer, the 4VTT had a nickel-steel crankshaft with needle-roller con-rod bearings. The move to needle-roller big-end bearings was a particularly significant one for Moto Guzzi and would now become a Guzzi feature. The cylinder head was bronze instead of cast iron and power was increased to 27 horsepower. The rear frame featured the strengthening first fitted on the European Championship C4V of 1924. The footpegs were more rear mounted, and the oil tank was located in front of a larger fuel tank. A tool box was fitted on the tank and there was a standard steering damper. The 4VTT also had larger tyres, a 2.75 x 27in on the front and 3.00 x 27in on the rear. The throttle was the hand-operated Binks type that had been used on the official bikes during 1926.

After the disappointment of 1926, Guzzi again decided to contest the Lightweight and Senior TT events at the Isle of Man. There were three entrants in the 250, and two in the 500, but the best result Guzzi could achieve was Luigi Archangeli's second place in the Lightweight. By now the 500, despite the four-valve cylinder head, was becoming uncompetitive, and 50 of

Guzzi's 62 victories during 1927 were achieved by the 250.

Surprisingly, given Moto Guzzi's increasing success, especially with the 250, the company announced a withdrawal from competition in February 1928. This was to concentrate on regular production and development of new models. High on the list of priorities was the expansion of the range of street motorcycles, which at that stage still only consisted of the Normale-based Sport, and the development of a three-wheeled commercial vehicle. The withdrawal from competition was unpopular with racing followers throughout Italy, but the range of catalogued racers was increased so that privateers could continue to promote the marque.

# THE 4VSS AND SS250

Revised and faster versions of both the 4V 500, the previously discontinued C2V, and the TT250 were made available. Although the 4VTT of 1927 continued through until 1929, the 4VSS superseded it with its slightly more powerful engine and drum front brake. Both models now had a triple-spring front fork and the oil tank moved to the top of the fuel tank. They also received a horn and provision for lights. The 4VSS was available in limited numbers through until 1934. The TT250 continued as before, but was supplemented by a faster SS250. With a bronze cylinder head the power was increased to 18 horsepower, enough to propel the SS to 125km/h (78mph).

SS250 Guzzis won Italian Championships in 1927 and 1930–33. As with the 500cc 4VSS, the SS250 was sold through until 1934, by which time the three-speed gearbox was also a limiting factor in its competitiveness as a racer, and the bronze cylinder head had reverted to cast iron. From 1934, racing 250s were reserved for factory riders only.

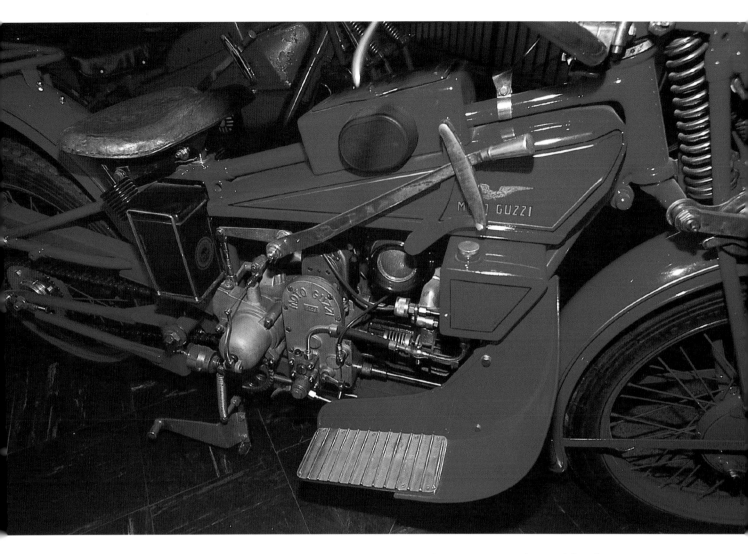

# THE G.T.

More significant than the few catalogue racers however, was the expansion of the range with the sprung-frame Gran Turismo. Launched in January 1928, only a few were built (78 between 1928 and 1930) as it was not popular. Once again it showed the company's capacity for original ideas and putting them into practice. When Carlo's engineer brother Giuseppe modified the frame of the 500 Sport to incorporate a swingarm operating four springs in compression by rods, both Carlo and Giorgio Parodi agreed to produce it. The springs were located in a pressed steel box underneath the engine.

Giuseppe, known by his nickname Naco, had officially joined the company in 1927, and was even more modest than Carlo. He was to be the impetus behind all of Moto Guzzi's significant frame development and was a champion of the sprung frame. This he had begun to design in 1925, and there were several versions. Unfortunately, the idea of a sprung frame was too advanced for the conservative motorcycle world and it would take later racing success to establish the merits of the idea. As with most of Moto Guzzi designs, it too was enduring, surviving through to the final Falcone of 1967.

One of the problems with the G.T. was its modest performance. The 13.2 horsepower engine now needed to propel 150kg (331lb), and the top speed was only 100km/h (62mph). This may have been fast enough in 1920, but higher standards of performance were expected by 1928.

In the meantime, Giuseppe made a trip to the Arctic Circle on his own development bike to promote the merits of the design. After this successful journey the G.T. was nicknamed the 'Norge' (Norway). This trip was only one of many that Giuseppe undertook on his prototype to test his designs, and the bike still exists. Giuseppe even re-registered it after the Second World War when he hid it from the Italian military that were confiscating all motorcycles over 250cc.

However, these trips still weren't enough to convince the buying public of the merits of Giuseppe's idea and

the unsprung Sport continued as the production mainstay. By 1928, production was around 50 motorcycles a week, a large number for the day. The Sport included a few modifications for that year, notably a drum front brake and a new cylinder and head with larger finning. By the end of the year a version appeared that looked much like the later Sport 14. This has become unofficially known as the Sport 13 although it is not listed in factory data as such. A luxury version of the Sport was also available with legshields and full lighting powered by a Bosch mag-dynamo (a magneto-dynamo combination).

## THE SPORT 14

By the end of 1928, the Sport had evolved into the Sport 14, with a new unsprung frame and the three spring forks from the racers. Soon there was an improved electrical system with a Miller dynamo separate from the magneto ignition. The Sport 14 was supplied with or without lighting, so the dynamo could be installed later if required. This provision for a dynamo was a significant step forward for Moto Guzzi and these models were characterised by the letter 'L' – representing 'Luce' (light) – in front of the engine number. New crankcases and crankcase cover, both with a bulge for the dynamo and dynamo gear, distinguished the Sport 14 from earlier varieties.

The engine had a larger cylinder barrel and head assembly and this construction would last through until 1946 on many production and military versions. The power was 13.2 horsepower at 3,800rpm with camshaft timing that differed to that of the Normale. The inlet opened 20° before top dead centre, closing 60° after bottom dead centre, and the exhaust valve opened 62°

before bottom dead centre, closing 26° after top dead centre. The compression ratio was 4.5:1 and carburetion was by an Amac 1in carburettor. The claimed top speed was 100km/h (62mph), although *Motociclismo* tested a restored Sport 14 in December 1980 and achieved only 87.5km/h (54mph) with the rider fully prone. The standing 400-metre (437yd) time was 25.294 seconds at 82.190km/h (51mph). Although this may seem slow by today's standards, the Sport 14 was one of the better-performing motorcycles of the period and was extremely popular. Weight was a moderate 130kg (287lb) and it was Guzzi's best-selling model of the 1920s.

Within ten years, Moto Guzzi had become one of Italy's premier motorcycle manufacturers, and in 1928 the company launched a unique vehicle that would be one of their most successful. With the front half of a 500cc Sport combined with a truck-like rear, the Type 107 Motocarri was created. While it may have seemed an incongruous concept, it once again showed Guzzi's capacity for originality and this model remained in production, later with Astore and Falcone-based engines as the Ercole, until 1980. From 1931 it was produced in two versions, the '125' Civile and the Militare. The front half was now roughly the later 500cc Sport 15 with a saddle fuel tank, and these 13 horsepower vehicles were produced until 1936.

At the Nations Grand Prix in September 1928, 250cc Guzzis had filled the first five places, and the company was again victorious at the Circuito del Lario that year. With these racing results from privateers surpassing expectations, Guzzi decided not to run an official team for 1929. The only official entry for that year was a return to the Isle of Man where Pietro Ghersi rode an SS250 in the Lightweight TT. As with previous Tourist Trophies, it was an unfortunate meeting for Guzzi with

LEFT The Sport 14 was
Moto Guzzi's most popular
model in the late 1920s.
Moto Guzzi

BELOW Replacing the C2V in 1930,
the 2VT was less of a pure racing
machine. The frame and saddle tank
were shared with the Sport 15.

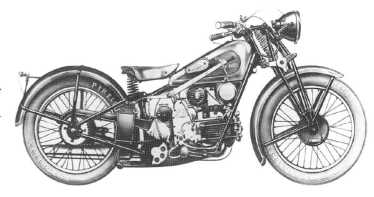

Ghersi retiring on the final lap while comfortably in the lead.

The catalogue 500cc and 250cc production racers (including the C2V 500) continued into 1929, as did the Sport 14 and the few GTs that were manufactured. The 4VSS 500 featured more chrome plating and dual silencers, and provided Guzzi its first victory that year when Mario Ghersi won the Targa Florio in April. As before, this season proved to be a good one for Moto Guzzi, culminating in Egidio Truzzi's victory in the 250cc Nations Grand Prix in September.

## THE 2VT AND G.T. 2VT

Only a few changes were made to existing models in 1930. The C2V 500cc racer was replaced by the 2VT ('Valvole Testa' – overhead valve), essentially the existing dual overhead valve C2V engine in a new Sport 15 frame with a saddle tank and front brake. Even the crankcases were the Sport 15 'L'-type, so it was only the overhead valve top-end that differed. The 2VT remained in production until 1934, by which time it had been supplemented by a sprung-frame version, the G.T. 2VT. Designed for longer distance events, this model first appeared in 1931 and used the chassis of the sprung-frame G.T. 16.

Neither the 2VT nor the G.T. 2VT was strictly a racing bike. Standard equipment included lighting, luggage racks and legshields, and they were really luxury versions of standard bikes. Weighing in at a solid 150kg (331lb), top speed of the G.T. 2VT with a 17 horsepower engine was only around 120km/h (75mph).

This was the final year for the C4V 500 TT and TT250, these being superseded in 1931 by the higher-performance SS. Factory racing 250s now had a pedal-operated three-speed gearbox (with new ratios) and Brampton forks, although the privateer versions retained the hand gearshift. By now, the 250 was developing 20 horsepower at 6,500–7,000rpm, a truly impressive figure for 1930. Continuous development saw the 250 overshadow the 500, with 36 out of 49 victories in 1930. Some of these were particularly impressive: 250 Guzzis filled the first five places in the Coppa Albano, coming first and second in the Targa Florio, while Truzzi again triumphed in the Nations Grand Prix.

## THE SPORT 15 AND G.T. 16

Most innovations appeared on the production Sport 15 of 1931, with a new frame (still unsprung) and a saddle-style fuel tank rather than the tank positioned on top of the frame tube. They were painted brown/amaranth until 1933. when a purple Lusso (luxury) version was added. This had more chrome on the tank, wheel rims and various cycle parts. Some were also painted red, and the Sport 15 was Guzzi's most popular production bike through the 1930s, remaining available until 1939.

The side inlet and overhead exhaust valve engine that had its origins with the Normale of 1921 was still used, but had been developed considerably. Carburetion was now by an Amal 6/142 and the needle roller big-end bearings of the C4V adopted to improve reliability. Another feature that carried over from the C4V was the introduction of a stronger 'I'-shaped con-rod in place of the weak 'O'-section tube type. The presence of 'L' crankcases, needle-roller big-end, and the 'I'-shaped con-rod are clues when dating pre-war Sports. In 1936, a Dell'Orto carburettor replaced the Amal, and 1937 saw new controls. The Sport 15 frame and saddle tank also made it to the sprung G.T., which in 1930 became the G.T. 16. However, for some reason the G.T. versions did not catch on and the G.T. 16 only lasted in production until 1934.

While many motorcycle manufacturers suffered after the Great Crash of 1929, Italian manufacturers, like those in Germany, were fortunate that their fascist governments saw motorsport as an important propaganda tool. So rather than being a period of depression, the 1930s were to be fruitful for Moto Guzzi, especially on the track. This success translated into Guzzi earning the status as the leading Italian motorcycle manufacturer by the end of the decade.

The supercharged four-cylinder
500cc engine of 1930. On top of the
engine is the transverse expansion
chamber, with the gear driven rotary
supercharger above the gearbox.

# 2 THE 1930s:
## A GOLDEN ERA

The onset of the new decade saw considerable development of the racing four-stroke engine, both in automotive and motorcycle applications. The appearance of superchargers and multi-cylinder engines had led to huge increases in power, and for 500cc racing motorcycles this indicated that the days of the naturally aspirated four-stroke single were numbered. However, this emphasis on horsepower was not initially matched by chassis development and it would be several years before the heavy, powerful, and complex multi-cylindered machines dominated the racing circuits.

## THE QUATTRO CILINDRI 500

Epitomising this lack of harmony was Carlo Guzzi and Oreste Pasolini's 500cc supercharged transverse four-cylinder racing motorcycle of 1931. Designed to be an answer to the four cylinder OPRA (later the Rondine and eventually Gilera) of Piero Remor and Carlo Gianini, the four was an amalgam of ancient and modern engineering practice. Thus it was disappointing and never achieved Guzzi's expectations.

The idea of four nearly horizontal cylinders and a one-piece alloy crankcase with the gear driven Cozette rotary supercharger bolted on to the rear of the gearbox was novel, as were the four separate and identical cast-iron cylinder heads and barrels. Yet there was still only a hand-operated three-speed gearbox. The supercharger fed a cylindrical expansion chamber mounted above the four 30mm inlet ports. This chamber was designed to maintain constant high pressure to the inlet ports and would be used again with the supercharged 250 single later in the decade. The exhaust ports were also 30mm and the ignition was by twin Bosch magnetos.

The engine was oversquare with dimensions of 56 x 50mm, and because it was to be supercharged the valve angle was widened. Whereas earlier racing engines had used narrow included valve angles and overhead camshafts, the four had its two overhead valves set 70° apart. These were operated by exposed pushrods and rockers driven by two camshafts situated inside the cylinder block. As expected with a supercharger, valve timing was very moderate with the inlet opening 10° before top dead centre, closing 50° after bottom dead

centre, and the exhaust opening 50° before bottom dead centre and closing 10° after top dead centre. Valve lift was 5.75mm for the inlet and 6.50mm for the exhaust.

In many respects the four was thoroughly up to date. The three-bearing crankshaft rods ran on roller bearings and the con-rods on needle rollers. The 4-litre lubrication system included an oil cooler mounted on the front frame downtubes, and there were two oil tanks, one for the engine (in front of the fuel tank) and one for the compressor (between the rear wheel and the engine). With a compression ratio of 5:1, 40 horsepower was developed at 7,800rpm with the supercharger operating at 0.75 bar. This was too much power for the rigid frame and small brakes (177mm front and 225mm rear) to handle, and the engine was considerably heavy at 80kg (176lb).

Giuseppe Guzzi's frame, although rigid and not strong enough for the powerful engine, was also quite advanced. More importantly, it featured some characteristics that would appear on later Guzzi racing frames, right through until the 1950s. The front part of the cradle frame was steel tubing, bolted to duraluminium plates underneath and on both sides of the engine. The triangulated rear steel tube section bolted to these plates. The use of duraluminium sheet metal as part of the frame was a new idea for Moto Guzzi but would become a feature of most racing Guzzis over the next 20 years.

First tested at Monza in September 1931, the 165kg (364lb) four-cylinder 500 was disappointing from the start and only raced once. This was at the Nations Grand Prix at Monza where three bikes were raced (with one spare), the riders being Terzo Bandini, Fumagalli and Moretti. Bandini battled for the lead with Piero Taruffi's Norton for 37 laps but all three bikes retired. However, Carlo Guzzi was not

completely disillusioned by the performance of the four and continued to test it with Siro Casali during 1932 before dropping the project that year. While not an unqualified racing success, it did spawn a three-cylinder road bike.

Racing duties throughout 1931 were still consigned to the SS250 and SS500. The biggest change to the 250 was the introduction of a foot-operated gearchange, and the front fork became a one-spring Brampton. Factory bikes were fitted with either a hand or foot gearchange, sometimes both. From 1932 the foot gearchange became an option on the 250SS and TT. Again, the 250 was victorious in the Nations Grand Prix, Alfredo Panella and Riccardo Brusi taking the first two places. Pietro Ghersi attempted the Lightweight TT at the Isle of Man once more but retired. Other victories during 1931 included Ugo Prini's win in the 250cc class of the Circuito del Lario, and Terzo Bandini's win in the 250cc Swiss Grand Prix held at Berne.

## THE TRE CILINDRI

The G.T. 16, a Sport 15 in a sprung frame had been introduced in 1930, and early in 1932 Carlo Guzzi produced a remarkable touring bike in a similar style. Following the disappointment of the four-cylinder racer, three of the cylinders were taken to create a compact 500cc in-line triple. With the four's 56mm pistons, the stroke was increased by 2mm to 67mm to give 500cc. The two overhead valves followed the four-cylinder's example by being operated by pushrods and rockers but now used coil springs instead of hairpins. Coil ignition was used, a distributor driven off the right side camshaft, together with a single Amal carburettor. With its 4.5:1 compression ratio, the three cylinder produced 25 horsepower at 5,500rpm. Despite the undersquare bore and stroke, this engine was very advanced. The flywheel was incorporated inside the engine cases as was the three-speed gearbox as usual. Running entirely on needle roller bearings the crankshaft had 120° crank throws creating a very smooth engine. The frame, in two parts bolted together, followed the form set by the racer apart from the inclusion of rear suspension with a new design of friction damper.

Unfortunately, the Tre Cilindri did not meet with universal acclaim, and because of its specification it

**BELOW** One of Moto Guzzi's more successful ventures during the 1930s was the expansion of the lightweight range. This is the P 175 of 1933.
Moto Guzzi

needed to be sold at a premium price. The conservative market was just not ready for such an expensive touring bike that could only provide modest performance. Even though the weight was only 160kg (353lb), top speed was merely 130km/h (81mph). Buyers still preferred the Sport 15 (especially at a price of 35 per cent less) and after one year the Tre Cilindri was discontinued.

# THE P 175, P 250, P.E. 250 AND G.T. 17

If the Tre Cilindri had been a marketing disaster, Guzzi's expansion of its range into the lightweight

segment was a brilliant success. With the release of the P 175 in 1932 some new features were introduced that would eventually find their way on to the 500cc production models, in particular, overhead valves. Typically for a Guzzi, the cylinder head design was very advanced, the two 32mm valves having a 62° included angle. The engine cases were also redesigned to make them more aesthetically appealing. Designed for an advantageous taxation class for lightweight motorcycles, motoleggere, the P 175 was produced until 1937. Still with a hand-operated three-speed gearbox, it was a sprightly little machine. While the 59 x 63.7mm engine only produced 7 horsepower at 5,000rpm, it only weighed 115kg (253½lb) and could achieve 100km/h (62mph).

In 1933, the Fascist government abolished the tax differences between light and regular motorcycles so the production range was expanded in 1934 with the addition of the P 250 alongside the P 175. Displacing 232.3cc, with its 68 x 64mm bore and stroke and pushrod-operated overhead valves, the P250 owed more to the P 175 than the racing 250s. With slightly larger, 33mm valves, power was only 9 horsepower at 5,500rpm and the top speed also around 100km/h (62mph). Unlike the P 175, however, the P 250 had a foot-operated gearbox and could be distinguished from the smaller model by its deeper mudguards and a frame that included a sheet metal section behind the engine.

The P 250 was soon joined by a sprung-frame P.E. (E for Elastico) that weighed considerably more, 135kg (298lb), but offered superior comfort and handling.

Also throughout this period, some of Guzzi's most successful ventures were military vehicles, in particular the G.T. 17. Based on the G.T. 16, this had the 500cc 13.2 horsepower opposed-valve engine, three-speed gearbox and sprung frame. Carburetion was now by a Dell'Orto MC 26F instead of an Amal, and a Marelli MLA1 magneto rather than a Bosch ZE1. The G.T. 17 also featured a double exhaust. The kickstart was on the right (left on the G.T. 16), and no battery was fitted. Instead of a battery there was a heavy-duty dynamo and voltage regulator. Single and dual seat versions were offered and there were a variety of options available, some including machine-gun mounting. The G.T. 17 was the first of a long line of Moto Guzzis built for specific military or police applications. Motor-tricycles also featured strongly in the production from 1931 until 1936. Two versions with the 500cc opposed-valve engine were produced, the '32' military version, and the '125' civilian version.

## THE 500 BICILINDRICA

With the four cylinder permanently retired, racing during 1932 continued with developed versions of the 4VSS and SS250. By now the 500cc 4VSS had a bronze cylinder head, and factory versions a twin Amal 6/011 carburettor with a single-float chamber on a V-shaped inlet manifold. Power was now 32 horsepower with a top speed in the region of 170km/h (105.6mph), but the rest of the bike was quite out of date, especially the hand-operated three-speed gearbox.

There was still one significant victory in store for the venerable 4VSS, the 1932 Milano–Napoli. Last run in 1925, this race was shifted to June (from September) and called the 'Mussolini Gold Cup'. On his 4VSS, Carlo Fumagalli won at an average speed of 93.084km/h (57.8mph) with Virginio Fieschi second on another 4V. Riccardo Brusi and Alfredo Panella matched this with a first and second in the 250 class. As usual, excellent race results continued for the 250 during 1932, victories by Brusi in the European Grand Prix and Fumagalli in the Swiss Grand Prix being particularly notable. Continued development saw the power up to 20 horsepower.

While the 4VSS 500cc racer was catalogued alongside the 250SS for 1933, it was clear that it was no longer competitive. Race victories were hard to come by and the Milano–Napoli event of 1933 was a disaster for Moto Guzzi. Fortunately Federico Susini on the non-factory 250 was victorious in its class, the only Guzzi to finish. All ten works bikes failed. There were other important 250cc victories however, in particular Walter Handley's win in the Swiss Grand Prix in July. Handley had observed Mario Ghersi in the Lightweight TT of 1933 (where he finished sixth) and also wanted to ride a Guzzi in that event but had not been able to due to his contract with Excelsoir.

Works 250s that year received a four-speed foot operated gearbox and were code-named the 4M for four marce (four-speed). Although Mario Ghersi retired in the Milano–Napoli, the 4M became the standard factory 250 after that event. It featured new crankcases, a cast-iron instead of bronze cylinder head, and an Amal 6/011 carburettor.

Needing a new 500, Carlo Guzzi, with characteristic originality, sought to combine two of his highly successful 250s to create a 500cc V-twin. The resulting Bicilindrica lived until 1951 and managed to blend the delicate balance between horsepower and agility. In the design of the Bicilindrica, Carlo Guzzi retained the horizontal cylinder of the SS250, and placed another cylinder 120° behind it. This cylinder had circular finning, both engines featuring a single overhead camshaft driven by a shaft and bevel gear. Thus the same bore and stroke was retained (68 x 68mm), as were the valves, 37mm for the inlet and 34mm for the exhaust with an identical 58° included valve angle. Initially, the cylinders and heads were in cast iron.

As expected, the aluminium crankcase contained the four-speed gearbox, operated by a foot change, and the 38/70 geared primary drive. The big-end and the crankshaft ran on 30mm roller bearings with a central main bearing. Separate crankpins were therefore used and spaced 120° apart to give even firing intervals. As the pins were integral with the crank webs the roller big-end bearings were unusual in that they were split diametrically. There was also the usual Guzzi external flywheel on the left side of the engine.

Carburetion was by two Dell'Orto 28.5mm carburettors, ignition by a magneto situated between the cylinders, and lubrication by dry sump. The original version had a rigid frame and Brampton forks and weighed around 160kg (353lb). First displayed in September 1933, power was 41 horsepower at 7,000rpm and the top speed was 186km/h (115.5mph). For the second version of 1934 the weight had been reduced to 151kg (333lb) and power increased to 43.35 horsepower. The three-part crankcase was now cast in electron rather than aluminium and featured a revised oil pump.

The racing debut of the Bicilindrica was on 15 October 1933 at the Rome Autodromo del Littorio in the Italian Grand Prix. Here three bikes were raced by Terzo Bandini, Guglielmo Sandri and the rising star, Omobono Tenni. Tenni crashed, Bandini retired, and Sandri finished second although Guzzi triumphed with the first three places in the 250cc event. It had been a very promising start for the new machine and once again Carlo Guzzi's originality had been vindicated. With more development the Bicilindrica could only improve and if it had not been for the rise of the supercharged 500s later in the decade, it would have been undoubtedly more successful. As it was, the Bicilindrica demonstrated its excellence by spearheading Moto Guzzi's 500cc racing programme for nearly 20 years.

With the addition of the Bicilindrica, things started to look up on the race tracks for Guzzi during 1934. Both the 250 and 500 were developed, the 250 now being reserved for works riders only. It also received a new frame (still with a rigid rear end), and new saddle-style fuel tank with an oil tank on top, Brampton forks and 19in wheels. The 500 Bicilindrica was essentially unchanged but for the 202mm brakes front and rear. The official team of Tenni, Bandini and Amilcare Moretti was also strengthened by the inclusion of Irishman Stanley Woods for selected international events, notably the Spanish Grand Prix in April, followed by the Isle of Man Tourist Trophy.

The Bicilindrica's first success was the Spanish Grand Prix at Montjuich Park, Barcelona on 22 April 1934. Stanley Woods rode to victory in both the 250cc and 500cc classes, nicknaming the Bicilindrica the 'monster' because of its evil handling. One month later, on the 20 May it was raced again at the Italian Grand Prix, again held at Rome's Littorio autodrome. Tenni took first place followed by Moretti. At this event Brusi also won the 250cc race. Tenni continued this success on the Bicilindrica to take the Italian 500cc Championship that year while Bandini won the Milano–Napoli event at an average speed of 98.370km/h (61mph). Brusi also led home four Guzzis in the 250 class. It had been a good year, with some important results, but 1935 would see Guzzi achieve what they had set out to do back in 1926, winning the most important road race in Europe, the Isle of Man Tourist Trophy.

Central to the improvement of both the 250 and 500 Bicilindrica for 1935 was the adoption of a sprung frame, designed by Giuseppe Guzzi. It was an unorthodox system with the rear fork pivoted near the engine and triangulated underneath. There were two springs in horizontal tubes alongside the wheel and damping was by friction dampers adjusted by a lever on the left side of the fuel tank and cable. Changes to the engine included narrower and stronger con-rods, and narrower valve stems. Power for the 500 went to 50 horsepower at 7,500rpm, with a top speed around 200km/h (124mph). This was amply demonstrated by Tenni at the Mellaha circuit at the Grand Prix of Tripoli at the end of March, which he won at an average speed of 178km/h (110mph). The 250 for

1935 received the 202mm brakes of the Bicilindrica, and also shared the engine improvements.

In the Milano–Napoli event of April 1935, Guzzi swept the board overall, in both the 500cc and 250cc classes. Tenni won, followed by Giordano Aldrighetti, Bandini, and Brusi on the 250. Tenni's winning average speed of 107.91km/h (67mph) indicated the superiority of the sprung frame. A similar victory followed one month later at Monza in the Gran Premio del Reale. This time the Bicilindrica was again triumphant, Bandini ahead of Tenni and Aldrighetti at an average speed of 164.678km/h (102.3mph). Aldo Pigorini took the 250 to its class victory. Tenni again won the Italian 500cc Championship, with Pigorini taking the 250cc Championship, these results doing much to publicise the new sprung frame.

The Tourist Trophy races that year were to be the most significant successes for Guzzi to that date. At 35 years of age Stanley Woods was a veteran of the Isle of Man course with six TT wins to his credit and both he and Tenni were entered on 250 Guzzis. Woods also had a Bicilindrica for the Senior TT. In the Lightweight TT on 19 June, Woods gave Guzzi its first Tourist Trophy at an average speed of 71.56mph (115km/h) in rain and very poor conditions. Tenni crashed and Woods winning margin was over three minutes from Tyrell Smith on the four-valve Rudge that had won the previous year.

The Senior TT three days later was a far closer race. Also held in atrocious conditions, Stanley Woods rode the race of his life to beat Jimmy Guthrie on a Norton. On the final lap Woods set a new lap record of 86.53mph (139km/h) to defeat Guthrie by four seconds. Despite the poor conditions, he also set a new race

record at 84.68mph (136km/h). It was a historic victory. Not only was it the first by an Italian motorcycle on the British manufacturers' home turf, but it signalled the end of the rigid frame and the big single for racing. These victories were especially important in elevating the status of Moto Guzzi as a world class, not just an Italian, motorcycle manufacturer.

Soon the Bicilindrica was also powering a four-wheeled Nibbio, designed by Count Giovanni Lurani and Carlo Guzzi's son Ulisse. On 5 November 1935, the 50 horsepower Nibbio broke kilometre and mile under-500cc vetturette records on the Firenze–Mare road. In May 1939, Lurani set more records, this time on a stretch of the Berlin–Munich autobahn, with a top speed of 174km/h (108mph).

# THE V, G.T.V., S, G.T.S., W AND G.T.W.

The production 500cc single-cylinder engine came in for a complete redesign for 1934, and was called the 'V'. While retaining the distinctive horizontal cylinder, 88 x 82 bore and stroke, and external flywheel, the valve layout followed that of the P 175 with two overhead valves operated by pushrods and rockers with external hairpin springs. The aluminium crankcase was also restyled along the lines of the P 175. The cast-iron cylinder head had twin exhaust ports, and with a 5.5:1 compression ratio and an Amal 27mm carburettor, power was up to 18 horsepower at 4,300rpm. Ignition was by a Bosch magneto with manual advance. The gearbox was now four-speed, and foot operated, and there was the usual 280mm external flywheel. All the gearbox shafts ran in ball bearings, there was a helical geared primary drive, and the big-end bearings were needle rollers. So sound was this design that it formed the basis of all later Guzzi 500 singles, including the magnificent Condor, Dondolino and Gambalunga competition machines.

The rest of the new 500 V followed a design similar to that of the earlier Sport 15, but with many variations. The frame was rigid but now included sheet metal plates behind the engine. The girder front fork now had friction dampers, and all the bodywork was new including the fuel tanks, mudguards and addition of toolboxes. Wheels were 19in and the V

was shorter than the Sport 15 with its 1,400mm (55in) wheelbase. A sprung-frame G.T.V. was also offered and this had a longer production run than the V, lasting until 1946. Surprisingly, given the more advanced specification of the V and G.T.V., the new engine was also built with the earlier side inlet and overhead exhaust valve cylinder head. The result was the S and its sprung-frame brother the G.T.S. Still making 13.2 horsepower as it had back in 1928, these four-speed variants were also offered with the option of a hand gearchange, and designed as a rugged workhorse rather than a sporting motorcycle. They were also more popular than the V, with nearly twice as many manufactured.

**LEFT** The Duke of Richmond
congratulates Tenni after his
1937 Lightweight TT victory.
*Moto Guzzi*

Despite the performance benefits offered by the V engine, the G.T.S. combination of the sprung frame with the earlier engine was also surprisingly popular, but this was related more to the reliability of the engine. If an overhead valve dropped on the S engine it did not end with catastrophic engine damage. The V would achieve 130km/h (81mph) against the 105km/h (65mph) of the S. It must also be remembered that the venerable Sport 15 with its opposed-valve engine and hand-change three-speed gearbox was Guzzi's production mainstay during the 1930s. It received some minor changes to colours, brakes, front suspension and carburettors, but continuing in production until 1939. The popularity of the Sport 15, especially given the alternative of the V and G.T.V., indicated the conservative nature of the motorcycle-buying public, something that continues to this day.

There were few changes to the range of production bikes in 1935. The W and G.T.W. joined the 500cc overhead valve line-up, being identical to the 18 horsepower V and G.T.V. apart from a higher performance, 22-horsepower engine. This was achieved through a slightly higher compression ratio (6:1), a new camshaft, and a 28.5mm carburettor. The W was produced through until 1939, and the G.T.W. until 1949. The higher horsepower engine brought the sporting G.T.W.'s performance up to the level of the lighter, unsprung versions, giving a top speed of 140km/h (87mph). There were now seven 500s in the production range: the Sport 15, V, W, and S with unsprung frames, and the G.T.V., G.T.W. and G.T.S. with sprung frames. Notwithstanding military and three-wheeled vehicles, this would remain the basic line-up until the outbreak of the Second World War.

Politics intervened during 1936 and affected Guzzi's racing involvement. Economic sanctions and fuel shortages due to the invasion of Ethiopia limited participation in international events to the Swiss and European Grands Prix. At Berne, Tenni won the 250 event but retired from the 500cc race, and, at the German event to coincide with the Olympic Games, the Guzzis were outclassed by the supercharged DKWs. In Italian events, however, Guzzi's dominance continued.

As usual in the Milano–Napoli race, a full factory team was entered, Aldo Pigorini taking out the 250cc and Tenni the 500cc classes. The Italian Grand Prix at Monza on 27 September also saw the Guzzi Bicilindrica triumphant, this time over the German invasion. Tenni took first and Aldrighetti second, ahead of the two supercharged BMWs. Results were similar in the 250 race, but with the places reversed, with Aldrighetti taking first place ahead of Tenni. The factory racing bikes were very similar to those of 1935, but for long trumpet-type exhausts. It was also significant in 1936 that the great engineer Giulio Carcano joined the company, as he would play an important role at Mandello through until the mid-1960s.

With a temporary reduction in international tension during 1937 there was a return to active competition on all fronts, not just in Italy. However, as early as 1934 the Bicilindrica had come under some pressure from the supercharged water-cooled four-cylinder Rondine. With Rondine selling this design to Gilera, which intended to race it during 1937, the Guzzi Bicilindrica's days of dominance looked limited. By the end of the year a prototype water-cooled supercharged Bicilindrica was produced, as well as a prototype supercharged 250, but only the latter would make it to the race track. Fortunately, Guzzi still had their venerable 250, and the remarkable Omobono Tenni, whose bravery and talent more than compensated for any deficiency of horsepower. At the Isle of Man in 1937 Tenni took the Lightweight Tourist Trophy. Stanley Woods had retired while leading, and Tenni set a new lap record at 77.72mph (125km/h).

For 1937, the North–South race was changed to Milano–Taranto, a distance of 1,283km (797 miles). Again it was a Guzzi benefit, Sandri winning at 104.013km/h (65mph), leading Guzzi 500s to 11 of the first 15 places outright. Nello Pagani took the 250 racing class. Sandri finished off the year with a win in the Italian 500cc Championship, while Pagani matched that with the 250cc Championship. Another project later that

year was an aerodynamic exercise on the 250 by the
aeronautical institute at the Turin Polytechnic. Under
Carcano's supervision, a fully faired motorcycle was
designed for record-breaking attempts, but did not get
past the model stage.

# THE 500 G.T.C., P.L. 250, P.L.S. 250 AND P.E.S.

Also in 1937, the 500 G.T.C. was introduced which was
a competition version of the 22 horsepower G.T.W.
Power was increased slightly to 24–26 horsepower at
5,000rpm and it had high rise exhausts, a 20in front
wheel and a rear mudguard seat pad, and was designed
for the production categories of races such as the
Milano–Taranto. The G.T.W.'s legshields were discarded
and both the fuel and oil tanks were larger.
Unfortunately, at 160kg (353lb) it was far too heavy for
this sort of competition and only had a modest top speed
of 150km/h (93mph). Production continued through
until 1939.

The P 250 became a 247cc in 1937 through a bore
increase to 70mm and was designated the P.L. (L for
Lamiera – the pressed-steel frame). Costs were kept
down through the use of this type of frame, a welded
steel girder fork and almost total absence of chrome. The
P.L., with its 22mm carburettor, produced 10 horsepower
and could achieve around 100km/h (61mph). The P.L.
replaced the P 250, but the P.E. (E signifying Elastico)
with a sprung frame and the 9 horsepower 232cc engine
continued through until 1939. A sporting version of the
P.L., the P.L.S. also appeared in 1937 which produced

slightly more power than the P.L., 12 horsepower,
weighed 105kg (231½lb) and by 1939 had evolved into
the Egretta.

The 250 range was expanded during 1938, with the
addition of a sporty version of the sprung frame P.E., the
P.E.S. With the 12 horsepower 70 x 64mm 247cc engine
of the P.L.S., and a three-speed foot-operated gearbox,
the P.E.S. weighed in at 135kg (298lb) and the top speed
was around 110km/h (68mph). However, when modified
for events such as the Milano–Taranto, the P.E.S. could
achieve up to 125km/h (78mph).

# THE SUPERCHARGED 250

While the development of the water-cooled Bicilindrica
prototype of 1937 was shelved, Carlo Guzzi proceeded
with the supercharged 250 for 1938. Initially, this was to
be for endurance record-breaking attempts, but it proved
eminently suitable for road racing.

The air-cooled 250cc single was fitted with a
Guzzi-manufactured Cozette supercharger above the
gearbox driven by gears contained in the primary drive
casing. In order to overcome the difficulties presented in
supercharging a single cylinder, an expansion chamber
was located between the supercharger and cylinder.
Supercharger pressure altered depending on the type of
fuel used and with the usual petrol-benzol mixture of the
day it was 0.6–0.8 bar, but on methanol pressure was
increased to 1.3–1.5 bar.

In the cylinder head of the supercharged 250, the
37mm inlet and 35mm exhaust valves were unchanged,
the inlet port being 33.5mm with the exhaust 29mm.
With a Dell'Orto 32mm carburettor power was

increased to 38 horsepower at 7,900rpm, or 45
horsepower on methanol. The supercharged 250 also
received a new frame in steel with an alloy rear section,
and wheels with alloy rims and electron hubs. The total
weight was 132kg (291lb) and top speed over 200km/h
(124mph).

It was immediately successful as a record breaker,
Nello Pagani setting a host of world records at Monza
on 30 September. These included an average of
180.81km/h (112mph) over 5km (3.1 miles) and
170.273km/h (106mph) over 100km (62 miles). On 30
November Tenni attempted more records, raising the
5km (3-mile) record to 187.832km/h (117mph) and
also setting a one hour record of 180.502km (112
miles).

Road racing duties throughout 1938 were
maintained by the Bicilindrica along with the
unsupercharged 250, and it was a difficult year for
Moto Guzzi. In the Milano–Taranto race Pagani
finished third overall on a 250 at a speed of
104.479km/h (65mph), faster than Sandri's winning
speed of a year earlier on the Bicilindrica. The G.T.C.
took out the production category, but the Bicilindricas
of Tenni and Sandri retired. While 500cc victories were
hard to come by, Pagani still managed to take the 250
Italian Championship, and there was no entry by Guzzi
at the Isle of Man that year. Even in the Nations Grand
Prix at Monza the Guzzis were defeated by the Benellis
and BMWs.

# THE CONDOR AND ALBATROS

There were also two new additions to the 500cc line-up
for 1938, a 500cc catalogue racer to replace the G.T.C.,
the Condor, and a new military motorcycle, the G.T.
20. Although not available until 1939, the Condor had
been raced in prototype form by Ugo Prini in the 1938
Circuito del Lario where it took a class victory. Called
the Nuova C, this still had a cast-iron cylinder and
head, but with a Dell'Orto SS 32mm carburettor, new
camshaft and 7:1 compression it produced 28
horsepower at 5,000rpm. The Nuova C weighed much
less than the G.T.C. at 145kg (320lb) with full electrical
equipment, and its encouraging performance saw it
being sold as the G.T.C.L. a few months later. By 1939,
it had become officially the Condor, one of the most
classically good looking Guzzis ever created, and the
first of many to carry the name of a bird.

Although descended from the G.T.V., the Condor
was such a purposeful racing machine that it looked as
if it shared very little with the mundane touring model.
By the time it made it into production there was an
aluminium cylinder head and barrel, electron
crankcase, straight-cut primary gears, a single exhaust,
and constant mesh type four-speed gearbox. Standard
versions produced 28 horsepower, but with special
preparation (as for Pagani in the 1939 Circuito del
Lario) the pushrod engine was tuned to produce 32

horsepower. This tuning included a lighter, 6.6kg (14½lb), 260mm flywheel, sodium-filled exhaust valve, and two-ring piston. The 39mm inlet and 35mm exhaust valves were inclined at 62°.

The lower and lighter composite frame was derived from that of the supercharged 250 and with 21in aluminium-rimmed wheels and cast electron brakes, the Condor weighed only 140kg (308lb) with full electrical equipment. Without lights and adapted for circuit racing the weight was less, at around 125kg (276lb). With a top speed in the region of 160km/h (99mph), the red Condor was undoubtedly one of the most competitive 500cc motorcycles available in Italy in 1939. Unfortunately, the outbreak of war that year halted Condor production and only 69 were manufactured between 1939 and 1940. Some even ended up being used as a mount by Mussolini's riding bodyguards. The Condor would, however, be resurrected in 1946 as the great Dondolino and Gambalunga.

Not only did 1939 see the introduction of the superb Condor, but it also saw the supercharged 250 take to the race track in addition to the record attempts. Carlo Guzzi now realised that both his 250 and Bicilindrica were being outclassed and while the new 500 supercharged racer would have to wait until 1940, it was a relatively simple matter to adapt the supercharged 250 for the race track. There were also some experiments with fuel injection, both electromagnetic and mechanical. The electromagnetic

injection was a joint design by Caproni-Fuscaldo but further development was interrupted by the war.

Entered in the Milano–Taranto, the supercharged 250s of Tenni, Pagani, and Sandri all retired, although amazingly, the prototype Caproni-Fuscaldo injected supercharged 250 of Raffaele Alberti finished second in the 250 class. This bike was called 'Gerolamo' by the factory design team. This was a nickname for 'The Hunchback of Notre-Dame' and referred to the shape of the engine with its expansion chamber sitting on top.

That year also saw Guzzi return to the Isle of Man with Tenni and Stanley Woods on supercharged 250s but both retired. Maurice Cann rode a Bicilindrica to ninth in the Senior TT but this machine was now totally outclassed by its supercharged competition. Further bad luck followed at the Dutch and European Grands Prix, but the supercharged 250 was to have more success in Germany in August. One month before the outbreak of war, Pagani and Sandri rode supercharged 250s, to victory ahead of the two-stroke DKWs.

On 20 October 1939, on the autostrada between Bergamo and Brescia, further world records were set by the supercharged 250. On this occasion, Alberti was timed over a flying kilometre at 213.270km/h (132mph). Sandri too now broke most of Tenni's records of the previous year, raising the 5km (3.1 miles) to 201.447km/h (125mph). After the war, too, the supercharged 250 continued to set records. On 28 February 1948 Luigi Cavanna attempted several new 350cc sidecar world records at Charrat-Saxon in Switzerland. The flying kilometre was achieved at 172.993km/h (107mph). To show how advanced the design really was Cavanna set more records with the supercharged 250 in 1952.

It was not only the supercharged 250 that achieved better results for Moto Guzzi during 1939 – the Condor too was proving a far more competitive machine than the earlier G.T.C. In the Circuito del Lario Pagani won, beating Serafini's supercharged Gilera four with more than twice the Condor's horsepower. Joining the Condor in 1939 for production racing was the 250cc Albatros, and this was also immediately successful. In the Circuito di Losanna (Lausanne) and Circuito di Bari, Massimo Masserini and Enrico Lorenzetti took out class wins on both the Condor and Albatros.

250cc "GEROLAM
Compressore ad inie
zione indiretta.
SPERIMENTALE .1938

BELOW Another classic catalogue racer of the 1930s was the Albatros. Originally intended for privateers, this assumed premier road racing status following the end of the Second World War. Moto Guzzi

BOTTOM The supercharged 250 was more successful when used for record attempts. In 1948, Luigi Cavanna set four world speed records with a resurrected pre-war supercharged 250. Moto Guzzi

BELOW Another classic catalogue racer of the 1930s was the Albatros. Originally intended for privateers, this assumed premier road racing status following the end of the Second World War. Moto Guzzi

hydronalium alloy rear section.

Other chassis parts too were shared with the Condor, in particular the 200mm electron brakes and 21in aluminium-rimmed wheels. With full electrical equipment the Albatros weighed 135kg (298lb), but specially prepared racing versions were only 115–120kg (254–265lb). Even more expensive than the Condor, Albatros production was severely affected by the outbreak of the war and only 25 were manufactured during 1939. Lorenzetti did however manage to win the 250cc Italian Championship (2nd Category) in 1940 before hostilities interrupted motorcycle competition.

Replacing the unremarkable P.E.S., the Albatros was even more sophisticated than the Condor, with a bevel-gear-driven single-overhead camshaft engine derived from the racing 250s. Designed by Carlo Guzzi with the assistance of Carcano, the Albatros had the usual 68 x 68mm dimensions, but with an 8.5:1 compression ratio, and Dell'Orto SS30M carburettor. With 33mm inlet and 31mm exhaust valves it initially produced 20 horsepower at 7,000rpm on a petrol-benzol mixture. The crankcases were the same as for the supercharged 250, cast in electron, as were the straight-cut primary gears. The frame was similar to the Condor with its

# THE EGRETTA, ARDETTA, AIRONE, G.T. 20, ALCE, TRIALCE AND ER

Regular production during 1939 was still centred on the same seven versions of 500cc machines as before, plus the cheaper 246cc P series. The P.L.S. became the Egretta (with the 12 horsepower P.E.S. engine), much the same as before but with an improved finish, and the basic P.L. became the Ardetta, with coil rather than

**BELOW** The G.T. 20 was built specifically as a military motorcycle but was short lived and was soon replaced by the Alce.
Moto Guzzi

magneto ignition. This very basic machine was the cheapest in the range and was available through a special hire purchase arrangement with fascist party clubs.

There was also one new P series machine for 1939 that would figure more prominently in later years, the Airone (Heron). This 246cc machine had Marelli magneto ignition, a four-speed foot-operated gearbox and a tubular (rather than pressed-steel) sprung frame. When it was launched it was still called a P.E., but this was soon changed to Airone. Power was up to 9.5 horsepower at 4,800rpm, giving a top speed around 95km/h (59mph). The Airone was quite popular in the year leading up to the war, with 997 being manufactured. The 1940 version of the Airone featured a pressed-steel frame derived from the Ardetta and P.L.

Like the Condor, production of the G.T. 20 military motorcycles in 1938 was on a limited scale, and it was really an interim model. From experience gained with the G.T. 17 during the war in Ethiopia in 1936, the G.T. 20 was designed for a more specific military application, in particular improved ground clearance. Although the basic 13.2 horsepower overhead exhaust and side inlet valve engine was retained, it was now derived from the S and featured a four-speed hand-operated gearbox. The new frame mounted the engine higher and the front and rear wheels were interchangeable. Although only a few were built, its successor the Alce was to be Guzzi's most famous military motorcycle.

Similar to the short-lived G.T. 20, the Alce had an oil pump automatic valve and alterations to the stand, exhaust pipes, and tool boxes. Produced until 1945,

still with the opposed-valve 13.2 horsepower engine, the Alce was the predominant vehicle for the Italian motorcycle corps. After the war it also continued to be produced in limited numbers until 1958, by which time it had evolved into the Superalce, with the V engine. The Alce was also produced in small truck form, the Trialce between 1940 and 1943. Some of these were designed to be parachuted from aeroplanes. Another significant three-wheeler was the civilian ER that was produced from 1938 until 1941. More a truck than a motorcycle, this featured the 17.8 horsepower V engine and had three forward speeds plus reverse. While its 1,000kg (2,205lb) carrying capacity was not much higher than before, the ER was a much stronger vehicle. It soon gained a reputation for being unbreakable.

As Italy did not enter the Second World War until June 1940, the Guzzi factory operated as normal until that year. There was even a Milano–Taranto event held on 6 May. This time, Guido Cerato rode a Condor to victory at 103.036km/h (64mph), with the supercharged 250 of Alberti finishing second. That month also saw the appearance of a bike that could have made Guzzi unbeatable in the 500cc class if the war had not intervened, the Tre Cilindri 500.

## THE TRE CILINDRI 500

Developed in 1939 as an answer to the supercharged Gilera, BMW and NSU, Guzzi's supercharged 500 triple again exhibited Carlo Guzzi's capacity for originality. Foremost was the use of aluminium for the cylinder head and barrels with cast-iron liners, an all

**RIGHT** The 500cc supercharged triple of 1940 was an extremely advanced design, with twin overhead camshafts driven by gears on the right-side of the engine. Inclining the cylinders forward allowed room for the supercharger.

**OPPOSITE**
Unfortunately, the triple was a victim of poor timing. Hostilities interrupted development and after the war superchargers were banned from competition.

enclosed valve system, and a five-speed gearbox. Inclined at 45°, the three-cylinder 59 x 60mm engine had twin overhead camshafts driven by a chain on the right side. Two valves per cylinder were used, inclined at 62°, and with an 8:1 compression ratio and a Cozette supercharger power was about 55–60 horsepower. This was despite Sandri enthusiastically claiming it produced around 85 horsepower at 8,000rpm after tests on the Bergamo–Brescia autostrada on 11 March 1940. Like the earlier three-cylinder, the four-bearing crankshaft had the cranks spaced at 120°. Lubrication was dry sump with the oil reservoir incorporated in the fuel tank, as was fairly usual Guzzi practice.

The composite frame featured a tubular top section with the engine hung underneath, and a hydronalium rear pressing with the usual Guzzi rear suspension. The Brampton fork, 21 inch wheels and electron brakes were from the Condor, and if there was a disadvantage to the new machine it was in the weight of 175kg (386lb). It was also longer than both the Condor and Bicilindrica with a 1,470mm (58in) wheelbase. Only raced once by Sandri, at the Lido di Albaro circuit at Genoa on 26 May, it retired but had showed promise. On this occasion the front brake was a much larger, 280mm unit. Unfortunately, the timing of its appearance could not have been worse. Italy joined the war and when racing commenced again superchargers were banned.

# THE 500U

By now Guzzi was almost totally committed to the production of military motorcycles, the Alce, Trialce, and from 1942, the Motocarri 500U. There were no resources for the manufacture of any other models and it was not until late in 1945 that normal production could be resumed. Some experimental work had continued during the war, notably the G.T.E. of 1942 that used a four-valve version of the 500cc single and produced 18.9 horsepower. The Motocarri 500U superseded the ER and was considerably more heavy duty than the Trialce. The U featured a fan-cooled overhead-valve 500cc V engine, the first time this unit was used in a military vehicle. It produced 17.8 horsepower at 4,300rpm allowing a 1,000kg (2,205lb) payload. A differential reduction provided six forward and two reverse gears.

This vehicle, with 1,608 manufactured in 1943 alone, formed the basis of production during the war. When the war finally ended however, Guzzi was fortunately more prepared than many other manufacturers. Being situated on Lake Como, away from the regular industrial centre around Milan, had saved the company from extensive Allied bombing. Moto Guzzi emerged from the devastation ready to take on the world in providing cheap transport. That in turn provided the company with the resources to become a major force in motorcycle road racing.

Descended from the
pre-war Condor, the
Dondolino was one of the
most successful privateer
racing Guzzis.

# 3 POST-WAR RACING: SUCCESS WITH EARLIER DESIGNS

As soon as motorcycle road racing resumed after the end of the Second World War, Moto Guzzi re-entered that world of competition. With supercharging banned by the FIM, both the supercharged 250 and 500 triple were rendered obsolete so that left the way open for the return of the pre-war Bicilindrica. Guzzi also decided to develop the pre-war single-cylinder Albatros and Condor.

Initially, these were catalogue racers in the style of the earlier bikes, but soon they were developed into more specialised machines. As the Albatros was a full racing design anyway this was not too difficult, but the Condor needed more serious treatment and evolved into the equally magnificent Dondolino and the official factory Gambalunga. Breaking from the tradition of using ornithological names, Dondolino meant 'rocking chair', because of its suspect road holding. Gambalunga, or 'long-leg', signified a longer-stroke engine.

## THE DONDOLINO

Faced with more intense competition, particularly from the Gilera Saturno that had appeared in 1940, the Dondolino of 1946 was essentially a tuned Condor. The frame was identical, but the rear suspension used only a single spring and as most Dondolinos were produced without electrical equipment, the weight was reduced to 128kg (282lb). Braking was improved by a 260mm front drum brake, with internal controls to improve streamlining, along with a 220 x 50mm rear brake. Most changes occurred in the engine. The inlet valve was 44mm, with a 40mm exhaust valve. The compression ratio was increased to 8.5:1, and with a Dell'Orto SS 35M carburettor, power was up to 33 horsepower at 5,500rpm. This gave the Dondolino a top speed around 170km/h (106mph).

The Dondolino was immediately a match for the Saturno and soon forced Gilera to release a 35 horsepower 'Sanremo' version. In its first race on 12 May 1946 Luigi Ruggeri finished second to Bandirolo's Saturno at the Circuito del Luino. One week later he won the second category at the Circuito di Regio Emilia. In the hands of factory rider Nando

**BELOW** Although closely related to the Dondolino, the Gambalunga had a different frame and leading link forks. Early versions were painted silver and each year saw further development. This is the 1947 version. Moto Guzzi

Balzarotti the Dondolino won the 1946 500cc Spanish Grand Prix at Barcelona. It was also successful in other 1946 events but the Dondolino's forte was really in second division championship races and the long distance events like the Milano–Taranto. Ruggeri took the 1946 500cc Italian Championship (2nd Category) and in the Milano–Taranto the Dondolino continued to be successful well after production had ended in 1951. When the Milano-Taranto race was recreated on 17 May 1950, it was the Dondolino of Guido Leoni that triumphed over Priamo's Gilera at an average speed of 102.033km/h (63mph).

Although not the fastest bike in its class, the Dondolino became renowned for its ruggedness and strength on these long events. Victories followed in 1951, 1952 and 1953; Bruno Franchisi won in 1951 and 1952, increasing the speed to 112.317km/h (69.75mph) and by Duilio Agostini in 1953. Sergio Pinza and Alberti Amaldo gave the Dondolino its final important results, class wins in 1954 and the last event of 1956.

The Dondolino was built in small batches for privateers from 1946 until 1951 (54 units). Each batch differed in small details, some had a spoiler under the engine, a stiffer rear spring, a smaller rear mudguard or a larger oil tank. In 1949 it was listed at a price twice that of the 500cc G.T.V. or G.T.W., so it was for serious racers only.

# THE GAMBALUNGA

In 1946, a Dondolino was developed into a works bike by Ing Carcano, and the result was the Gambalunga. In a manner typical of many Italian companies, the factory wanted to provide something special for an Italian rider who showed promise, in this case factory tester Balzarotti. By decreasing the bore to 84mm and increasing the stroke to 90mm, the Gambalunga was the first 500cc single-cylinder Moto Guzzi to break with the traditional oversquare bore and stroke. The longer stroke was used in an effort to reduce the stress on the main bearings by reducing the rod angularity. Running on the low octane fuel required of the period the compression ratio was 8:1.

Even though it produced more power than the Dondolino, 35 horsepower at 5,800rpm, the long stroke engine was not a total success and, for the 1948 Italian Grand Prix at Faenza, Guzzi reverted to the short-stroke engine on the factory-prepared Gambalunga. Now with an additional roller main bearing housed in the primary drive cover, this engine was known as the 'Tipo Faenza' which was also shared with the regular production Dondolino.

Where the Gambalunga really deviated from the Dondolino was in the use of leading link front forks, a particular favourite of Carcano, and something that

BELOW The 1950
Gambalunga had 20in
wheels and revised rear
suspension.

would feature on nearly all racing Guzzis over the next ten years. In an era where the telescopic fork was predominant, the use of leading link forks was another Guzzi trademark. In addition, there was a completely redesigned fuel tank, rear mudguard and slightly altered frame with different rear frame plates and front downtubes. The oil tank was mounted under the seat, but possibly the most striking thing about the Gambalunga was its colour: silver paint with blue lettering. The weight, too, was slightly reduced in comparison with the Dondolino, to 125kg (276lb).

Considering that the Gambalunga was still a single-cylinder with pushrod-operated overhead valves, it was surprisingly successful. In 1947 Lorenzetti won the Italian Grand Prix, following that with a victory in Geneva, while its most significant success was the 1948 European Grand Prix at Ulster. By then, most 500cc factory racing duties were assigned to the Bicilindrica, the lighter Gambalunga being kept mainly for the road circuits where its lack

of horsepower was more than compensated for by the light weight and ease of riding. After 1948, the Gambalunga was occasionally made available to privateers and continued to be developed, and won important events through until 1953. That year, Szabo won the Hungarian Championship and Jean Behra won successive French Championships from 1949 until 1951.

Although still strongly derived from the pre-war Condor, the Gambalunga had a thoroughly developed racing engine. The crankcases were cast in electron, and the cylinders and head in aluminium. All the engine components were manufactured from the finest materials available at that time. Features such as the uncaged big-end rollers were unusual but did not limit the reliability and life of the engine as the engine speeds were quite moderate. The con-rods were still bolted together to retain these 24 x 3mm rollers. The inlet valve was now 46mm and the sodium-filled exhaust valve was 40mm, these set at an angle of 60°.

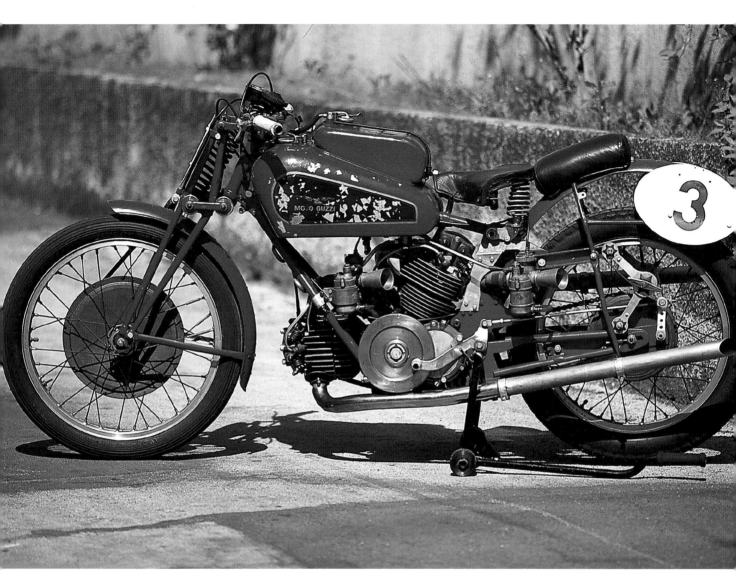

In 1950, the Gambalunga was lowered to improve streamlining. The rear mudguard was modified and 20in wheels replaced the 21in of the earlier machine. There was a revised frame, stronger around the steering head to cope with the increased forces of the leading link forks, but also included was a new swingarm, rear 'L' supports and upper friction damper mounting tubes. All these machines now had the short stroke engine so 'Gambalunga' was technically no longer the correct designation.

The following year the final Gambalunga appeared, now with another rear mudguard/seat unit and an engine with a 35mm remote float bowl Dell'Orto carburettor producing 37 horsepower at 6,000rpm. This final version was again red but the quest for aerodynamic efficiency had meant that the Gambalunga lost the classic lines of the Condor and Dondolino. There was a functional elegance about the design but not the beauty of those less exotic earlier machines.

## THE 500 BICILINDRICA

The banning of supercharging immediately after the war allowed the pre-war Bicilindrica to be brought out of retirement to resume racing duties. Limited to the 72 octane petrol available at the time, the maximum power was reduced to 42 horsepower, and the corresponding top speed to around 180km/h (112mph). This was not really enough to make the twin totally competitive; however the great rider Tenni still won the 1947 Italian Championship on a Bicilindrica.

There were only a few changes from the pre-war version with its Brampton forks. The cylinder heads and cylinders (with cast-iron liners) were cast in electron, the rear cylinder now having horizontal finning. In 1948, the Bicilindrica received a new frame, designed by Antonio Micucci, and telescopic forks. The frame was quite advanced, using the upper tube as an oil tank, and the Micucci-designed forks featured hydraulic damping and a leading axle. With its bulbous tank it was an unusual-looking motorcycle, but was exceptionally well engineered.

Tenni took it to the Isle of Man where he entered the Senior TT. This time he could not emulate his Lightweight win of 1937 as he was slowed by ignition problems after the fourth lap, but he still set the fastest lap at nearly 141km/h (88mph). This would be Tenni's final race as he was killed testing the experimental 250 twin in practice for the Swiss Grand Prix at Berne shortly afterwards. The Bicilindrica remained competitive in the Italian Championship, Bertacchini winning this in 1948. The Bicilindrica was also used to set several world records that year, in particular in Piero Taruffi's four-wheeled Bisiluro that achieved a top speed of 207km/h (129mph).

# THE ALBATROS

The 250 Albatros of 1939–40 was to be even more successful than the 500s in its transition to post-war competition. Still very much based on the 1926 TT250, unlike the Dondolino and Gambalunga, the Albatros was an uncompromised racing design from the outset. Following the failure of the new 250 Parallel Twin the Albatros also became the basis of the factory 250s, and during 1946–48 was almost unbeatable in its class.

Martelli won the 250cc Italian Championship in 1946, Tenni in 1947, and Lorenzetti in 1948. At the 1947 Isle of Man Tourist Trophy races, the first since the end of the war, Irish rider Manliff Barrington rode an Albatros to victory in the Lightweight TT at an average speed of 73.22mph (118km/h), with Maurice Cann second. Cann took out the event the following year at 75.18mph (121km/h).

Compared with the pre-war Albatros, the post-war version lost the electrical system and kickstart, and eventually the casting on the crankcase for the dynamo. This reduced the weight to around 120kg (265lb). Despite the low octane fuel, power was increased to 23 horsepower at 7,000rpm with a larger carburettor (32mm), and a larger inlet valve (35mm). Top speed was around 170km/h (105mph). However, by 1948 the Albatros, with its girder forks, pre-war brakes, and an obsolete chassis, was coming under some pressure from the resurrected Benelli. This would be rectified in 1949 with the Gambalunghino. Although the Gambalunghino usurped it as a Grand Prix racer, and the Albatros was not offered after 1949, it continued to have a highly successful life as a privateer 250 in Italy and other countries until 1954. Many were fitted with later Gambalunghino parts to keep them competitive. The Albatros was always an expensive motorcycle, on a par with the Dondolino, and only 34 were manufactured between 1940 and 1949.

# THE 250 BICILINDRICA (PARALLEL TWIN)

It had been intended to replace the 250 single with a new twin in 1947 but this did not happen. Two prototypes were constructed, one in 1947 and another in 1948, but they proved disappointing. The air-cooled double overhead camshaft parallel twin was an interesting design but with a 10:1 compression ratio could only manage 25 horsepower at 9,000rpm after some development. Designed by Antonio Micucci, the all-alloy engine had square dimensions of 54 x 54mm, dry sump lubrication with an external oil tank, and a four-speed gearbox. The cylinders were inclined at 60° from the vertical and the twin overhead camshafts driven by a train of five spur gears. The 360° crankshaft was in one piece with three main bearings. The cylinder head featured 29mm inlet and 23mm exhaust valves inclined at a wide 80° with two coil springs per valve.

The biggest handicap facing the Parallel Twin was that it was originally intended to be run with a supercharger, but these were banned before the design was completed. As with many other immediate post-war designs, few alterations were made to compensate. Thus the Parallel Twin was left with several features that were less than optimum for an unsupercharged engine, notably the wide valve angle and a heavy weight intended to withstand increased horsepower and rpm.

Technologically advanced materials were used throughout in the 250 twin. Electron for the crankcases, cylinders and brakes, hydronalium for the frame, and aluminium-bronze combustion chambers. With leading-axle telescopic front forks, and a light weight of only 125kg (276lb), it would have been expected to outclass the Albatros, but this was not the case. Testing only confirmed the superiority of the traditional Moto Guzzi layout that provided a lower centre of gravity for a better balanced machine, although two were taken to the Isle of Man in 1948. Manliff Barrington then showed that the twin was not a lost cause when he led the Lightweight TT for the first two laps at an average speed around 75km/h (47mph). Unfortunately, the death of Omobono Tenni while testing the Bicilindrica 250 a month later sealed its fate, and there was no further development.

In 1949 came the inaugural World Championship for motorcycles, an event in which Guzzi, like most manufacturers, was especially keen to participate. Prior to that year there had been only individual Grands Prix, and the European Championship. Thus, entries from the various manufacturers in Italy, Britain, and Germany were largely dependent on the particular event. Now there was an opportunity for all manufacturers to compete for one championship and it was the start of a golden era of racing. Taking the Albatros and transforming it into the Gambalunghino, as well as more development of the Bicilindrica, gave Guzzi the perfect machines for this new championship. As with the 1930s, the 1950s was to be one of the great decades for the company.

**LEFT** The final Albatros of 1949 included a Gambalunga-style rear mudguard but retained the girder fork. Moto Guzzi

**BELOW** Although technologically quite advanced, the 250 Parallel twin failed to meet expectations.

Replacing the Airone, the 235cc Lodola Gran Turismo offered performance, which was even more sedate performance than that of the 175. The overhead camshaft made way for pushrods and rockers, and weight was increased to 115kg (254lb).

# 4 EXPANDING THE CUSTOMER BASE

While it was race track glory that had always given Moto Guzzi its reputation, none of that success would have been possible without secure financial and managerial backing. Much of the production during the 1930s had consisted of the smaller P series, but it had been the venerable unsprung Sport 15 with the opposed-valve engine that had still dominated in terms of sales.

Production during the war had largely been limited to military vehicles of 500cc, but after the Second World War there was little demand for both military vehicles or larger capacity motorcycles. As with many other Italian motorcycle manufacturers, survival in those rather grim days relied on producing vehicles that people could afford. Immediately responding to market demands, there was now a distinct change in emphasis in the type of motorcycles manufactured.

With the release of the two-stroke 64cc Guzzino, Guzzi entered the world of mass production. Soon renamed the Motoleggera 65, this was so successful that production at Mandello increased from 4,518 in 1946 to 15,654 in 1947. By 1950, total Moto Guzzi production was 30,236 motorcycles, 22,115 of which were 65cc two-strokes. These mundane vehicles of transportation may have been of little interest to the enthusiast, but the revenue generated from their sales enabled Moto Guzzi to expand its racing programme and create expensive and sophisticated racing prototypes. Because of this they are extremely important in an historical context.

Guzzi was also fortunate in that, during the early part of the 1950s, it made very few marketing errors and most of its products were sound. Problems for Moto Guzzi occurred towards the end of the decade, and into the 1960s, when it failed to respond to the general downturn facing motorcycling.

Much of the initial credit for this great post-war revival of Moto Guzzi must go to Enrico Parodi, Giorgio's brother. Enrico had joined the company in 1942 while Giorgio was serving with the Italian forces. Injuries sustained to his eyes and arm saw Giorgio retire to Genoa in 1945, Enrico then taking over as day-to-day manager, even though he still spent much time in Genoa. By this time, Emanuele Vittorio, and his nephew, Angelo, had died. Giorgio still maintained an interest in what was happening at Mandello, but died suddenly in August 1955.

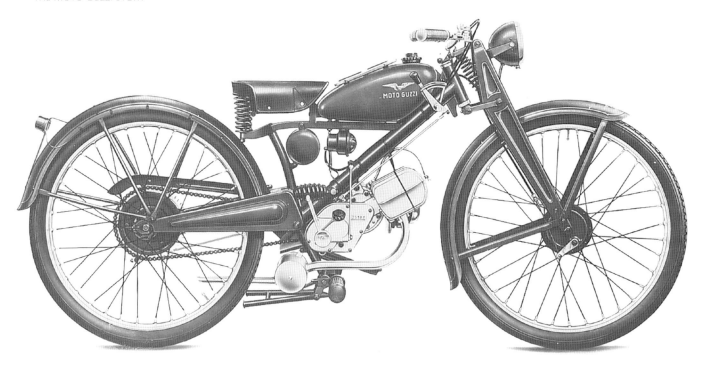

Unfortunately, while undoubtedly a brilliant man, Enrico later lost direction and foresight, contributing to the crisis the company faced during the 1960s. When Carlo Guzzi also died in November 1964 Enrico was left to salvage what he could but by then it was too late. By 1966 the Parodi fortune had been lost and the company was put into receivership.

# GUZZINO, MOTOLEGGERA AND CARDELLINO

Enrico Parodi always saw cheap and basic transportation at the lower end of the market as the key for survival. Sensing this demand even before the end of the war, he had Carlo Guzzi initially design a 38cc two-stroke engine that could be mounted on a bicycle in the manner of Ducati's Cucciolo. Soon this idea, the Colibrì (Hummingbird), was replaced by one that incorporated a 65cc two-stroke engine in a complete frame and running gear, and thus the Guzzino was born. With Carlo Guzzi now assuming an elder statesman design role, other engineers were given more responsibility. Carcano was involved in developing the Gambalunga, and Antonio Micucci the Guzzino. Micucci had joined the company during the war as a two-stroke specialist, and had started work on the Guzzino as early as 1944.

Where the Guzzino really succeeded was that it looked and operated more like a motorcycle than its competition, which in 1946 were primarily bicycles with engines attached. Although it had 26in wheels the blade-type front forks were sprung, as was the pressed-steel swingarm. Both wheels featured lateral drum brakes. The frame was an excellent and simple design, consisting of a single, straight 50mm tube connecting the steering head with the swingarm. A subframe supporting the 6.5-litre fuel tank and solo seat was attached to this frame tube.

The engine mounted underneath the frame. This too was quite advanced for its day, being a 64cc two-stroke with rotary valve induction. Cast entirely in aluminium, with the cylinder inclined 30° to the horizontal, the 42 x 46mm engine produced a modest 2 horsepower at 5,000rpm. Because of the poor fuel available the compression ratio was only 5.5:1, with the cylinder fed by a Dell'Orto MA13mm carburettor. In typical Guzzi fashion the primary drive was by gear (initially straight-cut but soon helical) and the clutch a wet multi-plate type. The gearbox was a hand-change three-speed. Weighing only 45kg (99lb), the top speed was hardly earth-shattering at 50km/h (31mph). The most significant aspect of the Guzzino was that it was cheap and reliable, and hence hugely popular in an era where basic transportation was in demand.

With a name change to Motoleggera 65, production continued virtually the same through until 1949 when it was fitted with a stronger swingarm, reinforced forks, and a cast-iron cylinder. On 28 February 1948, Guzzi once again attempted several world speed records, one with a modified Motoleggera. Raffaele Alberti set a 75cc flying mile record at 59.7mph (96.072km/h) amongst others. On the Charrat-Saxon road in Switzerland Luigi Cavanna also set several 350cc records at the same time with the supercharged 250. Later at Montlhéry further records were set with a 73cc version (46 x 46mm) of the Motoleggera. In September 1950, ridden by Gianni Leoni and Bruno Ruffo in addition to Alberti, a total of 33 75cc and 100cc records were established.

The little Motoleggera had such a following during those years immediately after the war that in 1949 Moto Guzzi organised a rally at Mandello for Guzzino owners. This was so successful that 14,000 people attended, with over 12,500 bikes, causing a traffic jam all the way to the nearby town of Lecco. Gradually the price and specification was reduced until 1954 when the Motoleggera became the Cardellino (Goldfinch). As with all successful Guzzi designs, the basic Guzzino of 1946 was to have a

long production run, the Cardellino finally ending in 1963. The success of the Motoleggera resulted in it being also built as a joint venture with Moto Guzzi Hispania of Barcelona. The bikes were identical, but for tank and side cover decals.

With buyers now turning towards larger displacement motorcycles, the Cardellino initially remained at 65cc but with a lower price and specification than before. Most noticeable was a reduction in wheel size to 20in and a rear subframe that included a mudguard attachment with adjustable friction shock absorbers. The Cardellino received telescopic front forks and revised styling in 1955, and by 1957 the engine had grown to 73cc.

Now in two versions, the Lusso (Luxury) and Turismo, the 45 x 46mm engine produced 2.6 horsepower at 5,200rpm with a 6.4:1 compression ratio. The Lusso had a larger, 8.5-litre fuel tank and had gained some girth over its predecessor, weighing in at 60kg (132lb). The Turismo weighed slightly less at 57kg (125lb). Finally, the hand-gearchange was replaced by a foot-operated type. In 1958, the Nuovo Cardellino featured the 73cc engine with the aluminium cylinder and hard-chromed barrel that had been pioneered on the Zigolo.

The final development of the Cardellino was the 83cc version of 1962. Boring the 73cc engine to 48mm and increasing the compression to 7:1 saw the power increase modestly to 2.9 horsepower at 5,200rpm. The 83 Cardellino also featured twin shock-absorber rear suspension and weighed around 58kg (128lb). Production ended in 1963 with 3,732 units constructed that year. By that time the design was beginning to show its age. It was still a three-speed two-stroke single that could barely top 65km/h (40mph). Not surprisingly, there was little demand for such basic transportation, especially considering the recession facing the motorcycle market in general. To further seal the Cardellino's fate, the company was in crisis in the mid-1960s.

## THE GALLETTO

Following the success of the Guzzino rally in 1949, Carlo Guzzi decided the time was right for a slightly larger utilitarian motorcycle. An unusual and highly successful motorcycle/scooter hybrid, this was called the Galletto (Cockerel). Indicative of Enrico Parodi's intuitive feeling for the market during those post-war years, the Galletto was neither a true scooter nor a motorcycle. It was designed so that a woman could operate it wearing a dress, hence the enclosure of the engine and large rear mudguard. Other practical features called for the Galletto to turn almost around its axis. While Ducati failed miserably with their ambitious scooter, the Cruiser of 1953, Guzzi found a niche with the Galletto. After a peak of 12,305 in 1950, production settled down to around 4,000 a year before declining in the early 1960s.

Distinguished by interchangeable, 17in wheels (including an optional spare), the Galletto offered the limited weather protection of a scooter, with a tubular and pressed-steel frame incorporating the steering head and fuel tank. The spare wheel could be mounted in front of the engine and also functioned as a crash bar. For those Gallettos without a spare wheel there was an aluminium cover. Many of the other body parts too were aluminium, in particular the instrument mounting plate, engine side cover plates and leg shields on the early versions.

The overhead-valve four-stroke engine was designed by Carlo Guzzi specifically for the Galletto and was initially 150cc with a bore and stroke of 60 x 53mm. The crankcase, cylinder and cylinder head were cast in aluminium. It was a typical Guzzi horizontal single with an external flywheel, but it had the crankshaft unusually incorporated in the left crankcase with only one flywheel. By the time it went into production the engine had grown to 160cc (62mm bore) and this size lasted until 1952. The 26mm valves were operated by pushrods and rockers, and lubrication was dry sump. With a

5.6:1 compression ratio and a Dell'Orto MA 18 BS 1 carburettor, 6 horsepower was produced at 5,200rpm. The three-speed gearbox was operated by a pedal. The front suspension was by leading link forks, and the rear by a single-sided swingarm with horizontal coil springs and an eccentric chain adjuster. The standard colour was an ivory-beige, and with a weight of 107kg (236lb) the 160cc Galletto was capable of around 80km/h (50mph).

Barely two years later the Galletto was uprated to 175cc by boring the engine to 65mm. The compression ratio was increased slightly to 6:1 and a four-speed gearbox fitted. This version lasted two years before the engine grew again in 1954, to 192cc. By lengthening the stroke of the 175 to 58mm and increasing the compression ratio once again (to 6.4:1), 7.5 horsepower was now developed at 5,200rpm. The cylinder was now cast iron instead of alloy with a liner. On the 192 the flywheel magneto was deleted and a dynamo mounted above the engine along with battery and coil ignition, which meant a higher engine enclosure. Other small changes were a smaller rear mudguard and larger

headlight. In this guise the Galletto remained unchanged through until 1960.

The final version appeared in 1961, still with the 192cc engine but now with 7.7 horsepower and a 7:1 compression ratio. In an endeavour to compete with the new compact cars that were becoming more affordable, a Marelli 12-volt 75-watt dynastart was attached behind the engine and connected to the flywheel by a V belt for starting. New bodywork included an aluminium headlight enclosure and load adjustable hydraulic shock absorbers accompanied the electric start that unfortunately was not the most reliable system. It was mounted behind the engine where it was susceptible to debris thrown from the rear wheel.

There was also a considerable increase in weight due to the added electrical equipment, to 134kg (295lb), but the top speed remained in the region of 85km/h (53mph). The cosmetic facelift and electric start still was not enough to save the Galletto and production ended in 1965 when only 1,500 were manufactured. Problems with the electric start notwithstanding,

the Galletto over its 15-year production established itself as a well-designed and well-engineered vehicle with exceptional reliability. A tribute to its excellence is that in the small towns of Italy, and particularly those around Lake Como, Gallettos are still a regular sight on the roads. That is something that cannot be said about too many other utilitarian motorcycles nearly 50 years old.

## THE ZIGOLO

In 1953 the two-stroke line was also expanded with the addition of the 98cc Zigolo (Bunting). This was a new design intended to fill the gap between the Motoleggera and Galletto and was also unusual in that it featured partially enclosed bodywork. The Micucci-designed rotary-valve two-stroke differed considerably from that of the Motoleggera. Not only was the cylinder horizontal, but there were completely new crankcases. With square engine dimensions (50 x 50mm) and a 6:1 compression ratio, the first Zigolo produced 4 horsepower at 5,200rpm.

With its 19in wheels the Zigolo looked more like a motorcycle than the Motoleggera, but offered a very basic specification. The front suspension was by undamped telescopic forks, while the rear swingarm used a rubber element in compression with Hartford-type friction dampers. Underneath the bodywork was a spine frame and while weighing in at 75kg (165lb), the three-speed Zigolo could achieve 76km/h (47mph). To emphasise the utilitarian nature of the machine it was painted grey, even the wheel rims. There was no chrome and the rear friction dampers and silencer were blued.

With initial production of 6,107 in 1953, Moto Guzzi was so encouraged by the reception to the Zigolo that a more powerful dual seat Sport version was planned for the following year. This did not happen, but 1954 saw the Lusso, with much more attractive red paintwork and a chromed fuel tank. Although the engine was unchanged, the Lusso also had a dual seat and was distinguished by 17in wheels. Introduction of the Lusso saw production of the Zigolo more than double to 14,793 in 1954 and 15,800 in 1955. It was interesting that during this heyday period of racing for Moto Guzzi, when total production was around 40,000 machines a year, the Cardellino, Galletto, and Zigolo accounted for the entire output other than 2–3,000 Airones and a few hundred Falcones.

In 1958, the Zigolo Series II was introduced. While only in production for two years, this now featured a light alloy cylinder with a hard chromed barrel that had been pioneered on the Grand Prix racing four-strokes. It was a significant technical advance for two-stroke engines and soon found its way to the Cardellino. Later it would feature on four-stroke Moto Guzzi engines, in particular the later V7. This new cylinder allowed the compression ratio to be increased to 7.5:1 and power to 4.6 horsepower at 5,200rpm. With the 17in wheels of the Lusso, the Series II weighed 77kg (170lb) and had a top speed of around 80km/h (50mph).

The final version of the Zigolo appeared in 1959 and ran through until 1965. Now with a bore and stroke of 52 x 52mm, the 110cc Zigolo with a compression ratio of 7.5:1 produced 4.2 horsepower at 5,200rpm. The carburettor was now a Dell'Orto MAF 18 B1 (up from 15mm), the exhaust became a canister type underneath the swingarm, and the telescopic front forks

now featured oil damping. Weight was much the same as before at 78kg (172lb), but the three-speed Zigolo 110 was still pressed to achieve 80km/h (50mph). By 1965, this modest performance was no longer satisfactory and although 110 Zigolo production had initially peaked at 12,310 in 1960, by 1965 only 1,925 were manufactured. The motorcycle was not only obsolete by that stage, but also one out of tune with the marketplace.

# THE LODOLA

Since the inaugural World Championship of 1949, Moto Guzzi had been one of the foremost names on the racetrack. By 1956 the company had won a considerable number of world and national championship events and was pouring considerable energy and resources into its racing programme. Yet in terms of production Moto Guzzi was still manufacturing two-strokes of 65cc and 98cc: the utilitarian Galletto, and the ageing Astore and Falcone. There seemed to be no correlation between the magnificent racing motorcycles and the Moto Guzzis available to the consumer.

The first Giro d'Italia, a road race for motorcycles up to 175cc took place in 1953, and proved exceptionally successful, even rivalling the traditional Milano–Taranto event. Seeing the domestic demand for lightweight sporting motorcycles increasing, Enrico Parodi encouraged Carlo Guzzi to design one last engine before retiring. The result was the Lodola (Skylark), a 175cc overhead camshaft four-stroke single that sported many new features for a Moto Guzzi.

Even though the Lodola was not really envisaged as a competition machine in the manner of the contemporary Mondial and Ducati, market demands dictated that Carlo Guzzi incorporate an overhead camshaft in the design. Driven by a chain rather than the more expensive bevel gears as used by other manufacturers, the cylinder was inclined at 45° rather than horizontal. The camchain also featured a novel chain tensioner via a rocker and steel plate near the camshaft. This was intentionally designed to compensate for different rates of expansion. With oversquare dimensions of 62 x 57.8mm, the entire engine was cast in aluminium alloy. The 34mm inlet and 31mm exhaust valves used enclosed coil springs rather than the usual hairpin type and with a 7.5:1 compression ratio and a Dell'Orto UB 22 BS 2A carburettor, 9 horsepower was developed at 6,000rpm.

In many other respects the Lodola engine continued Guzzi traditions. The lubrication was dry sump and the flywheel was still outside the crankcases, although now hidden underneath an aluminium side cover. Primary drive was by helical gear, the clutch a wet multi-plate type, and there was a four-speed gearbox. The crankshaft was a three-piece affair with roller big-end and ball main bearings.

The frame was a full-duplex cradle type with oil damped telescopic front forks and a swingarm with twin shock absorbers. Brakes were a pair of single cast-iron drums laced to a pair of alloy wheel rims, an 18in on the front and a 17in on the rear. Weighing in at 109kg (240lb), the first Lodola was capable of around 110km/h (68mph). Unfortunately, this modest performance left the Lodola overshadowed by the competition from other Italian manufacturers, and in 1958 a Sport version was made available.

Although an increase in compression to 9:1 saw power up to 11 horsepower, the Sport was still a relatively sedate performer with a top speed of around 120km/h (75mph). Changes from the first Lodola included larger brakes and a dual seat. The shock absorbers could be adjusted into two positions: forward for solo and upright with a passenger. By 1958, production of the Lodola was 4,900, down from the 6,120 of the previous year. Moto Guzzi needed the model to be successful as they had tooled the plant at Mandello at considerable expense. Thus 1959 saw an increase in engine size to 235cc, the larger bike being titled the Gran Turismo and replacing the ageing Airone.

The increase in engine size also brought some major changes in the design. The single overhead camshaft was replaced by valves operated by pushrods and rockers, and the alloy cylinder by one of cast-iron. Both the bore and stroke were altered to achieve the increase in capacity, with the dimensions now being 68 x 64mm. Although less sporting than the 175, the 235 Lodola soon gained a reputation for solid and reliable, if not exciting, performance. It was also in a lower state of tune than the 175, and with its

7.5:1 compression ratio still produced 11 horsepower. Contributing to this milder tune was an air cleaner inside an airbox in front of the oil tank. With an increase in weight to 115kg (253½lb), the Gran Turismo had a similar performance to the earlier 175 Lodola Normale, and a top speed of around 110km/h (68mph).

After a hiccup in 1961, when only 650 Lodolas were produced, the Gran Turismo continued through until 1965. Although a prototype 247cc Sport version was displayed at the 1965 Milan Show, by then economic rationalisation meant that production of the Lodola was finished. It was indicative that the crisis at Moto Guzzi during the mid-1960s coincided with the departure of the four model lines that had sustained them so admirably during the 1950s. Unfortunately, the company also let these basic motorcycles run well past their 'sell-by date' and this undoubtedly contributed to the difficulties faced in 1966.

The Lodola did however have a competition life as a trials motorcycle. Following their withdrawal from road racing at the end of 1957, Moto Guzzi entered prepared Lodolas in selected trials events during 1958 in preparation for a more serious attempt the following year. Both 175cc and 235cc machines were developed (with overhead camshafts), the 175 weighing 107kg (236lb) and developing 12 horsepower at 7,500rpm. The 235 weighed 108kg (238lb) and produced 14 horsepower at 7,500rpm. In the International Six Day Trial (ISDT) held in Gottwaldov, Czechoslovakia in 1959, Guzzi riders took four gold medals, helping the Italian team to be placed second overall.

For 1960, the 235cc Lodola Regolarità was offered to privateers and while it featured a similar engine to the previous year's factory 235, the weight was up slightly to

110kg (242½lb). The factory continued to develop the Lodola for trials. Victories followed in the Italian Valli Bergamache Trials Championship, and six gold medals at the 1960 ISDT of Bad Ausee in Austria. In 1961, the capacity was increased to 247cc (68 x 68mm) with a five-speed gearbox. With an 11:1 compression ratio, 16 horsepower was now produced at 7,500rpm, enough for a string of successes and several gold medals in the 1961 and 1962 ISDTs.

The high point for the Lodola was the 1963 ISDT held in Spindleruv Mlyu, Czechoslovakia. With Guzzis comprising the entire Italian entry (five Lodolas and five Stornellos), Italy won the Silver Vase and all ten riders gained gold medals. In a world increasingly dominated by two-strokes, Moto Guzzi had shown the benefits and qualities of a well-developed four-stroke. At the end of that year, Guzzi withdrew from international trials competition and that was the final curtain for the Lodola Regolarità. The Stornello however, lived on a little longer.

## THE STORNELLO

At the same time as the Lodola lost its overhead camshaft for the cheaper solution of overhead valves operated by pushrods and rockers, Moto Guzzi decided to enter the world of the basic lightweight four-stroke with the Stornello (Starling). Given his first production bike since Guzzi's withdrawal from racing, Giulio Carcano designed this new machine to be intentionally cheap to manufacture. It incorporated many features unusual for a Guzzi. The single cylinder was only tilted 25° forward and the two overhead valves were mounted parallel and operated by pushrods and rockers. The lubrication was wet sump and the bore and stroke under square at 52 x 58mm.

The primary drive also had three helical gears so that unlike other Guzzis, the engine rotated forwards. The gearbox was four-speed, the clutch the usual multiplate type, and ignition by a flywheel magneto. It was also the first four-stroke engine to feature pressure die-cast crankcases. Hardly a high performance design, the 123cc Stornello Turismo of 1960 had an 8:1 compression ratio and a Dell'Orto ME 18 BS carburettor. Maximum power was 6.8 horsepower.

The duplex frame used the engine as a stressed member and telescopic forks, twin rear shock absorbers, and 17in wheels were fitted. Offered with either a single or dual seat, it made for a very small and light machine at 92kg (203lb), and with a 100km/h (62mph) top speed, performance was sprightly. Offering similar performance to the 235cc Lodola at a price 44 per cent less, the Stornello was immediately successful, and 5,610 were produced in 1960. Still, as a performance machine it was overshadowed by the competition and the end of 1961 saw the introduction of the Stornello Sport.

For the Sport there was a new cylinder head, now with inclined rather than parallel valves. The compression ratio was increased to 9.8:1, a Dell'Orto UB 20 B carburettor fitted, and power was up to 10 horsepower. Other changes included fitting lower handlebars, a racing-style seat, and 17in alloy wheel rims. The Sport ran through until 1967, by which time it had been slightly restyled but was essentially unchanged.

From 1965, many variations on the Stornello theme appeared. It was the only lightweight Guzzi to survive the rationalisation of 1966, and the first versions were a Scrambler, the F.S. (Fuori Strada) and Regolarità. The 125 Regolarità was derived from the prize-winning 1963 ISDT bikes and with a 24mm carburettor and 11.3:1 compression produced 12

horsepower at 8,000rpm. In 1965 and 1966 460 of these purpose-built competition machines were produced. These were joined during the latter year by the Sport America (or Sport USA), and the Scrambler USA. Some of these US bikes were also sold in Europe, including a few to the Italian police.

In 1968 the Stornello grew to 153cc (58 x 58mm bore and stroke) and the 160 was born. The magneto went for an alternator with battery and coil ignition and the weight increased to 107kg (236lb). The engine now featured a large bulge on the right crankcase cover for the alternator. Developing 12.6 horsepower at 7,500rpm, the 160 had a top speed of 118km/h (73mph).

Both the 125cc and 160cc versions of the Stornello came in for a redesign in 1971 and the range was rationalised to three versions: the 125, 160 and 125 Scrambler. These continued through until 1975 but only modest numbers were manufactured. To incorporate a five-speed gearbox the engine cases were redesigned with ugly alloy outer covers and both the 125 and 160 now featured inclined overhead valves. An increase in compression, to 9.6:1 for the 125, saw power increase to 13.4 horsepower at 7,400rpm. The 160 now had a 9.5:1 compression ratio and produced 16.2 horsepower at 7,400rpm. While there was also a corresponding increase in weight, to 113kg (249lb), the performance of the new five-speed versions was improved. The 125 could achieve 117km/h (73mph) and the 160 managed 122km/h (76mph). The Scrambler weighed slightly more at 117kg (260lb).

There was completely new suspension and bodywork for the new versions. However, by 1974 with Alejandro De Tomaso at the helm, it was obvious that the new range of smaller Moto Guzzis would be Benelli derived. Also regulations were beginning to call on all motorcycles to have a mandatory left-side gearshift and this meant another redesign. The final 1,040 Stornellos rolled out of Mandello in 1974, after a 15-year production run. From now on all small, single-cylinder Moto Guzzis would be two-strokes.

## THE DINGO

As he had been immediately after the war, Enrico Parodi was convinced, even in the early 1960s, that with the severe downturn affecting the industry, the future for Moto Guzzi lay in the production of motorcycles for the lower end of the market. Thus in 1963, as the Cardellino was being discontinued, the Dingo was born.

Produced in two versions, the Turismo and Sport, the 49cc Dingo two-stroke had a bore and stroke of 38.5 x 42mm and with a Dell'Orto SHA 14.9 carburettor produced 1.4 horsepower at 4,800rpm. A very basic machine, it featured a three-speed hand-change gearbox and a pressed-steel frame. In 1966, these two versions were joined by the Dingo Cross and the Dingo Super with a tubular steel frame, but most development occurred from 1967. Now the engine featured a four-speed foot-operated gearbox, and a GT version joined the Cross.

By this stage, Guzzi had become part of SEIMM, a government-controlled holding company (see Chapter 7). Despite the rationalisation that saw four models disappear, the unremarkable Dingo not only continued, but was developed further. In 1968 came a Dingo Supersport, and in 1970 the entire range was restyled. The three-speed Turismo (3V) returned, and there was a new version, the MM (Monomarcia) with an automatic centrifugal clutch and pedals. Unremarkable it may have been, but the Dingo was moderately successful. Even while it is not exactly the most fondly remembered Guzzi of the late 1960s and early '70s, the Dingo contributed to the commercial viability of the company prior to the De Tomaso era. Production continued until 1976.

## THE TROTTER AND CHIÙ

An even more basic machine emerged from Mandello in 1966, the 41cc Trotter. An entry-level, the two-stroke moped, it initially had an engine with a bore and stroke of 37 x 38mm. As cheap transportation it was a concept reminiscent of the Motoleggera but with its rigid frame and 16in wheels was even less of a real motorcycle. The Dell'Orto SHA 14.9 carburettor was mounted in front of the engine and a fitted with an automatic centrifugal clutch. In 1970, the Trotter grew to 49cc (38.5 x 42mm) and the cylinder was placed horizontally. There was now also the Trotter Special M with leading link front suspension, the Trotter Special V with a stepless transmission powered by a V-belt, and the Trotter Mark M with a rear swingarm.

Finally, there was the Trotter Mark V with the stepless transmission and the sprung frame. These four Trotters continued in production until 1973, by which time De Tomaso was more interested in promoting the Benelli two-strokes, and the Trotter evolved into the Chiù. The Trotter too, like the earlier Zigolo and

Dingo, was also produced in Spain as a Moto Guzzi Hispania.

With a new horizontal 49cc two-stroke engine (40 x 39mm), the Chiù was a much more modern looking machine than the Trotter. It had mechanical telescopic front forks and swingarm rear suspension and a more powerful, 1.5 horsepower, engine than the Nibbio and Cross 50s, also introduced in 1974. It continued as a Moto Guzzi until 1976, remaining as the Benelli Elle until the early 1980s.

## DE TOMASO BIKES: THE 250TS, 125, CROSS 50, NIBBIO, MAGNUM, 350/400GTS, 254, 125 2C 4T, 125 C AND 125 TT

The De Tomaso purchase of Moto Guzzi (see Chapter 8) saw the range expand to include a number of re-badged Benellis that were only superficially associated with Mandello del Lario. The first of these was the 250 TS that was produced from 1973 until 1982. Very much a Benelli 2C, this five-speed 56 x 47mm two-stroke twin was almost identical but for chrome cylinder bores and a larger, Dell'Orto VHB 25 B, carburettor. With a 10:1 compression ratio, 30 horsepower was produced at 7,400rpm. This gave the 129kg (284lb) TS sprightly performance and a top speed of around 150km/h (93mph).

The first version came with a twin leading shoe front drum brake which was replaced by a single 260mm Brembo front disc in 1975. That year it also gained electronic ignition and an ugly, square instrument panel. While the Benelli and Guzzi were similar, the Guzzi was sold as a more upmarket version, but both lacked convenience features like automatic oiling. Thus neither was successful against the Japanese in the market for middleweight two-strokes.

Shortly after the release of the 250 TS came three Benelli-inspired two-stroke 125 singles, the Trial, Tuttoterreno (a trail bike) and the Turismo. Like most of the Benellis that Guzzi inherited from De Tomaso, these were poorly designed and executed

motorcycles that did not compare very well with the
Japanese competition. Although sharing the same
120cc two-stroke engine and five-speed gearbox, the
Trial produced 14 horsepower at 6,500rpm, while the
Tuttoterreno and Turismo produced 15.4 horsepower.
They all shared a Dell'Orto VHB 22 BS carburettor
and while the off-road versions weighed 98kg (216lb),
the Turismo came in at 78.5kg (173lb). Another feature
of the Turismo was a single Grimeca 220mm front disc
brake. A few 125 Turismos were also sold in England
as Meriden's badge-engineered 'Co-Uno'.

After these 125s, there was the Cross 50 and
Nibbio, both with five-speed 50cc two-stroke engines,
which were in production from 1974 until 1982.
The Cross 50 underwent a number of modifications
and developments during its lifespan, notably a later
high-rise exhaust system and ABS bodywork. The
Nibbio was a touring version, styled along the lines of
the 125 Turismo. In 1976 the 50cc Magnum minibike
joined the range, but this only lasted until 1979.

One of De Tomaso's first projects with Benelli
had been to produce a single overhead camshaft
four-cylinder engine, which was in nearly every
respect a copy of a Honda design. In 1974 the 350cc
version became the Moto Guzzi 350 GTS. This was

closely based on the excellent Honda engine, but
with quality Italian chassis components and Bosch
electrics, and could have been a successful motorcycle.
Unfortunately, as with the Benelli 500 four, the Guzzi
was perceived as being too closely derivative of the
Honda. The 350 (50 x 44mm) produced 38 horsepower
at 9,500rpm and featured four Dell'Orto VHB 20 D
carburettors.

In 1975 the 350 gained a 300mm Brembo front disc
brake, and also grew to 400cc. Power from the 50 x
50.6mm engine was up to 40 horsepower. Weighing
in at 175kg (386lb), it was no lightweight but was a
smooth and sophisticated machine. However, at that
time Honda also released its CB400F but the world
was not ready for either bike. The Guzzi 350/400 GTS
lasted only until 1979.

Another of De Tomaso's more unusual projects
was the 254 of 1977. Also shared with a Benelli – the
Quattro – the Guzzi version had some unorthodox
features including the instruments mounted on the
fuel tank and plastic bodywork. The tiny four-
cylinder engine had cylinders reminiscent of the
earlier 500cc racing V8, but with a shorter stroke,
the bore and stroke being 44 x 38mm. The five-speed
single overhead camshaft 231cc engine was fed by

four Dell'Orto PHBG 18 B carburettors and with a 10.5:1 compression ratio produced 27.8 horsepower at 10,500rpm. A 260mm Grimeca front disc brake was fitted, the 254 running 18in cast alloy wheels front and rear. Although only fitted with 2.75in and 3.00in tyres the wheels looked almost too large for the 117kg (258lb) 254. The top speed was around 150km/h (93mph).

An oddity, the 254 remained in production until 1981 but was not a particularly practical motorcycle for the street. From 1979 the 254 had a Brembo front disc brake and a more conventional Le Mans-style instrument panel. De Tomaso also had plans for a Moto Guzzi version of the Benelli six-cylinder. A prototype engine is on display in the Moto Guzzi museum but this project was shelved before anything came of it.

From the 254 emanated the 125 2C 4T (two-cylinder, four-stroke) of 1979. With a 45.4 x 38mm engine displacing 123.57cc, this too featured a chain-driven single overhead camshaft and two valves per cylinder, a 22.5mm inlet and 18mm exhaust. With a compression ratio of 10.65:1 and two Dell'Orto PHBG 20 B carburettors, 16 horsepower was produced at 10,600rpm. This little five-speed engine was placed in a 254 chassis so the dimensions were identical, except that weight was reduced to

110kg (243lb). The claimed top speed was around 130km/h (81mph). Lasting until 1981, it may not have seemed like a recipe for success, but the 125 2C 4T was a highly agreeable little commuting motorcycle that thrived on high revs.

The final Benelli-inspired Moto Guzzis were a pair of particularly uninspiring water-cooled two-strokes, the 125 C (Custom) and 125 TT (Trail). Introduced at the 1983 Milan Show, it was not until 1985 that they became available, only being produced until 1988. The 123.15cc (56 x 50mm) single-cylinder engine now featured automatic oiling, reed valves and a six-speed gearbox. With a Dell'Orto PHBL 25 BS carburettor, 16.5 horsepower was produced at 7,000rpm. Both featured a monoshock rear suspension and the 125 C included a windscreen and a ridiculous 16in front wheel, a real tribute to the fashion of the day. The 125 TT, with its 35mm offset axle Marzocchi forks and 21in front wheel, was a more effective motorcycle but it still failed to offer a superior alternative in this competitive market segment.

Overall, the Benelli experience at Moto Guzzi was not successful. The motorcycles did not fit into the Mandello ethos and often the products were either inferior or too unusual for the marketplace. Fortunately, De Tomaso let Guzzi maintain its individuality with the V7 series.

# THE ERCOLE, EDILE, ERCOLINO, AIACE, DINGOTRE, FURGHINO, 3 X 3, MOTOZAPPA AND MOTOCOLTIVATORE

It must also be remembered that over a very long period some of the most significant Guzzis, in terms of production if not technical interest, were the three-wheeled commercial vehicles. From the Type 107 of 1928 these were developed into a wide range of models powered by the various engines that were used

in motorcycles at the time. Production of this type of vehicle lasted until 1980.

The first commercial vehicles to appear after the war were the Ercole and Edile, both using the 500cc V engine. The Ercole (Hercules – the first Guzzi to use a Greek mythological name) was to be one of Guzzi's production mainstays for 30 years. Initially having a 17.8 horsepower V engine, the major appeal of the Ercole was its car-type five-speed gearbox (plus reverse) and shaft drive. Fully sprung and able to carry 1,500kg (3,300lb), performance was still only moderate with a top speed of 60km/h (37mph). The Edile on the other hand was only produced during 1946 (150 were manufactured) but with a 16 horsepower engine, a weight of 1,350kg (2,977lb), a 25km/h (16mph) top speed, and no suspension it was not popular. However, the Edile with its enormous, 3,600kg (8,000lb) payload provided more carrying capacity than any other Moto Guzzi three-wheeler.

Throughout its life, the Ercole was developed continually. In 1950, the engine received a light alloy cylinder and head with enclosed rocker gear, and in 1952, an automatic advance magneto. A variation with a cab appeared in 1955, and hydraulic brakes were adopted in 1956. In 1959, an electric start and coil ignition was introduced, and later there was a version adapted to run on methane. Throughout the difficult period of the early 1960s Ercole production was maintained at around 2,000 units a year, before tapering off at a few hundred a year in the early '70s. By that stage the 500cc single-cylinder engine could not provide the level of performance expected even from basic commercial vehicles.

With Moto Guzzi at the peak of its success in the mid-1950s, the 192cc engine of the Galletto was used to create a smaller goods vehicle, the Ercolino. With a four-speed gearbox, plus reverse, and a payload of 350kg (772lb), this was also a successful model for the company, production lasting until 1971. It received 10in wheels in 1958 in place of the earlier 14in and 15in, with an increase in carrying capacity to 560kg (1,235lb). It was also available with an electric starter.

Following the use of the Galletto engine was the 110cc two-stroke Zigolo engine in the Aiace covered truck of 1961–63 and the three-wheeled agricultural Motozappa 110 of 1965. Even smaller versions appeared later in the 1960s. With the 49cc Dingo engine came the Dingotre of 1965–68, and the Furghino of 1968–70, with a covered cab. None of these underpowered vehicles was very successful.

A more interesting machine was the 3 x 3 Autoveicolo da Montagna (mechanical mule) of 1961. Powered by Carcano's new 745cc (80 x 75mm) 90° V-twin engine, this three-wheel-drive vehicle was originally intended for the Italian Ministry of Defence. It was an ambitious engineering exercise, but the 20-horsepower 3 x 3 didn't

perform as well as expected. However, this engine concept would spawn the later V7 even though there were only a few similarities between the two designs (see Chapter 7).

The intention had been to create a vehicle that could cope with a variety of terrains. By having a shaft drive to each of the three wheels it had an amazingly complicated drive system. Drive was provided to the front wheel by a shaft and bevel gear from the steering head, and behind each rear wheel was a smaller wheel that could be adapted for a caterpillar track. The engine was air-cooled, assisted by a fan in front of the engine, and incorporated a gearbox with six forward speeds plus reverse. Although it could be used almost anywhere, and in the most adverse weather conditions, ultimately the 3 x 3 was unnecessarily heavy and complicated for the performance it could offer.

There were also three types of agricultural tractors produced in the 1960s: the Motozappa G2, Motocoltivatore, and for 1965 the MZ0. The Motozappa G2 was produced from 1961 until 1965, and used the 49cc Dingo engine while the Motocoltivatore used a short-stroke 'F 100' four-stroke single (80mm stroke yielding 486cc) with the cylinder inclined 25°. These were manufactured from 1964 until 1966. It is beyond the scope of this book to exhaustively detail these vehicles, but they need to be included as they were produced with a Moto Guzzi trademark.

The Airone was restyled along the lines of
the Falcone in 1952. The Sport initially had
black-painted tank panels and in 1954,
received a new round silencer and automatic
advance magneto, as pictured here.

# 5 SYMBOLIC SINGLES:
## AIRONE, ASTORE AND FALCONE

If any models of Moto Guzzi have come to symbolise the marque, it has been the post-war Airone, and its larger brothers, the Astore and Falcone. Although not produced in anything like the numbers of the Cardellino, Galletto or Zigolo, or even the Stornello, it was because they had such long and distinguished production runs that they have become representative of Moto Guzzi in the post-war period.

The 250cc Airone made a brief appearance during 1939 and 1940, with 122 even manufactured during the war, but it was not until the end of 1945 that regular production resumed. It was much the same with the 500cc G.T.S., G.T.W., and G.T.V. Although production had continued on a very limited scale until 1942, these did not become available again until 1946. Even then they were in short supply because the Mandello plant was largely being used for the hugely successful, and profitable, Guzzino.

When the Airone made its appearance again after the war it was largely unchanged from the final version of 1940. That was strongly derived from the sprung-frame 250 P.E. but with the pressed-steel frame of the 1940 version instead of the tubular type that had appeared on the first Airone.

Although one 500cc G.T.S. with the opposed valve 13.2 horsepower engine was produced in 1946, this engine was finally discontinued after the war. Starting life in the Normale of 1921 it had had a long and fruitful production run, but it was now of insufficient power and was obsolete. The sprung-frame G.T.V. and G.T.W. were the only versions of the seven 500s of 1940 to be resurrected and these, with the V engine, were to form the basis of the new Astore and Falcone, a few years later. The Falcone would also benefit from the development the venerable overhead valve engine received from racing as a Dondolino and Gambalunga.

## THE AIRONE

With 875 manufactured in 1945, the 246cc Airone made up half of that year's total production. It looked a utilitarian type of vehicle with its pressed-steel frame, swingarm, and parallelogram forks, and provided very modest performance. Still with the pre-war 9.5 horsepower engine, the 135kg (298lb) Airone could barely achieve a speed of 95km/h (59mph). After one year however, the Airone was updated with upside-down-type telescopic front forks and hydraulic rear shock absorbers, still with the springs mounted underneath the engine, the new version appearing in 1947.

With demand increasing (1,100 produced in 1947), the Airone received continual development. In 1948, the cylinder head and barrel were cast in aluminium, and the previously exposed rocker gear enclosed. At the same time a Sport version was introduced. This used the pressed-steel frame with a tubular rear section and saw a return to the friction dampers. The engine of the Sport featured a different camshaft, thicker valve springs (4.5mm instead of 4.2mm), 25mm Dell'Orto carburettor, and an increase in compression to 7:1. The power increased to 13.5 horsepower at 6,000rpm. Completing the sporting profile were 19in Borrani alloy wheel rims, 200mm alloy drum brakes, lower and narrower handlebars, alloy friction dampers (rather than the Turismo's steel ones), and a rear pad on the mudguard to allow the rider to adopt a crouched riding position. The top speed of the 137kg (302lb) Airone Sport was around 118km/h (73mph).

Both the Airone Turismo and Sport came in for a complete restyle in 1952, together with the introduction of a specific Airone Militare. With styling along the lines of the larger Falcone, they looked more modern but there were also several changes to the engine and final drive. The manual advance magneto became automatic and a ⅝ x ¼in chain replaced the earlier ½ x ³⁄₁₆in type. The Turismo now shared its frame with the Sport, but the Turismo still retained the 9.5 horsepower engine through to its demise in 1958. The weight had increased however, to 140kg (309lb), fortunately only marginally, denting the Turismo's already sedate performance. The top speed was around 94km/h (58.4mph).

With the restyle of 1952 came a lower state of tune for the Sport. Now with 12 horsepower produced at a lower 5,200rpm, this was not enough of a drop to hurt the performance dramatically. After all, even by the standards of the early 1950s the Airone was a sedate motorcycle. Other Sport features such as the thicker valve springs and Borrani alloy wheel rims remained. The Airone Militare differed in a number of small details to the Turismo, notably the fitting of standard legshields, pillion seat, and 3¼ x 19in tyres.

By 1956, the Sport was deleted, the Turismo and military versions continuing until 1958. The Airone briefly resumed production for the police in 1951 with 201 built.

Those first few years of the early 1950s were the peak period for production of the Airone, which at this stage, outnumbered the larger Falcone and Astore by a factor of four to one. By 1952, 3,375 were produced annually and there was only a small drop to 3,450 in 1953. With sales at such buoyant levels, there were only minor changes to the Sport for 1954. The Sport and Turismo were now visually distinguished by the Sport's chromed kneepads in the fuel tank in place of the earlier rubber pads, and the Turismo's black kneepads. Chrome was very much in demand and expensive so this gave the Sport an air of quality. The distinctive but loud fishtail silencer was replaced by one with a rounded end that was also quieter. Unfortunately, 1956 saw the popularity of the Airone plummet. The poor performance was beginning to affect sales and only 75 were produced in 1957, most of these military versions. That was also the year where the Lodola was established. Offering similar performance to the Airone but in a more modern, smaller, and lighter package at a price considerably less, it virtually made the Airone redundant. It was an inauspicious end to a model that had been so successful only a few years earlier, but the spirit of the Airone lived on in its larger brother, the Falcone.

# THE G.T.V., G.T.W., ASTORE AND SUPERALCE

Production of the Airone had recommenced in 1945 and it was joined in 1946 by the sprung-frame 500cc G.T.V. and G.T.W. As before, the G.T.W. had a higher-performance engine (20.5 horsepower at 4,300rpm), and the G.T.V. the 18.9 horsepower version. These were essentially the same as the pre-war models but for red rather than amaranth paint and with a single exhaust also in the cylinder head. The parallelogram girder forks were retained but were changed to telescopic when both models were updated in 1947 following development of the Airone. Production during 1946 and 1947 was 1,620 G.T.V.s and 133 G.T.W.s.

**BELOW** The Astore of 1950
was an evolution of the G.T.V.
Moto Guzzi

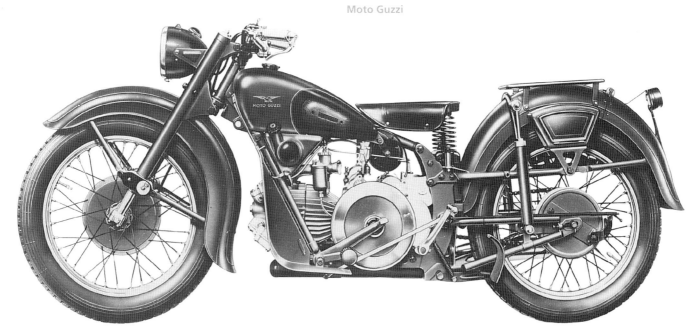

**BELOW** Prior to 1953 the Falcone had chromed tank sections and oil tank knobs.

**BELOW** Prior to 1953 the Falcone had chromed tank sections and oil tank knobs.

**RIGHT** The Falcone Turismo replaced the Astore in 1954.

With the telescopic forks came hydraulic rear dampers, a deeply valanced front mudguard and an increase in weight to 190kg (419lb). The G.T.W. was slightly sportier with lower handlebars, alloy wheel rims, and larger brakes, but both models shared the cast-iron barrel and cylinder head with exposed valve gear. Performance was however, still very much at pre-war levels, the G.T.V. managing 120km/h (75mph) and the G.T.W. 130km/h (81mph).

Further Airone features filtered through to the larger model late in 1949 when the G.T.V. evolved into the Astore (Goshawk). Production began in 1950, and it replaced both the G.T.V. and G.T.W. Although essentially unchanged from the final version of the G.T.V., the Astore now had an aluminium barrel and cylinder head, with enclosed valve gear. There was also a new Dell'Orto MC 27F carburettor but the power output was unchanged at 18.9 horsepower. It was quite successful, with 1,250 produced in 1950, but the Astore still looked very old-fashioned and was slightly restyled for 1951 with a red fuel tank with black panels. It was also offered with an optional sidecar but production was halved, to 662, in 1951. This was probably due to the introduction of the sportier Falcone, but economic factors dictated that sales of large displacement motorcycles during this period were considerably less than that of smaller bikes. The final year for the Astore was 1952, when 800 were constructed. By now it had a fuel tank styled along the lines of the Falcone, but the Astore continued with hydraulic rear dampers and leg shields.

During this period the wartime military Alce evolved into the Superalce. Released in 1946, this was almost identical to its predecessor except for the use of the V engine. The Superalce remained available to the Carabinieri and military until 1958 but was only ever produced in relatively small numbers. To the end it retained the girder forks but gained a magneto with an automatic advance in 1952. Until 1955 it always featured a distinctive double silencer exiting on the left.

## THE FALCONE

By 1950, the Astore had replaced the G.T.V., but Guzzi now needed a more sporty motorcycle to fill the space occupied by the unremarkable and ageing G.T.W. With very few modifications, the Astore was transformed into the Falcone (Hawk). It was an extraordinary transformation because the Falcone was to have one of the longest production runs of any motorcycle, not just a Moto Guzzi. It also became a symbol of the

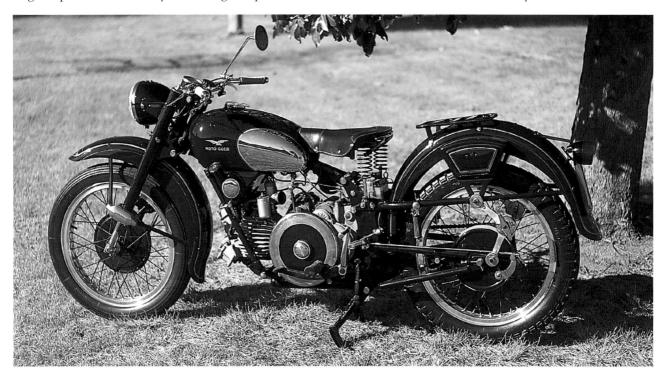

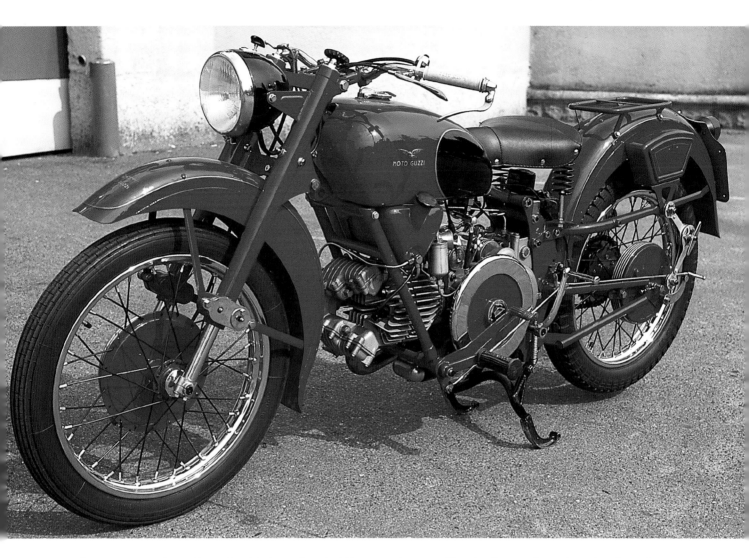

production Guzzi throughout the 1950s and early '60s. This is despite only a few hundred generally being produced each year, mostly for police use. In terms of production nearly three times as many Cardellinos were made in 1950 (22,115) as Falcones between 1950 and 1968. Thus the Falcone is one of the rarer production Guzzis.

The success of the Falcone was undoubtedly due to the purposeful styling and its relationship with the catalogue racers, the Condor and Dondolino. Smaller mudguards, a rounded 17.5-litre fuel tank, while friction instead of hydraulic dampers gave it a much more sporting profile. It also shared the G.T.W.'s alloy wheel rims and lower handlebars, and in line with the Airone Sport, a rear seat pad that allowed the rider to assume a racing crouch.

The biggest changes to the Falcone came in the engine. Finally, racing developments found their way through to the production line and the Falcone engine was virtually a detuned version of a Condor or Dondolino unit. The crankcases were cast in aluminium rather than electron and the cylinder head had enclosed

valve gear like the Astore, but otherwise the Falcone engine was that of a Condor. The gearbox was the Condor four-speed constant-mesh type and the crankshaft and con-rod lighter than that of the Astore. The 43mm inlet and 40mm exhaust valves were inclined at 60° and a Dell'Orto SS 29A racing type carburettor used. For all that, the Falcone still only had a 6.5:1 compression ratio and produced marginally more horsepower than the GTW 23 horsepower at 4,500rpm.

Where the Falcone differed was that with a little modification it could be made to provide similar performance to that of a Dondolino, and a Dondolino camshaft was easily installed. Considering that the Falcone in 1950 sold for half the price of a Dondolino, it made it an attractive proposition for those seeking a performance motorcycle.

The first Falcone was a range-leading sporting motorcycle with a chromed fuel tank. An improved 6-volt electrical system included a more powerful (Marelli DN 19G 30-watt) dynamo and a battery, but the ignition was still by magneto with a manual advance and retard. The weight was reduced considerably on

BELOW A 1956 Falcone Sport outside the factory at Mandello. After some years with black tank sections these were again chrome. The quieter, cylindrical silencer hurt performance.

that of the G.T.W., to 176kg (388lb), and consequently top speed increased to around 135km/h (84mph).

Although only 300 were manufactured in 1950, with a further 512 the following year, the Falcone was immediately successful as a spearhead for the entire line-up. In 1952 two versions of the Falcone were produced, both with minor changes. The Falcone appeared at the January Milan Show with less chrome, an oil tank with black knobs, and many other black-painted components. Another version was displayed at the Milan Show in November, this featuring a Marelli MCR 4E magneto with an automatic advance, new handlebars and switches.

There were more changes for 1953. In April, at Milan, a Falcone was introduced with an Airone-style oil tank without knobs, and a new pillion seat. The biggest development however was seen at the Milan Show in November. Here, a detuned version was shown to replace the Astore, and following the example of the Airone, there were now two varieties of the Falcone. The earlier Falcone became the

Sport, and the new bike the Turismo. Although the Turismo shared its major engine components with the Sport (including the constant-mesh gearbox), it basically had the engine of the Astore. This was a 5.5:1 compression ratio, a 42mm inlet valve and a Dell'Orto MD 27F carburettor. Maximum power was the same as for the Astore, 18.9 horsepower at 4,300rpm and the performance of the Turismo was predictably sedate.

With the frame and suspension of the Sport, the Falcone Turismo gained the Astore's handlebars, leg shields and more forward-mounted footrests. The chromed knee sections in the tank became black and the front tyre a 3.50 x 19in, also from the Astore. The Turismo also featured steel wheel rims and the rear mudguard carrier of the Astore. There were a few further changes over the next few years, but basically the Falcone in both its forms, weathered the problems that Moto Guzzi faced towards the end of the 1950s. Also, at no point during that decade did Falcone production exceed the high point of 700 manufactured in 1957.

**BELOW** Strongly reminiscent of the racing singles, few motorcycles embodied the Moto Guzzi spirit like the Falcone Sport.

In 1956, both the Turismo and Sport gained quieter (and uglier) silencers, similar to that of the Airone, dropping the noise level to 84 dBA as well as hurting performance. A specific police model with a higher headlight mounting to allow the fitting of a siren on the forks appeared in 1958. In response to police request the 30-watt dynamo was replaced by a 60-watt Marelli DN 36C in 1961. Production of the Falcone increased slightly in the 1960s, with a peak of 1,150 produced in 1960. The end of the Sport, and regular Turismo production, occurred at the end of 1963, although ten were built in 1965.

If it hadn't been for the police and military, the Falcone would have ended there, but it was relaunched again in 1967. Now only in one version, the Nuovo Turismo, this featured a Falcone Sport engine (6.5:1 compression) but with the Turismo's Dell'Orto MD 27F carburettor. The resulting power was 19.4 horsepower at 4,450rpm. Unlike the Turismo there was now a speedometer, and a new, more rounded fuel tank. The seat mounting was also changed and the Nuovo Turismo had wide handlebars. It still came with the Turismo-style legshields. As it was intended for official use, the Nuovo Turismo came with the higher headlight mount with a siren fitted underneath. Weight was up to 192kg (423lb), along with a corresponding decrease in performance and it could only manage about 125km/h (78mph).

It was not that successful and only 405 were produced in 1967, with a further 390 in 1968. These were the final Moto Guzzi horizontal 500cc singles with the external flywheel. Throughout its life the Falcone was produced in several special versions for the police, notably the Guardia di Finanza and the Corpo dei Corrazieri (Presidential Guard) of 1952, and the now sought-after Corpo dei Corrazieri of 1957. Amongst many specific features these had 12-volt electrics, dynastart and extra batteries.

The most extraordinary thing about the Falcone was that, even when production ended in 1968, it was still basically a pre-war motorcycle. The engine and running gear were still very much that of the G.T.W. and riding a Falcone was really an experience of a different era. The heavy flywheel meant that acceleration was leisurely and even the constant mesh sliding gearchange was very slow compared with more modern designs. Friction dampers combined with the unique Guzzi springing under the engine were very much an anachronism. It was still similar to the type of rear suspension that had appeared on the ill-fated Three Cylinder of 1932, certainly vindicating the expertise of Giuseppe Guzzi.

Fortunately, Guzzi was not relying on the Falcone for survival and they were able to produce and sell such a motorcycle with its proud ancestry essentially unchanged for many years. Because of its long production run, it has earned itself a classic status, and has become a representative model for the marque. This is not that surprising as while the Falcone may have always been obsolete, it retained clear bloodlines to some of the most significant racing Guzzis, the Condor, Dondolino, Gambalunga, and of course the G.P. of 1920.

## THE NUOVO FALCONE

Continued demand for the Falcone by the police and military saw Moto Guzzi release the Nuovo Falcone in 1969. Although only eight were built that year, this soon proved extremely popular, with many more being produced than the earlier Falcone. A total of 2,946 were built in 1970, with production peaking at 3,775 in 1971. At that stage more Nuovo Falcones were being constructed at Mandello than any other single model, including the V7.

By combining many of the traditional features of the earlier Falcone in a more modern chassis Guzzi managed to create an uninspiring workhorse that was eminently suitable for the police and military. Much of the engine was similar to before and it still had the 88 x 82mm bore and stroke of the very first Moto Guzzi, the horizontal cylinder with radial finning, and the external flywheel (although this was now hidden underneath an alloy side cover).

Where the Nuovo Falcone really departed from its predecessor was in the change to wet sump lubrication and a redesigned four-speed gearbox. No longer with magneto ignition and a separate dynamo, the Falcone finally came of age with a 12-volt electrical system and coil ignition. There was even an optional dynastart. A more modern square-slide Dell'Orto VHB 29A carburettor was used, but with a 6.8:1 compression ratio the Nuovo Falcone was barely more powerful than a Falcone Sport – 26.2 horsepower being developed at 4,800rpm. Civilian versions had a lighter flywheel than military models.

The chassis too was completely updated with an orthodox tubular steel double-cradle frame, enclosed

**LEFT** The Nuovo Falcone had an unusual twin exhaust arrangement, but was neither powerful nor fast.
Moto Guzzi

**BELOW** The enclosed flywheel and electric starter were modern features of the Nuovo Falcone, but the classic horizontal single was largely unchanged.
Two Wheels

telescopic forks and twin rear shock absorbers. The wheels were reduced in size to 18in (3.50 x 18 tyres front and rear) and a 200mm twin leading shoe drum brake fitted on the front. Unfortunately, this modernisation saw the weight soar to 214kg (472lb). This meant that the Nuovo Falcone was barely able to match the performance of a Falcone Turismo, and had a top speed of only 127km/h (79mph). The Nuovo Falcone was not a motorcycle suited to the Autostrada and gave a new meaning to the word 'plodder.'

However, as a military motorcycle it was extremely successful, particularly in Italy. In 1970 and 1971 so many were sold that the following year it was also made available to civilians. It was intended to be the motorcycle for those enthusiasts eager for an update but still offering the nostalgic look of the previous Falcone. However, as it was neither ancient nor modern this new model was a disappointment. The more modern instrument layout was shared with the V7 Special, as were many of the ancillaries. The styling of the civilian white Nuovo Falcone was unusual, particularly the twin silencer emerging from a single exhaust. In a world where performance levels were increasing the Nuovo Falcone began to struggle in the marketplace. Production however was still up

considerably on that of the earlier Falcone, and 2,293 were built in 1973.

In 1974, the Nuovo Falcone was given a new colour scheme (dark red and matte black) with stainless steel mudguards, along with an additional version, the Sahara. Painted beige, the Sahara was essentially a military bike sold for civilian use. It featured a sprung single seat, panniers, and a noticeable absence of chrome. The compression ratio was increased slightly to 7:1, and power up marginally to 27 horsepower, but as this was still a very heavy motorcycle it could still only manage about 130km/h (81mph).

By 1976, demand for the Nuovo Falcone had dwindled and the model finished that year. Except as a military motorcycle it had never lived up to its expectations, and it was also a victim of increasing worldwide legislation. All motorcycles were beginning to share uniform left-side gearshifting and converting such a basically ancient design was not economically feasible. Although nearly twice as many Nuovo Falcones were manufactured as Falcones, the newer model has never achieved the classic status of the original. The marriage of an older style engine with a modern chassis and styling was never going to be a recipe for success. It was an inauspicious end to a great engine line.

Moto Guzzi continued to develop
the Bicilindrica, installing a leading
fork in 1949 and an anatomically
sculptured fuel tank in 1950. It was
last raced in 1951.

# 6 THE SECOND GOLDEN AGE

While the 1930s had been a wonderful period for Moto Guzzi, even this decade was eclipsed by the magnificence of the 1950s. From 1949, until their dramatic withdrawal at the end of 1957, the Moto Guzzi racing department, headed by Giulio Cesare Carcano, created and developed a series of unequalled Grand Prix machines. These were not only highly individual, but also portrayed Carcano's ideology. Unlike the competition, Carcano placed greater importance on aerodynamics, minimal weight, and weight distribution. He was committed to the leading-link front forks and the development of the existing flat single. When forced to seek more horsepower Carcano's answer, the V8, again was totally unique. Aided by a sympathetic management, and with considerable financial backing, some of the greatest racing motorcycles of all time emanated from Mandello during this period.

## 1949

For the new World Championship Moto Guzzi was better prepared than most manufacturers. By developing their two excellent pre-war designs in the years immediately following the end of the Second World War, they had competitive offerings in both the 250cc and 500cc categories for the 1949 season. The 350cc class was one historically associated with British manufacturers but it would not be long before Guzzi would also successfully contest this category. With the 250 Parallel Twin shelved, the successful but ageing Albatros was transformed into the Gambalunghino (Little long-leg).

The combination of the Albatros engine with a Gambalunga, leading link front suspension and front brake, gave the venerable single overhead camshaft 250, which had first appeared in 1926, a new lease of life. The success of the Gambalunghino over the next few years really showed how good the concept of the compact horizontal single, with its geared primary drive and external flywheel, had been in the first place. What was really more surprising, especially given its incredible success over the next few years, was that no-one copied it. For the 500cc class the venerable Bicilindrica was further developed, but was not to be as successful against stronger, four-cylinder, competition.

**LEFT** Moto Guzzi's racing success during the 1950s was largely due to the genius of its great engineer, Giulio Carcano.

suspension, brake, fuel tank and a more streamlined tail section. Painted silver and later red, the early Gambalunghino looked very much like the Gambalunga.

Although the weight was similar to that of the final Albatros at 122kg (269lb), the Gambalunghino was a more effective racing machine because of its better brakes and front suspension. Where the Gambalunghino really succeeded over the competition was not so much in its superior speed, but in its reliability. The first race on the calendar was the Isle of Man TT. Here, Manliff Barrington on a Gambalunghino won the Lightweight TT at 77.93mph (125km/h), ahead of Tommy Wood also on a Gambalunghino.

At the Swiss Grand Prix at Berne, factory rider Bruno Ruffo took his only Grand Prix victory of the season and at Ulster Maurice Cann rode an Albatros to first place ahead of Ruffo's factory Gambalunghino. With only four events counting towards the 250 World Championship Ruffo became World Champion, and Guzzi won its first manufacturers' title.

For the 500cc class Moto Guzzi continued to develop the Bicilindrica. While the telescopic-forked Micucci version of 1948 had performed well, particularly at the Isle of Man, the machine was considerably revamped for 1949. Carcano's influence became more apparent and the result was one of the best-looking racing machines of the era. Development of the engine saw the use of Dell'Orto carburettors with detachable float chambers, and megaphone exhausts. Power on the low octane fuel was up to 45 horsepower at 8,000rpm.

While the frame, with the oil reservoir, and rear suspension with a single spring came from the 1948 version, the leading-link forks were similar to that of the Gambalunga. The front brake was a full-width drum. One of the more unusual features of the 1949 Bicilindrica was the fuel tank, which extended forwards in front of the steering head to improve streamlining. With this model the weight was reduced to 145kg (320lb) and, unlike the Gambalunghino, the Bicilindrica was painted red.

Unfortunately, the Bicilindrica could not match the success of the Gambalunghino in the World Championship. At the Isle of Man, Bob Foster was leading the Senior TT before the clutch failed, and there were no results of any significance during 1949. In the Italian Championship however, Lorenzetti (now a factory rider) rode a Bicilindrica to victory in the 500cc class.

The first Gambalunghino had come about at the beginning of 1949. Enrico Lorenzetti was racing in the 250cc class for Moto Guzzi on an Albatros. After collecting the bike from the racing department at Mandello, it was badly damaged when the trailer broke away from the car as it was being towed. Returning to Mandello, the mechanics found the frame was too badly damaged to repair, so in order to get the bike ready to race in time they simply installed the Albatros engine in a Gambalunga chassis. Lorenzetti won the race and the resulting hybrid took him to victory in the Italian 250cc Championship

The factory also adopted it for the inaugural World Championship in 1949. While the 68 x 68mm engine shared much with the Albatros, including the bevel-gear driven single overhead camshaft and four-speed gearbox, power was increased to 25 horsepower at 8,000rpm. This was primarily through the use of a Dell'Orto SS 35mm carburettor. For the official Gambalunghino, the twin downtube frame and rear suspension came from the Albatros, the Gambalunga supplying the leading-link front

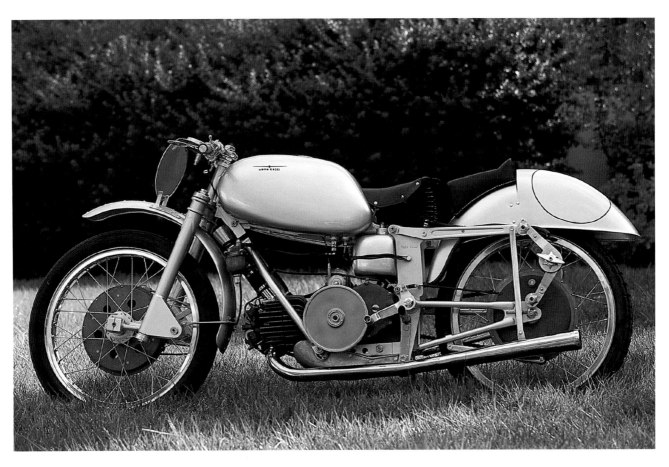

# 1950

Although victorious in the 250cc class in 1949, Moto Guzzi faced increased competition during 1950, this year being their least successful of the period. It did, however, prompt further development of both the 250 and 500, as well as a 350. To counter the Benelli of Dario Ambrosini, the Gambalunghino was further improved. More power was required, so the valves were increased to 38.5mm inlet and 33mm exhaust. A special inverted 37mm Dell'Orto carburettor was fitted to a down-draught manifold and the power increased to 28 horsepower at 8,000rpm. There was now a large rubber connecting tube between the engine and carburettor, a feature that would last through on the racing singles until 1957. Other developments included a new, more-streamlined, seat, and friction rear dampers mounted backwards to improve the handling under hard braking. In order to lower the machine, 20in wheels were fitted.

Despite this development, the Gambalunghino was outclassed by Ambrosini's Benelli and Guzzi withdrew official works entries before the conclusion of the season. This saved some of the embarrassment of a comprehensive defeat, and also allowed development of a double overhead camshaft four-valve Gambalunghino that would make a brief appearance in 1951.

The only Grand Prix win for the Gambalunghino in 1950 was Maurice Cann's victory at Ulster, and Cann eventually finished second in the 250cc World Championship. Guzzi however did manage to fill the minor placings, with Fergus Anderson coming third and Ruffo fourth.

Following the disappointment of the 1949 season, the Bicilindrica was not officially entered by the factory in Grands Prix during 1950. Despite this, there was still some development, mainly along the lines of the Gambalunghino, the front Dell'Orto carburettor being mounted in a similar downdraft style. Styling was again altered, with an unusual fuel tank shaped to

accommodate the rider's arms when crouched. Foster again rode the Bicilindrica in the Senior TT at the Isle of Man but could not match his pace of the previous year. He was in sixth position before being forced to retire with the engine misfiring at the end of the sixth lap after he holed one of the rubber carburettor connecting tubes.

More significant was the creation of a 350 single during 1950. Following the poor showing of a 350cc Bicilindrica by Bruno Bertacchini in 1949, Guzzi decided to build a double overhead camshaft 350 single. This 78 x 73mm engine displacing 349cc soon produced 31 horsepower at 7,000rpm, and weighing only 116kg (256lb) showed considerable potential. It also featured an unusual arrangement of quadruple hairpin valve springs. Several innovations were tested, notably a water-cooled exhaust valve. Lorenzetti first rode the new five-speed 350 at Mettet in Belgium and later, Cann tested it at the Isle of Man. Guzzi also supplied Cann with a 310cc single overhead camshaft Gambalunghino-inspired version for the 1950 Junior TT, which he preferred and eventually rode in the race.

During the race the 310 expired, but even prior to that it could not challenge the leaders. Both prototypes were then retired.

The construction of the famed wind tunnel at Mandello was undertaken in 1950. It is still operational and is located behind the original buildings of 1921. Further world speed records were set at Montlhéry in September on the Gambalunghino. Anderson, along with Ruffo and Gianni and Guido Leoni, set ten 250cc world records up to 8 hours, including 2 hours at 160km/h (99mph). A few months earlier, on 9 May, Gino Alquati used a Gambalunghino engine to power a racing boat to a new flying start kilometre record of 80.181km/h (50mph).

# 1951

After a disappointing season in 1950, Moto Guzzi was again strongly represented in both the 250cc and 500cc categories for 1951. The official works team now included Anderson alongside Ruffo, Lorenzetti, Gianni

Leoni and Sante Geminiani. This was a highly successful year for the Gambalunghino, and after the French Grand Prix, where Ambrosini was killed, Moto Guzzi was untroubled in the 250 category. Guzzi won four of the five 250cc races and Ruffo again took the championship, with Tommy Wood second and Lorenzetti fourth. Tommy Wood won the Lightweight TT and also raced in the 350 class in Spain (there was no 250 event), giving Guzzi their first 350 GP victory.

Further development saw the Gambalunghino gain a five-speed gearbox and hydraulic rear shock absorbers for some circuits, but generally the four-speed gearbox was still used. A four-valve twin cam 250 had been produced in the latter part of 1950, featuring twin Dell'Orto remote float bowl carburettors and enclosed coil valve springs. This engine had a slightly longer stroke (68 x 68.5mm) and a longer con-rod, 140mm eye-to-eye. A short stroke version (70 x 64mm) was also constructed but the four-valve engine did not show any superiority over the single camshaft model and, while it made further brief appearances in 1952 and 1953, was eventually discarded.

More successful was Maurice Cann's home-built double overhead camshaft two-valve 250. During practice for the Lightweight TT, Cann's bike was as fast as the factory Gambalunghinos and the Guzzi engineers had a very close look at it. It would be this engine that would influence the eventual double overhead camshaft 250 Bialbero.

This was the final year for the Bicilindrica and it featured a few more improvements. Power was increased to 47 horsepower at 8,000rpm and the remote float bowl Dell'Orto SS carburettors were mounted on long manifolds, the rear carburettor situated close to the rear wheel. Even in its final form the 500 Bicilindrica was not as highly developed as the Gambalunghino. Valve sizes were 35mm for the inlet and 33mm for the exhaust. There was return to the rear friction dampers (in place of the hydraulic unit under the engine) and a redesigned seat and rear mudguard. One more significant victory was in store for the Bicilindrica when Fergus Anderson dominated the rain-soaked Swiss 500cc Grand Prix of 1951. Winning at an average speed of 80.16mph (129km/h), Lorenzetti took another Bicilindrica to third place.

While the 250cc results were excellent, 1951 was a particularly tragic year. Besides Ambrosini, Guzzi riders Gianni and Guido Leoni, Geminiani, and Raffaele Alberti died in accidents.

The Gambalunghino was also used in several long-distance record attempts at the Montlhéry autodrome in France. On 17 September, Anderson, Lorenzetti and Ruffo continued where they had left off in 1950, setting 1,000-mile and 9, 10, 11, and 12-hour 250 records.

# 1952

The development of the racing Guzzis took an important turn in 1952 that would continue to see them dominate. With the commissioning of the wind tunnel, aerodynamics started to play as important a role as engine development. This immediately influenced the shape of the Gambalunghino, resulting in a considerable redesign. The fuel tank was derived from the anatomical design of the final Bicilindrica and as it incorporated the numberplate, it indicated the way of the future and the eventual integral fairing. There was a new frame and the rear suspension was now by twin hydraulic shock absorbers with external springs. To improve the frontal area the wheels were now 18in instead of 21in. There was not much more development to the single overhead camshaft engine except for a new Dell'Orto carburettor. This featured a special float to stabilise mixture strength while cornering, braking and accelerating. At 7,500rpm, 27 horsepower was developed and the compression ratio was now 8.7:1. The bike weighed 116kg (256lb) and still used a single leading shoe front brake.

With the Bicilindrica pensioned off, Guzzi contested only the 250cc class in 1952, with three riders, Anderson, Lorenzetti, and Ruffo. The Guzzis won five Grands Prix, only beaten in Germany by the DKW after all the factory Gambalunghinos retired. With two victories, Lorenzetti took the title ahead of Anderson (also with two wins). Ruffo distinguished himself at the Isle of Man where he comfortably led the Lightweight TT but slowed on the last lap to obey team orders that allowed Anderson and Lorenzetti to overtake him. In the process, Ruffo set a fastest lap of 84.82mph (136km/h). The Ulster Grand Prix was won by Cann on a 250 Gambalunghino with his own designed and built twin overhead camshaft cylinder head.

During the season, Lorenzetti tested various experimental four-valve Gambalunghinos but they were never as effective as the two-valve version. Even

Cann's home-built effort was superior. That August also saw further successful world record attempts, with the pre-war supercharged 250 and a sidecar on the Monaco–Ingolstadt autobahn in Germany. With new streamlined bodywork designed in the Guzzi wind tunnel, Gino Cavanna took the supercharged 250 to a record speed of 221.226km/h (137mph) over a flying kilometre. Seven further records were also set.

# 1953

With the company buoyant from the sales of Guzzinos, Moto Guzzi decided to expand the racing programme beyond the 250cc category. There were no changes to the team for 1953, but Guzzi now provided works entries in both the 350cc and 500cc classes. It was the new 500 that caused the most interest. At the final event of the 1952 season, the Italian Grand Prix at Monza, the racing world was stunned by the unveiling of the replacement for the 500cc Bicilindrica, a new in-line four, for the 1953 season. By this stage the four-cylinder MVs and Gileras were beginning to dominate 500cc racing and the Guzzi design was refreshingly different. Unfortunately, unlike the earlier Bicilindrica, which was also an original and unique design, the four was unsuited to a racing motorcycle application. It was also uniformly disliked by the riders.

At the instigation of Giorgio Parodi, the great Carcano was bypassed when it came to the design of the four-cylinder. Although Parodi had approached him as early as 1948, in 1951 the four-cylinder was given to the Rome-based engineer, Carlo Gianini who

worked for the Giannini company. Parodi felt it was time for some fresh ideas in the racing department and underestimated Carcano's brilliance. This may have seemed a slight on the racing team at the time but the failure of the four would eventually give Carcano the sanction for the V8.

Gianini had impressive credentials. Together with Piero Remor he had been responsible for the four-cylinder OPRA 20 years earlier that had become the Rondine and eventually the supercharged Gilera four. This was the engine that had inspired the ill-fated Guzzi four of 1931, and Gianini's new four would also prove to be a disappointment.

In an effort to be different to the other fours, and also reduce frontal area, the new engine was a longitudinal four-cylinder that closely followed automotive practice. In the era before streamlined fairings it made sense to keep the engine narrow. However, by 1954 this was not really important as wider engines could be more easily accommodated under the dustbin fairings and ultimately, the disadvantages of an inline four outweighed the advantages. It was not only the torque reaction from the crankshaft that caused problems, but also the engine-speed clutch made gear changing difficult. The clutch was also too small and not strong enough, but to fit a larger one would have required an expensive redesign of the rear of the engine.

Technically however, the four was a beautiful racing engine in the best Italian engineering tradition. Designed without too much regard for the cost, it was oversquare (56 x 50mm) with a displacement of 492cc, and featured double overhead camshafts driven by straight-cut gears from the crankshaft. One-piece

con-rods with single-row roller big-end bearings were
used with a built up 180° crankshaft. The big-end
journals were locked in place with serrated Hirth
couplings, and the crank itself ran on five ball and
roller bearings. With the two valves set at a wide
included angle of 96°, the three-ring pistons required a
very high dome to achieve the 11:1 compression.

Although designed to allow for larger valves, this
1930s practice of a wide included valve angle
ultimately limited potential horsepower, and was one
area where Gianini's design was obsolete. Valve sizes
were 32mm for the inlet and 30mm for the exhaust,
each valve having three coil springs, the camshafts
operating directly on caps over the valve springs.

An unusual feature was the seating of the valves
directly in the cylinder head without inserts. The clutch
was a multiplate type splined to the crankshaft without
any reduction. A compact four-speed gearbox was
incorporated in the engine casting with drive to the
rear wheel by a shaft in the left side of the swingarm.
The bevel drive for the magneto sat within the gearbox
shell with the oil pump in the sump situated in the
lower crankcase.

Undoubtedly the most unusual feature of the four
was its induction system. So as to minimise engine
width by not mounting four carburettors to one side of
the engine, a pressurised system using a Roots-type
blower housed in the gearbox shell supplied air to four

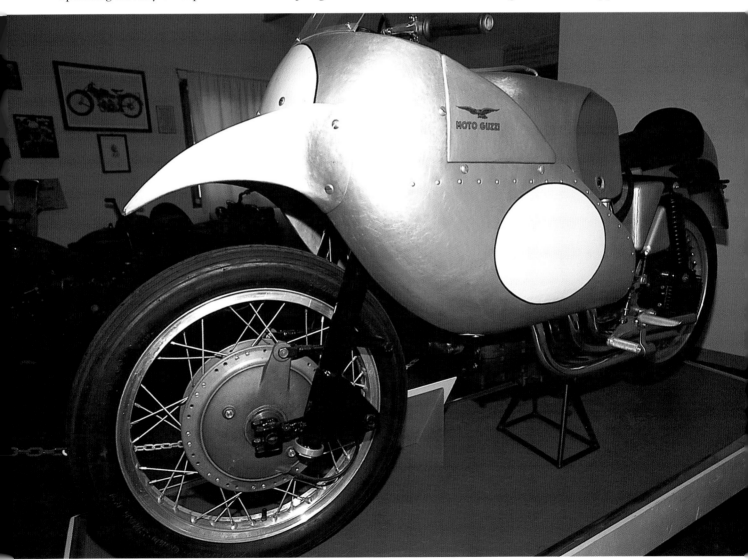

was very slow, mainly because the engine was built in Rome and modifications made in Mandello. The frame too was a Giannini design but by the time the bike was ready for the 1953 season there was much Guzzi influence in the design.

After its showing at Monza, Lorenzetti tested the four at Ospidaletti in San Remo in February 1953, and it made its debut at Siracusa together with the new 250 Bialbero. Things looked promising when Lorenzetti won an international event at Hockenheim on 10 May at an average speed of more than 173km/h (107mph), with Anderson setting a fastest lap at 182.4km/h (113mph). Yet while it occasionally showed bursts of speed, the four was extremely unreliable and difficult to ride. Guzzi did win a 500cc Grand Prix in 1953, the Spanish, but it was not with the 500 four. Here, Anderson amazingly defeated a field of Gilera and MV fours with the new 350.

It was in the 350cc class that Guzzi found their greatest success that year, and one that they would dominate until 1957. After several years of testing various prototypes, Carcano finally discovered the right formula. Earlier 350s were simply a bored and stroked Gambalunghino, and this was initially what Fergus Anderson persuaded Carcano to do late in 1952. As a Scot, Anderson wanted to compete with the Nortons and AJSs, the traditional leaders of the class. By enlarging the 68 x 68mm Gambalunghino as far as the crankcases would permit, and moving the crankpin as close to edge of the crank webs as seemed safe, a 317cc (72 x 78mm) version was created. A longer, 155mm con-rod was used in the longer stroke engines.

The cylinder head design followed that of the Gambalunghino with a 60° included valve angle, which was still very narrow for the day. Valve sizes were 38.5mm for the inlet and 33mm for the exhaust and with a 10:1 compression ratio power was 31 horsepower at 7,700rpm. This was the same horsepower as the short-stroke 350cc double overhead camshaft prototype of 1950. A 35mm Dell'Orto carburettor was used, on the usual long induction tract with a steep 33° down-draught angle. The crankshaft too followed Gambalunghino practice by being pressed up in three pieces with a caged roller big-end bearing.

This engine was then placed in a 1953 250 Bialbero chassis with the 'bird-beak' streamlining of that year. Wheels were both 19 inch, a 2.75 x 19in tyre on the

atomisers in the inlet tracts. These air valves were opened by additional cams on the inlet camshaft and fuel was continually fed by a pump. Excess fuel was returned to the tank by another pump, and later by gravity. This mechanical fuel injection system was a variation on experiments carried out on the supercharged 250cc 'Gerolamo' Milano–Taranto machine of 1939. Even with water-cooling it was a very clean-looking engine with the water pump mounted on the front of the engine near the radiator.

The power developed from this compact 500cc motor was 55 horsepower at 9,000rpm, and it was housed in an original trellis frame with Bicilindrica leading-link forks and twin leading shoe front brake. Wheels were 19in at the front and 18in at the rear, and the 500 weighed in at a respectable 145kg (320lb). Thus it maintained the noted Guzzi favourable power-to-weight ratio and was capable of 230km/h (143mph). It was also surprisingly compact and the wheelbase was a moderate 1,400mm (55in). When it appeared early in 1953, it featured the 'bird-beak' style fairing that typified 1953 racing Guzzis. Development

front and a 3.00 x 19in tyre on the rear, and unlike the 250 Bialbero the front brake was a twin leading shoe. This 317 was entered in an international meeting at Hockenheim in May, and Anderson easily won the 350cc race. It was also an extremely successful day for Guzzi, as it was the same event where the 500 four was also victorious.

So encouraging had been the 317's performance at Hockenheim that Anderson organised a last-minute entry for the Junior TT at the Isle of Man three weeks later. He came home third at 89.41mph (144km/h), convincing Carcano that Guzzi should contest the other rounds in the 350cc World Championship. For the next event at Assen, Carcano redesigned the engine cases to accept a 75mm piston, and Lorenzetti went on to win. Throughout the rest of the 1953 season, both the 317cc (72 x 78mm) and larger, 345cc (75 x 78mm) engines were used.

Both these engines had a one-piece crankshaft with uncaged needle roller big-end bearings and two-piece con-rods. For the larger bore (75mm), the valve sizes were increased by 2mm to 37mm inlet and 32mm exhaust, and the compression ratio reduced slightly to 9.5:1. Although a 37mm carburettor was tested, the 35mm proved more satisfactory and the engine produced 33 horsepower at 7,500rpm. Weighing 122kg (269lb), and with a top speed of around 210km/h (130mph), the Guzzis took the opposition completely by surprise. With victories in France, Belgium and Switzerland, Anderson won the 350cc World Championship from Lorenzetti, who had wins in Holland and Italy.

However, with several retirements, the success of the 350 was tempered by constant reliability problems during 1953. The engine suffered excessive oil consumption as the cast-iron liner was so thin that both it and the piston distorted. Also the uncaged rollers were unsuitable for high-speed big-end bearings and contributed to premature big-end failure. Both of these problems would be rectified for the 1954 season.

Despite their move into the 350cc category, Guzzi continued to contest the 250cc class. Double overhead camshaft two-valve and four-valve versions were

tested by Lorenzetti and Anderson at Ospidaletti early in the year, and box-section swingarms tried. However, as had happened earlier, the two-valve cylinder head gave better results and this was used during 1953. This was based on Maurice Cann's DOHC design of 1951, but Guzzi made it lighter and more compact with a different valve angle. Like the larger bikes, the 250 had the 'bird-beak' fairing that year and a low fuel tank that required a fuel pump. Both single and double overhead camshaft versions were raced during 1953, and they shared a slight increase in stroke (to 68.4mm). This had been tried on the 1950 double overhead camshaft bike and saw the capacity increase to 248.2cc. The double overhead camshaft 250 Bialbero produced 28 horsepower at 8,000rpm with a 9.5:1 compression ratio and a huge, 40mm Dell'Orto carburettor. As with the 350, 19in wheels front and rear were used on the Bialbero.

Although now outclassed by Werner Haas on his NSU Rennmax twin, the 250 Bialbero managed to win three events in 1953. Fergus Anderson again took the Lightweight TT, this time at 84.73mph (136km/h) after Ruffo had crashed badly in practice, ending his career. Lorenzetti won two 250 Grands Prix, the Nations at Monza and the Spanish at Barcelona in October. These were also the first races for Australian

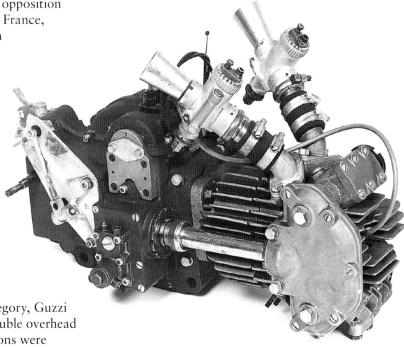

Ken Kavanagh on a factory Moto Guzzi after Fergus Anderson had approached Norton's Joe Craig to secure his services as a replacement for the injured Ruffo. Anderson believed Kavanagh had assisted him in his victory in the 350cc Swiss Grand Prix, giving him the World Championship over Lorenzetti.

With the championship decided, Norton had resolved not to contest the final two rounds, and they were interested to know how good the Guzzi really was. After a poor start and being black flagged in Monza, Kavanagh responded with a second in the Spanish 250 race. The 250 results were disappointing for a team that had been dominant for the past few years. Anderson ended up third in the 250cc Championship, with Lorenzetti fourth. Although the results in the 250cc World Championship were disappointing, in European Championships the 250cc Guzzis continued to succeed. National championships were won in Italy, Austria, France, Great Britain and Switzerland. However, while they maintained an interest in the 250 class, Guzzi would concentrate more seriously on the larger categories in the future.

# 1954

Enrico Parodi offered Kavanagh a full works ride for 1954 alongside Anderson, Lorenzetti, Montanari and Ruffo. An indication of the financial buoyancy of the company at that time was his incredible salary of £3,000 plus expenses and prize money, with a condition to strictly follow team orders. As Kavanagh said 'Compared with Norton, Moto Guzzi had an enormous racing department and seemed to have an unlimited budget.' Reserve riders included Duilio Agostini, who had won the 1953 Milano–Taranto race on a Dondolino, and Alano Montanari. The dustbin fairings, developed with the aid of the wind tunnel, were first seen in 1954. Initial testing for that season was again undertaken at Ospidaletti at the end of February. All works riders tested the 250, 350, and 500s, including Ruffo in what was his last ride on a racing machine.

Although it had not had a very spectacular debut year, the 500 four continued to be developed, mainly by Kavanagh, despite almost universal dislike by the riders. The metal dustbin fairing incorporated 28-litre side fuel tanks, the upper tank being replaced by a rather ugly metal bulkhead. The four was also fitted with a linked braking system and Kavanagh's single front brake lever but was unable to even repeat the moderate success of the previous year. Apart from a minor victory by Anderson at Mettet in Belgium, where the injection system was replaced by four carburettors, the four was spectacularly unsuccessful. After all the expense of design and development there were no Grand Prix victories, and Carcano's racing programme was vindicated.

All the riders preferred the less-powerful 500cc single and the last race for the four was at an international race at Hockenheim on 9 May 1954 where Anderson was defeated by Kavanagh on the new 500 single. In a staged race the four towed the fragile single and then threw its rear tyre tread at 250km/h (155mph). Not only did this frighten Anderson but the four's defeat convinced Parodi that Carcano should persevere with the 500 single. While it was no longer raced by Guzzi, the four-cylinder design continued to be developed by Gianini for car racing. Uprated to 750cc, the Giannini G2 powered many highly successful Italian racing cars.

Sharing the same engine dimensions as all the classic Moto Guzzi 500cc singles (88 x 82mm), the 500cc Grand Prix single initially had a single overhead camshaft and was developed from the Gambalunghino. This was the bike that Kavanagh rode to victory at Hockenheim at an average speed of 182km/h (113mph) with a fastest lap at 188.8km/h (117mph). With a 45mm Dell'Orto carburettor 42 horsepower was developed at 7,000rpm. This engine proved very unreliable, much of it as a result of Carcano's obsession with weight saving, and many parts broke through being too light.

At the Imola Gold Cup the clutch lever simply snapped off its pivot lugs because they were designed for 250 clutch springs. These problems were largely overcome when the 500 was redesigned as a larger engine. It received a double overhead camshaft cylinder head like the 250 and 350 of 1954, with an increase in power to 45 horsepower at 7,000rpm. Valve sizes were 47mm inlet and 42mm exhaust, and the 500 used a 165mm con-rod. Twin spark plugs and battery and coil ignition was employed.

While the 500 single may have been an expression of Carcano's ideology and tribute to excellent aerodynamics, it was never a match for the significantly more powerful Gilera and MV fours. Kavanagh managed a second place in Belgium and Spain, eventually finishing third in the 500cc World Championship. These results would see him as the principal development rider for Guzzi's next 500cc contender, the V8.

After many years of riding Nortons, Kavanagh initially found the Guzzi singles strange to ride. 'The front brake plate was anchored to a flange on the front axle so that when the brake was applied the front of the bike would lift. This was especially disconcerting going into a curve a little too quickly because by backing off nothing happened. It was the first thing I had changed on my Moto Guzzis. I also had the two front brakes balanced by the front hand lever, then fitted to all the racing bikes. The Guzzis had a much wider powerband than the Nortons, more like a touring bike. What made the Guzzis so good were the weight and the streamlining.'

As it was the 350cc Championship that Guzzi was defending, most development went into this engine. In an effort to overcome the reliability problems during 1953, the 350 was redesigned over the winter of 1953 for the 1954 season. As before, both 72 x 78mm and 75 x 78mm engines were raced and later there was also a 79mm stroke version displacing 349cc. However, information from Umberto Todero indicated the 78mm stroke was generally used. Many of the developments were carried over from the 1953 250 Bialbero and were eventually shared with the 500. These included a double overhead camshaft cylinder head with enclosed valve gear and single coil valve springs, the twin camshafts still being driven by a shaft and bevel-gear and five straight-cut gears. The cams operated directly on bucket-type tappets without skirts and the fuel and oil pumps were driven from the ends of both camshafts.

A five-speed gearbox was also standard for 1954, which was a confusing year in the documentation of the 350, but Umberto Todero states that three versions were used (317cc, 345cc and 349cc), and both single and double overhead camshaft cylinder heads were fitted, depending on the circuit. The Monalbero engines were lighter than the Bialbero and were preferred on the slow tracks. The 317cc engine was only used at the beginning of the season and by the end of 1954 a completely new short-stroke 350 was also developed. This was used in a few races towards the end of the season.

The reason for the continued use of the 317cc (72 x 78mm) engine early in the season was the problem of excessive oil consumption with the larger bore. During 1954 the 345cc engine (75 x 78mm) received a thicker cylinder liner and stronger piston to alleviate this problem. The compression ratio was reduced to 9.4:1 and valve sizes were increased yet again, to 39mm inlet and 33mm exhaust. With a 37mm carburettor 35 horsepower was developed at 7,800rpm.

Another important change was a return to a three-piece built-up crankshaft with caged roller big-end bearings. Ignition was no longer by the magneto that had occasionally caused problems, but now consisted of two individual circuits of twin coils and twin 10mm spark plugs operated by twin distributors. One ignition circuit provided less advance and was used for starting only. For the TT, two batteries were used with two independent circuits, one as a backup with two switches on the handlebar. Over long bumpy races the batteries would fail and the 6-volt ignition system required a high current. These features were also incorporated on the similar, 79mm stroke version but

generally the 78mm stroke predominated during 1954.

Other significant developments occurred in the design of the frame and fairing, and these too were shared with the 250 and 500. The dustbin fairing, constructed of hand-beaten electron, carried the fuel in two pannier tanks, one on either side. This was done because only frontal resistance, and not lift, could be tested in the wind tunnel and Carcano wanted as much weight on the front as possible to minimise a back flip. There was also a completely new trellis frame built from small-diameter tubes. This extended over the front wheel to support the fairing, making the fairing integral in the design of the motorcycle for the first time. It was a revolutionary idea, and one that would ensure the 350's superiority. With only 35 horsepower, the 123kg (271lb) 350 of 1954 was capable of an amazing 220km/h (137mph), purely because of the compactness of the motorcycle and aerodynamic efficiency of the dustbin fairing. The fairing also contributed to extraordinary fuel consumption.

During the course of the season the fairing design was developed continually, Anderson sometimes racing

LEFT Australian rider Ken Kavanagh was signed by Moto Guzzi for 1954, riding the 250, 350 and 500 singles. All three capacities were visually similar and this is Kavanagh on the 250 (not 350, as stated on the photograph).
Moto Guzzi

BELOW For 1954, the factory bikes featured a full-coverage front fairing. This initially incorporated twin fuel tanks, but during the season these were replaced by a cylindrical tank above the engine, as on this version. The rear streamlining was less successful.
Moto Guzzi

with rear streamlining, although this was unsuccessful. One of the duties expected of the riders was the development of the frame and improving the overall handling, which in those days was done by trial and error. Various combinations of fuel tank were tested as with the pannier tanks the rear wheel would sometimes lift under braking. The pannier tanks also used to split due to the vibration, and for the Isle of Man TT they were replaced by a cylindrical tank over the engine, together with an interconnected fuel tank on top.

After the TT, for other Grands Prix, only the cylindrical tank was used, held by steel straps against wooden supports and it could be moved forward and backwards to alter weight distribution. From November 1953 until September 1954, most of this development was undertaken by Kavanagh. Both Anderson and Lorenzetti felt that at their age (45 and 43 respectively) they had better things to do. In Anderson's case this was golf, while Lorenzetti had many business interests in Milan.

Not content with the 75 x 78mm, or even the 75 x 79mm engines, Carcano wanted to improve breathing at high rpm and also reduce piston speed. Already the 75mm bore had stretched the 250-based design to its limit, so Carcano created the short-stroke 350 by reducing a 88 x 82mm 500. The stroke was shortened

to 69.5mm, and a bore of 80mm took the capacity to 349.345cc. This new 350 could fit larger valves, a 41mm inlet and 36mm exhaust and with a 40mm Dell'Orto carburettor the power was increased to 38 horsepower at 7,400rpm. The cast-iron cylinder liner was replaced by a hard-chrome aluminium cylinder, also reducing weight.

The 1954 350cc Grand Prix season started very poorly for Moto Guzzi and there were no good results in the first three rounds, France, the Isle of Man and Ulster. At the Belgian Grand Prix however, the 345cc Guzzis showed that they were in a class of their own, Kavanagh leading home Anderson. With victories in Switzerland, Holland, Italy and Spain, Anderson comfortably retained his 350cc World Championship. The 350 Grand Prix at Monza was a triumph for Moto Guzzi in front of their home crowd, with works bikes filling the first four places.

The 250 Bialbero continued to be raced during 1954, although a short-stroke version (70 x 64.8mm) was produced, the NSUs continued to dominate. The new short-stroke engine had a 38.5mm inlet valve and 33mm exhaust valve, and still used the 140mm con-rod. This was the final 250 Bialbero engine which was also used during 1955. First raced by Lorenzetti and Montanari at a national meeting at Monza, even with

the new engine results were not forthcoming in the 250cc category. The first Grand Prix was the Isle of Man and Fergus Anderson could only manage fifth in the Lightweight TT, his streamlining having broken with the vibration and had acted as an air brake.

Assen was the next Grand Prix, and it was also the last official race for a works 250. Here, Kavanagh finished fourth. For the Italian Grand Prix at Monza much effort was spent on getting more speed out of the bike but when NSU's Rupert Hollaus was killed in practice NSU withdrew from the event. In a spirit of sportsmanship Moto Guzzi also withdrew, Arthur Wheeler taking the 250cc victory on his private machine. The official 250 was retired After Monza, but nevertheless. The 1954 season was extremely successful for 250cc Moto Guzzi in various national championships with wins in Italy, Austria, Great Britain, Holland and Switzerland.

By the end of 1954 the 350 was still dominant in its class, and with the new short-stroke engine the prospects for the following season looked promising. However, both the 250 and 500 singles were struggling

and after the disappointment of the 500 four, Carcano wanted a new challenger for the 500cc crown. This would be the V8 that would appear during 1955.

# 1955

Enrico Parodi was now worried about the age of two of his leading riders and offered Fergus Anderson the position of racing team co-ordinator. Anderson thus retired from active racing, and Lorenzetti, only slightly younger than Anderson, having disobeyed the finishing order in the previous year's 350cc race at Monza, was replaced by Duilio Agostini. Completing the team alongside Kavanagh was Dickie Dale and the reserve rider, 1954 Italian Champion in the 2nd Category, Giovanni Rocchi. With no official factory representation in the 250 class, Lorenzetti, Roberto Colombo, and Cecil Sandford were provided with 1954 works bikes, Lorenzetti winning the Italian Championship in 1955. Lorenzetti also had a 1953 350 fitted with 1955 streamlining.

From September 1954, all the testing was done by Kavanagh, and he would spend two or three days a week at Monza. Dale still lived in England and Agostini was involved in riding instruction at Mandello for the police. However, Agostini was the standard rider for the wind tunnel tests. When Bill Lomas joined the team after the Isle of Man TT he was only a freelance rider and still rode an MV in the 250 class.

Soon however, there was considerable tension between Anderson and the rest of the racing department, much of it centring on Anderson's continued role as a journalist for *The Motor Cycle* and his first test of the V8. This is recounted in the section covering the V8 and ultimately led to Anderson's position as team manager not being renewed. By 1955, Enrico Parodi too was becoming concerned about the cost of running the racing programme, which by now also included the V8.

The 350 for 1955 was the short-stroke (80 x 69.5mm) version that was raced a few times at the end of 1954. The frame was virtually unchanged from 1954 but there was more development in the wind tunnel. The result was a new fairing that had a better drag factor, leading to higher speeds. In order to save weight, Carcano would not allow the electron fairings to be painted a final colour, instead, leaving the fairing in the anti-corrosive green protective paint. This would become as distinctive

for racing Guzzis as the earlier red. The barrel fuel tank was supplemented by a normal one above the top frame tube giving a fuel capacity of 30 litres. By now the 500 single was barely competitive, and development of the V8 continued throughout the year.

The first official meeting with Anderson as team manager was the annual Shell Gold Cup at Imola at Easter. It was an eventful meeting. Kavanagh won the 350 race at an average speed of 83.98mph (135km/h), but the event was marred by the death of Ray Amm on the MV. In the 500cc race Agostini's 500 single caught fire, the electron parts causing a spectacular fireball. At Hockenheim shortly afterwards, Kavanagh and Lorenzetti completely dominated the DKWs, Kavanagh winning at 154.5km/h (96mph). He also finished second in the 500 race.

It was a vintage year in 1955 for Moto Guzzi in the 350cc World Championship, the green streamlined singles winning every race; Agostini in France, Dale in Italy and Kavanagh in Holland. However, it was new-recruit Bill Lomas who took the title with victories

ABOVE The 350 was unbeatable in 1955, and the first victory of the season was in the hands of Kavanagh at the Easter Imola Gold Cup. *Moto Guzzi*

BELOW Although only a freelance rider for Moto Guzzi, Bill Lomas won the 350cc World Championship on the short-stroke DOHC single. *Moto Guzzi*

in the Junior TT, Germany, Belgium and Ulster. To prove there was still life left in the 500 single, Lomas won the 500cc Ulster Grand Prix, his efforts earning him a two-year works contract.

A single overhead camshaft 1953 350 was also used to set several world records during 1955. On 23 March, Anderson, Agostini, Dale and Kavanagh, took the 350 to Montlhéry in France where they set 8, 9, and 10-hour records, plus the 1,000-mile in 350cc, 500cc, 750cc and 1,000cc categories. Further solo and sidecar records were set in October and November by Anderson, Lomas and Dale. Shortly after that Lomas and Dale went to Australia with a 350 and 500 to compete in selected events, winning races as far afield as Perth and Mildura. Giorgio Parodi, one of Moto Guzzi's founding fathers, died on 28 August leaving Enrico firmly in control.

# 1956

Now at the peak of their success, the venerable singles were coming under increased competition from the four-cylinder opposition. Again Carcano's brilliance was demonstrated with further domination in the 350cc class, although Guzzi still struggled in the 500s. For 1956, the official racing team consisted of Lomas, Kavanagh, Dale and Agostini. Rocchi was again retained as the reserve. With Anderson gone, Mondo Michelli once again became team manager.

Enrico Parodi immediately instigated a new set of guidelines regarding prize money and starting money. This gave the company even more control over the outcome of the races and the company, rather than the riders, would negotiate starting money. Also, it was agreed that all prize money would be shared between the three riders.

In the 500 class the single was still campaigned but was now totally outclassed. The ignition was changed to a magneto and single spark plug. The only placing the 500 achieved was Lomas's fifth in the Senior TT at the Isle of Man. Carcano was hoping that the V8 would provide success in the 500 category, but development was slow and hampered by problems with the handling and reliability. It was with the 350 that most hopes were placed, but now the venerable single was coming under increased competition from the four-cylinder Gileras and MVs.

While the engine remained much as for 1955, it received new camshafts to improve the torque, and different gearbox ratios. The camshaft timing was now inlet opening 77.04° before top dead centre, closing 63.39° after bottom dead centre, and exhaust opening 63.87° before bottom dead centre, closing 44.37° after top dead centre. For a racing engine the overlap of 121° was very moderate, as was the inlet duration of 243° and exhaust duration of 288°. With a compression ratio of 11.7:1 the 1956 engine still produced 38 horsepower at 7,400rpm on 90/100 octane fuel, but with a wider spread of power. Even though the power peaked at 7,400rpm, the engine would run safely to 8,200rpm. The contact breaker for the dual ignition was now mounted on the right side of the crankcase, above the geared oil pump.

More development work was concentrated on the chassis and streamlining, with particular emphasis on reducing the weight even further. Carcano knew that only through a combination of superior aerodynamics and an improved power-to-weight ratio could the 350 single beat the fours. The fairing for 1956 also featured a small air intake to cure what Carcano suspected was a breathing problem. Although the fairing was noticeably

LEFT With successive 350cc World Championships from 1953 until 1957, the 350 Bialbero was the most successful racing Moto Guzzi. Carcano's obsession with saving weight saw them finished only in green protective paint. This is Kavanagh's 1956 350, with the Isle of Man TT number 72. The air intake in the fairing has been covered but is clearly visible.

**BELOW** Kavanagh is seen in practice at the Isle of Man in 1956. He went on to win the Junior TT that year, at an average speed of 89.29mph (143.67km/h) with a fastest lap of 93.15 mph (149.88km/h).
Ivar de Gier

**BOTTOM** Dickie Dale (34) and Duilio Agostini (12) lead Bill Lomas in the 350 Nations Grand Prix at Monza 1956. This time, the Moto Guzzis were outpaced by Liberati's Gilera.
Moto Guzzi

**RIGHT** No longer an official factory rider, veteran Enrico Lorenzetti still provided Moto Guzzi with third place in the 1956 250cc World Championship.
Moto Guzzi

Throughout the season the bikes of the other riders had been plagued with detonation and ignition failures but the cause was not located until the end of the season. Each frame had its own coil ignition as did the Heenan & Froude test bench. Tracing the problem to faulty ignition systems attached to the frame led to the coil ignition being discarded for the nest year. Another problem was the bucket tappets with the cam riding directly on the valve collar. After Lomas dropped a valve at Hockenheim these were replaced with those from the 500 four, in either steel or duraluminium, along with a larger valve guide.

In October 1956, a single overhead camshaft 350 was used for more standing start record attempts. On the airstrip at Montichiari, Enrico Lorenzetti set both standing kilometre and standing mile world records. Lorenzetti also continued to campaign a 250 Bialbero special with more up-to-date streamlining. Created with the assistance of Luigi Lunardon and Eugenio Canova, Lorenzetti's five-speed 250 Bialbero featured the barrel-type fuel tank and a tubular backbone frame. Although he did not win any classic events, Lorenzetti ended third in the 250cc World Championship. An amazing result given he was 45 years of age and the Bialbero, its roots in the TT 250 of 1926, was struggling against the MVs. After his final

sleeker, the frame too reverted to the 1953 type with a single, large-diameter main frame tube that also acted as an oil tank. The engine hung from a trellis and there was a completely new rear subframe consisting of short triangulated tubes. The leading link forks were now from the V8, and featured Girling sprung dampers. The reduced drag, combined with lower weight and higher overall gearing (17/43 final drive sprockets), saw the top speed increase to around 230km/h (143mph).

Lomas and Dale returned from Australia in time for the Imola Gold Cup at Easter. Here, Kavanagh led the 500cc race on the V8 before it overheated, but won the 350 event. Shortly afterwards, at the non-championship event at Floreffe in Belgium, Fergus Anderson, after such a distinguished career with Moto Guzzi, was tragically killed on a BMW. The first World Championship event was the Isle of Man Tourist Trophy. Kavanagh won the Junior TT but that was to be his only Grand Prix victory that year. Lomas went on to take victories in Holland, Germany, and Ulster. It was enough to give him his second 350cc World Championship.

race, the 1957 Nations Grand Prix where he finished third, Lorenzetti retired to his business in Milan, where he died in July 1989.

It was at Senigallia on 30 July that another Australian rider, Keith Campbell was offered his first ride on a factory 350cc Moto Guzzi. Campbell was being tested along with Eddie Grant (who was killed the following weekend), and the politics of racing took over. Campbell, with a faster machine and under team orders, won the race ahead of the official works riders Kavanagh and Dale. Mandolini on an indecently fast 1953 bike finished second, creating further tension within the team. This resulted in the eventual signing of Campbell for the 1957 season and led to Kavanagh leaving Moto Guzzi for MV. In the meantime, Campbell took a pair of racing singles to Australia and competed in several events over the southern summer, winning the Australian Senior TT.

During the period from March 1956 until 1958 Count Giovanni Lurani used a single overhead camshaft 350cc powered four-wheeled Nibbio II to set several distance records at Monza. In 1960, it was fitted with a 1954 DOHC 250cc engine, the final version being the 1963 Colibrì (Hummingbird) of Piero Campagnella and Angelo Poggio.

# 1957

This was the final Grand Prix season for Moto Guzzi and was one of the more difficult, but ultimately rewarding. In a season marred by serious injuries, this year saw the 350 Bialbero reach the pinnacle of its development and the V8 finally achieve some success. For the Italian Championship of 1957 Lomas, Dale and Campbell were joined by newcomer Giuseppe Colnago. Development of the V8 continued slowly but the machine still had some way to go before it was a championship contender. A 350 V8 was also considered, but it was with the 350 single that Carcano still saw Guzzi's racing future in that class.

With ever-increasing competition, especially from the Gilera, Carcano set out to lighten the 350 even further, and alter its power characteristics. In so doing

he created the ultimate racing single, and one that
could defeat the far more powerful competition
because it could corner and brake more effectively.
There was no better example of Carcano's genius than
the magnificent 350 of 1957. This existed in two
versions, one with a 78mm stroke and the other with a
79mm stroke, although they were essentially similar.

After testing a 1954 version and its 1956 counterpart
at Modena, Carcano found the earlier bike lapped
faster because of its better acceleration out of slow
corners. The priority on reducing weight as much as
possible, and increasing low-speed torque saw a return
to the 1954 engine dimensions of 75 x 78mm (345cc),
with a corresponding reduction in valve sizes to 39mm
inlet and 33mm exhaust. The carburettor size was
increased to a 45 mm Dell'Orto and while the torque
was increased, power was unchanged at 38
horsepower. This was now produced higher up the rev
range at 8,000rpm. Even with single-coil valve springs
(to reduce weight further), the engine was safe to
8,400rpm. The rest of the engine followed the
tried-and-tested formula that had worked so well since
1954. The one-piece connecting rod ran on a caged
big-end consisting of 16 5mm roller bearings on a
36mm crankpin.

With the reliability problems of 1956 traced to the
coil ignition, there was a return to a magneto with a
single 10mm spark plug. Similar to that of the 500
single of 1956, this also saved the weight of two
batteries, coils and contact breakers. Everywhere there
was evidence of considerable attention to weight saving
with aluminium and magnesium used throughout.
Even the front brake was now a single leading shoe
instead of the earlier double. Such careful attention to
lightness resulted in a race weight of 98kg (216lb)
while for the TT, which required a larger fuel tank and
fatter tyres (2.75in and 3.00in) the weight was 102kg
(225lb). Halfway through the 1957 season the stroke
was lengthened to 79mm, giving 349cc, but all the
other engine specifications were unchanged, as was the
power of 38 horsepower at 8,000rpm.

The weight-saving measures of the 350 were also
passed on to the 500 single. Although the power
remained at 46 horsepower, the carburettor grew to
50mm and the weight of the 500 reduced to 100kg
(220lb). These were astonishing figures considering
that this was before the era of plastic components.
With streamlining, the 500 was capable of nearly
250km/h (155mph). On the track it meant that the 38
horsepower 350 was more than a match for the 45
horsepower Gileras, even on fast circuits like
Spa-Francorchamps, but with only four more
horsepower than the 350 the 500 was more
disadvantaged against the fours.

However, Carcano had already designed a
replacement 500 single that he fully expected to run
during 1958. This new engine was eventually produced
in 1965 and had an even longer stroke (84 x 90mm).
With an 11:1 compression ratio, four valves set at a
narrow included angle, and a 45mm carburettor, the
power was 47 horsepower at 7,000rpm. This five-speed
500 was eventually raced with some success by
Giuseppe Mandolini nearly ten years later.

The 1957 350 season got off to poor start for the
Guzzi team when Lomas was injured, first at the Easter
Imola Gold Cup, then more seriously on the V8 in
practice for the Assen TT, effectively ending his career.
He did not race in any Grands Prix that year. Dale also
crashed at Assen on the 350 Bialbero, finishing his
season. The first classic event was the Isle of Man TT
where the Guzzis were defeated by Bob McIntyre's
Gilera, although Campbell did come second in the
Junior TT. After that Campbell completely dominated
the rest of the season, winning the 350 Grands Prix of

Holland, Belgium and Ulster. He ended up winning the championship, Guzzi's last. Another Australian, Keith Bryen, had joined the Guzzi team in Belgium where he finished third, following that with a second at Ulster.

It was at the end of September, shortly after the final race of the season at Monza, that Dott Rag Bonelli, Moto Guzzi is general manager, announced that the company would be withdrawing from Grand Prix racing. Moto Guzzi's withdrawal, together with that of Gilera and Mondial, signalled the end of the golden era. While the racing success had been a wonderful advertising exercise, the motorcycle market was undergoing a severe downturn and the cost of running the racing department was difficult to justify. By the end of 1957 all three works riders were severely injured, and 1958 would see the end of the dustbin fairings, one of the advantages that Guzzi had over other companies. Although they had planned to approach John Surtees to ride in 1958, this did not materialise. With 14 World Championships, 47 Italian Championships and 3,329 victories since 1921, a long tradition had come to an end.

Keith Campbell reverted to racing private Nortons in 1958, suffering a fatal crash at Cadours in France in July on a 500 after winning the 350 race. However, the single-cylinder Guzzis were raced by privateers for several years afterwards. Giuseppe Mandolini raced the long-stroke 500 in the Italian Championship and some Grands Prix from 1965 until 1970, his best result third in the Spanish Grand Prix in September 1970. Prior to that, however, he had finished second to Giacomo Agostini in the 1965 Italian Championship. Arthur Wheeler also continued to campaign 250s and 350s, his best result being a victory in the 250cc Argentina Grand Prix of 1962. Wheeler was third in that year's 250cc Championship.

# THE V8

Nothing represents the resources and technical expertise available to Moto Guzzi during the mid-1950s more than the 500cc V8. More than 50 years on it stands alone as an example of engineering luxuriance. In designing the V8 Carcano was given a free hand, as did the regulations then governing 500cc motorcycle racing. The result was an engine clearly too advanced for the frame and tyre technology of the day, and one that also showed huge potential for further development. While it did not achieve any memorable racing success over its three-year lifespan, it was truly representative of the Moto Guzzi racing department at that time. A brilliant concept let down by a reluctance to face up to the problems it created.

The V8 story began after the Nations Grand Prix at Monza in 1954. Although Guzzi had triumphed magnificently in the 350 race, Kavanagh could only manage sixth behind the Gileras and MVs on the 500 single. On the drive back to Mandello Carcano suggested to Kavanagh the best solution to defeat the fours was either a straight air-cooled six or a water-cooled V8. With the dustbin fairings engine width was a crucial factor and Carcano calculated the maximum width of the engine to be 500mm. He set about designing the most powerful engine he could within those parameters.

A meeting was held to put the idea to the directors of Moto Guzzi. Carlo Guzzi was not very enthusiastic about the project, preferring Carcano to build a single-cylinder to test first, but Dott Enrico Parodi supported Carcano and overruled Guzzi. Enrico Cantoni was given the project to draft as Umberto Todero was involved with the short-stroke 1955 350 Bialbero. The design proceeded in secrecy, with the bike appearing by surprise at the French Grand Prix in May 1955. In the meantime Fergus Anderson had become racing manager and in a letter of 1 February 1955 sent the news of the V8, along with a preliminary drawing, to the press. When the picture was published in *The Motor Cycle* on 10 February 1955 the tension between Anderson and the rest of the Guzzi racing department increased. It also hurt Guzzi's relationship with the Italian press, and the V8 was no longer a secret.

The water-cooled 90° V8 was an amazing design, with many unusual features. The crankcase consisted of a one-piece magnesium casting mounted transversely across the frame and incorporating a six-speed gearbox. When it was found that the flexibility of the engine did not necessarily require the six speeds, a five-speed, and finally a four-speed gearbox was used. Cast-iron cylinder liners were screwed into the engine cases, these being grooved to provide a larger surface area for cooling. With a bore and stroke of 44 x 41mm the engine was slightly oversquare and each cylinder had a 23mm inlet and 21mm exhaust valve set at an included angle of 58°.

The valve stems were a very narrow 5mm and thus not grooved for collets. The tops of the stems were

enlarged, meaning that the aluminium-bronze valve guides needed to be split to allow for assembly. This valve collet retaining system would also cause problems and was later modified. The valves were operated by double overhead camshafts driven by six straight-cut gears, and like the earlier 500 four, they were seated directly in the cylinder head with no inserts. As expected, the primary drive was by straight-cut gears, the reduction being 2.7647:1 (34/94), and the dry multi-plate clutch mounted outside the primary drive cover. This large reduction was in response to the problems that had occurred with the engine speed clutch of the 500 Four.

Water-cooling was essential to cool the rear cylinders, and the radiator was situated in front of the crankcase. The water pump was driven by one of the timing gears but the cooling system was not pressurised. Lubrication was dry-sump, the 5 litres of oil being retained in the frame top tube. On the left of each inlet camshaft was mounted a C.E.V. distributor for the coil ignition to that bank of cylinders. For the first engine the firing order (right to left starting at the front) for the 10mm spark plugs was 1, 8, 3, 6, 4, 5, 2, 7.

The initial design of 15 November 1954 featured a one-piece 180° crankshaft. This was essentially an in-line four with dual con-rods side by side on the crankpins. While the 180° crankshaft had perfect primary balance and was chosen for simplicity of construction, there was some secondary imbalance. The crankshaft itself was supported by five roller bearings, the middle three having split outer races and split cages. The one-piece crankshaft also required the big-end bearings to be split. This was an unusual move, especially considering the unreliability of split cages in the 350 Bialbero during 1953, and would be one of the major causes of engine failure during the next two years. Eye-to-eye con-rod length was 90mm, giving a long rod-to-stroke ratio of nearly 2.2:1.

Carburetion was by eight 20mm Dell'Ortos controlled by a single cable and two cross-shafts, initially with a single float chamber for each bank. In this form, with a 10:1 compression ratio, 68 horsepower at 12,000rpm was produced at the rear wheel. When placed in a duplex cradle frame with leading link forks and swingarm pivoting at the rear of the engine cases the total weight was 150kg (331lb), of which the engine and transmission comprised 56kg (123½lb). The front forks used two external Girling shock absorbers similar to those at the rear, while the brakes were a 240mm four leading shoe at the front and a 220mm single leading shoe at the rear. Tyre sizes were 2.75 x 19in on the front and 3.00 x 20in on the rear, although occasionally, a 19in rear wheel was used.

Development proceeded very quickly and by 14 April 1955 the first prototype was ready. On the road outside the factory Kavanagh briefly ran the bike in front of a crowd of onlookers that included everyone of importance at Moto Guzzi. They were to take it to Monza the next day but this time it would not run on all cylinders because of an ignition problem, so the first test session was at Modena on 18 April. It was still the intention to present the bike unexpectedly at Reims in May and hopefully have Kavanagh lead the Gileras. Reims was chosen because it had three very long straights and would not place too many demands on the handling. This would have been purely as a publicity exercise and the V8 may not have been raced again, existing only to represent the engineering and technological superiority of Moto Guzzi.

Although he had shown little interest in the V8 project, Anderson arrived unexpectedly at Modena and demanded to be the first to test the new machine. Despite being set up for the much smaller Kavanagh, Anderson tested it against the wishes of the technical department and immediately crashed. The bike was destroyed, including the engine as the broken swingarm had damaged the crankcases. As every part was unique the entire project was postponed. From that moment Anderson had a difficult relationship with the racing department and barely communicated with Carcano.

The first race for the V8 was thus at Spa for the Belgian Grand Prix where Kavanagh retired when all the crankcase studs snapped. Immediately after Belgium larger bearing studs were installed. Kavanagh then raced the V8 again twice in 1955, at Senigallia and Monza. In both these races the valve collars became unscrewed. At this stage the crankshaft was still in one-piece, but in an effort to overcome balance problems a one-piece 90° crankshaft was designed and installed on 8 September 1955. This was followed shortly afterwards by an evolutionary 90° crankshaft on 5 October 1955. With the 90° crank came a revised firing order of 1, 5, 4, 8, 6, 3, 7, 2. The 90° crankshaft also used lighter flywheel discs because the pistons now contributed to crankshaft inertia.

RIGHT The magnificent V8 in its final form. Even in 1957, after three years of development it still had many problems.

A winter redesign saw the V8 ready for the 1956 Easter Imola Gold Cup. Here, Kavanagh retired with water pump failure while leading. At Hockenheim shortly afterwards, he retired after five laps when the big-end cages broke, again while leading the race. He did however demonstrate the speed of the V8 when he set a lap record of 199km/h (124mph). At Assen, he retired after a collision with Umberto Masetti's MV on the third lap. Until Assen, Kavanagh was the only rider to race and test the V8, but for the Belgian Grand Prix at Spa, Lomas also rode one. Here, a longer swingarm was tried and Lomas worked his way up to third before retiring, once again demonstrating the V8's impressive speed.

Kavanagh found the bike frightening on the long fast curves at Spa, and after a confrontation with Carcano over the handling no longer raced it. Lomas then rode the V8 at Solitude where it overheated when in second place behind Geoff Duke. At Senigallia, the same event that saw Keith Campbell's first Guzzi works ride, Lomas crashed the V8 while dicing with George Monneret's Gilera. At Monza Lomas crashed the 350 single, breaking his wrist, and Campbell raced the V8 but retired after ¾ of a lap with a big-end bearing failure. On 25 October at the Montichiari aerodrome near Brescia, Dickie Dale set some world records on the V8, for a standing-start kilometre at 144.8km/h (90mph) and a standing-start mile at 185.99km/h (115.5mph).

The one-piece crankshaft was used up until Monza 1956, and despite Dale's world records, the V8 had still not finished a race. The persistent crankshaft problems finally led Carcano to Hirth-Welle in Germany where he had them design a 90° pressed-up crankshaft with one-piece con-rods and caged big-end bearings. The crankpin was increased to 30mm, and the big-end used 15 5mm rollers. Con-rod length increased significantly to 110mm. The new crankshaft consisted of nine separate parts united by radially serrated Hirth couplings.

On 4 December 1956, the new engine was drafted and most of the engine reliability problems solved. Other small changes were the relocation of the oil pump to the rear exhaust camshaft and the carburettors that now had individual float chambers. The carburettor size was increased to 21mm and with the new crankshaft came revised camshafts. Valve timing was: inlet opening 76° before top dead centre, closing 67° after bottom dead centre and exhaust

opening 62° before bottom dead centre, closing 40° after top dead centre. With valve overlap of 116° these were still very moderate figures for a racing engine. The compression ratio remained at 10:1 (it was the same from 1955 until 1957) and the V8 now produced 73 horsepower at 12,500rpm (at the rear wheel), with strong power from 7,000rpm. Crankshaft horsepower was approximately 7 horsepower more and torque was 4.85kgm at 9,300rpm. An indication of the success with the development of the engine was when Lomas set new speed records on 26 February 1957 at Terracina near Rome. Lomas's standing-start 10km (6.2 miles) speed of 234.572km/h (151mph) stood for more than 30 years.

Not long afterwards the V8 had its first victory. On 19 March 1957, Colnago won the 500cc Italian Championship race at Siracusa in Sicily. That was followed by the V8's greatest moment, the Imola Gold Cup at Easter. Three V8s were entered (Dale, Lomas and Colnago), Dale taking the victory. With Lomas out after a crash on the 350 at Imola, Dale and Campbell rode the V8 in the German Grand Prix at Hockenheim. Dale finished fourth and Campbell retired after four laps with engine trouble. In the Isle of Man Senior TT, Dale again rode the V8, now with a dolphin rather than a dustbin fairing. He finished fourth at 94.89mph (153km/h), the engine only running on seven cylinders. Lomas was back for Assen but crashed in practice, serious head injuries ending his career. Dale also crashed in the 350cc race at Assen, breaking both ankles, so he was out for the rest of the season.

With the loss of two star riders the final Grand Prix for the V8 was the Belgian event at Spa. It was almost the V8's final hour as Campbell set a new lap record at 190.130km/h (118mph) and was timed at an incredible 286km/h (178mph) on the Masta straight. While leading the race convincingly the V8 came to a halt with a broken battery lead. For the final event of the season at Monza, Campbell crashed the V8 at the notorious Ascari curve in practice, breaking his pelvis; he did not race again until 1958. Bryen also practised on the V8 at Monza but refused to race it. Two machines sat in the pits but there was no-one left to race them, all of Guzzi's works riders being injured. Shortly after came the announcement that Guzzi were withdrawing from competition.

After three years the development of the V8 was starting to pay off, but while the engine was finally producing reliable horsepower, it was not quite the same with the handling. Although always stable enough in a straight line, the V8 never earned the reputation as a good handling motorcycle. Kavanagh, with much experience on Nortons, wanted to try telescopic forks and was worried about the narrowness of the swingarm bearing at the rear of the crankcase. The leading link forks worked well the 350 but the V8 was considerably heavier and more powerful. Dale too thought the bike had a front-end problem but Lomas suspected it was weight distribution and he sometimes tested and raced the V8 with lead weights on the swingarm.

There was also probably an aerodynamic problem. The wind tunnel only measured frontal resistance and provided no data on the effect of lift. According to Kavanagh, on slow and banked curves the V8 was magnificent, but on the 240km/h (149mph) left-hand Ascari test curve at Monza, the V8 had a terrible weave. So bad was the handling on fast curves that

Carcano even invited the 53-year-old Stanley Woods to test the V8 during 1956. After testing at somewhat less than racing speeds Woods described the motorcycle as perfect and Carcano felt vindicated. What is indisputable is that the V8 nearly killed several top-line riders, including World Champions Lomas and Campbell.

A 350cc V8 was also built, but never raced. This 36 x 41mm engine produced 48–52 horsepower. By using the stretched front cylinders of the V8, a significantly lighter 350 four was also built, producing 48 horsepower. If developed further this could have been the most successful of all Carcano's multis.

While Carcano's V8 was an incredible engineering exercise, over its three-year period it still did not achieve any victories in classic events. If the handling difficulties had been overcome in the same way as the crankshaft problem the V8 would have probably been invincible. Nearly 50 years on the V8 remains a unique example of the abilities of an extraordinary engineer and a small dedicated racing department, in a time of unparalleled economic prosperity.

By 1968, the V7 was painted white
and firmly entrenched as a police
vehicle. This photograph from 1970,
shows a V7 as used by the Italian
municipal police.

# 7 THE V7

As soon as Moto Guzzi withdrew from racing at the end of 1957, Ing Giulio Cesare Carcano started designing a new V-twin engine. The first sketches appeared late that year and work continued during 1958, initially as an academic exercise, but many of the design features would eventually find their way to both the 3 x 3 and a sporting engine for the Fiat 500 motor car.

Built initially as a 500 in 1959, then 650cc, this Fiat engine can really be considered the predecessor of the V7. With forced-air cooling and twin carburettors, it soon produced 34 horsepower, enough to propel the tiny car to 140km/h (87mph). The Fiat project was then abandoned, but many of its characteristics continued on the unsuccessful 3 x 3 Autoveicolo da Montagna that had been developed in parallel. The 3 x 3 engine was, however, designed by Micucci and apart from being a 90° V-twin, shared little with the eventual V7; the crankcases, displacement, cylinder head and lubrication system all being different. It was the tender for a new police motorcycle to replace the Falcone which would see a more satisfactory outcome for Carcano's V-twin.

Since the 1920s, Moto Guzzi had been the primary supplier in Italy of police and military vehicles, so it was with some surprise that a tender was announced. For the continued prosperity of the company during the depressed 1960s it was vital that Moto Guzzi secured this tender. In May 1963, Carcano and Todero, assisted by Micucci and Soldavini, began serious work on the project. The requirements were for a faster and more powerful machine than the Falcone, with a powerful electrical system and a service life of 100,000 kilometres (60,000 miles).

Taking the Fiat engine as a basis, it was decided to double the power output of the Falcone and place the engine in a tube and pressed-steel frame. This was soon considered too expensive to produce, and was replaced by the cradle frame of the V7. The prototype was produced during 1964 and testing began over the winter of 1964–65. In the meantime, a civilian version was also developed, the first model being displayed at the Milan Show in November 1965 where it was the star of the show. Testing by the Italian police and military began in 1966, the V7 initially only completing 31,000km (19,000 miles) before Guzzi's

A 90° V-twin all alloy design, like the earlier Fiat and 3 x 3, the V7 had pushrod-operated overhead valves with the camshaft situated between the cylinders. The camshaft timing was inlet opening 24° before top dead centre, closing 58° after bottom dead centre, with the exhaust opening 58° before bottom dead centre and closing 22° after top dead centre. Lift for both inlet and exhaust valves was a moderate 6.6mm. This camshaft would also be used on the later V7 Special, Ambassador and 844cc Eldorado, and was driven by helical gears from the crankshaft.

Unlike most motorcycle engines of the time, the one-piece steel crankshaft used plain big-end and two plain main bearings. Many of the design features would remain unchanged through the entire production life of the engine. These included the con-rod length of 140mm, the 22mm gudgeon, and 44mm crankpin. The plain bearings necessitated a high-pressure lubrication system, the three litres of oil being contained in a detachable sump underneath the engine. Unlike the 3 x 3 that had an oil filter, the V7's only oil filter was a wire gauze located at the bottom of the crankcase directly connected to the oil pump. Replacement of the lower-end bearings could be done without removing the engine from the frame.

The bore and stroke of the first version was 80 x 70mm, giving an unusual displacement of 703.717cc, again quite different to the 3 x 3. In line with other Moto Guzzis chrome cylinder bores were used. Two overhead valves, a 38.5mm inlet and 34.5mm exhaust, were set at an included angle of 70° and used single-coil springs. An unusual feature was the four-ring piston that carried a second oil scraper ring underneath the 22mm gudgeon. The compression ratio was 9:1 (7.5:1 on the police version) and carburetion was by two Dell'Orto SS1 29mm carburettors. Ignition was by battery and coil, an automotive-type Marelli S 123A distributor being driven off the rear of the camshaft. Power was 50 horsepower at 6,300rpm, with 32 horsepower at 4,500rpm for the police model.

The clutch and final drive followed automotive rather than traditional motorcycle practice. Bolted to the rear of the crankshaft was a flywheel housing a twin plate dry clutch, and the final drive was by shaft inside the right side of the swingarm. A universal joint was connected to the gearbox layshaft

own testers rode a further 55,000 kilometres. With minimal engine wear the V7 won the contract ahead of offerings from Benelli, Gilera and Laverda.

The designation V7 came from the V layout and the capacity of 700cc. The civilian and police varieties were similar (the police version in a lower state of tune), and the basic layout adopted would prove so successful that it continues in production today. As a large-capacity reliable motorcycle the V7 was a wonderful design, but it was far removed from Carcano's fabulous racing engines only a decade earlier. The huge V7 was the antithesis of the final 350 Bialbero that had taken a balance between minimal weight and power to new levels. However, while it was no lightweight performance machine, the V7 was a very clever design, with careful attention paid to accessibility for servicing and long-term reliability. These qualities distinguished this next generation of Moto Guzzi and the V7 would build a loyal following. Eventually too, the V7 would evolve into some of the most impressive sporting motorcycles of the 1970s, '80s and '90s.

and the rear of the drive shaft to a pair of bevel gears. It was a robust design well suited to the police use that was the motorcycle's prime intention. More motorcycle in design was the four-speed constant-mesh gearbox that bolted to the rear of the crankcase.

Other areas where the V7 departed from usual motorcycle practice was in the electrical and starting system. A 12-volt electrical system incorporating a 300-watt Marelli DN 32 M dynamo and 32Ah battery was used and starting was electric only. A massive Marelli MT 40 H 0.7 horsepower starter motor made the fitting of a kickstart unnecessary. The only instrument fitted to the V7 was a speedometer.

The chassis was more conventional in its layout. Although constructed more for strength than lightness, the frame was a tubular steel double-cradle type with a single 48mm backbone tube. Telescopic forks and swingarm rear suspension completed the specification. Because the forks were enclosed by top covers these too looked massive, but the fork tubes were only a marginal 35mm in diameter and they were very heavy as the fork legs were steel. Wheels were alloy Borrani 18in front and rear, fitted with large 4.00 x 18in Pirelli tyres. This was also an unusual feature for the time as most motorcycles were fitted with narrow tyres on 19in rims.

The brakes too were marginal, even though the front was a full-width 220mm twin leading shoe with a 220mm single leading shoe at the rear. The weight of 243kg (536lb) was just a little too much for the brakes and although the factory claimed a top speed of 170km/h (105mph) with the rider fully prone, the early V7 was hardly a performance machine.

As the V7 was a totally unique motorcycle it was greeted favourably by the press. Not only was it a refreshing design but it also offered a level of quietness and sophistication that was rare for motorcycles in 1966. Handling was surprisingly sure-footed for such a large motorcycle and as a touring motorcycle the V7 was unequalled. Performance however, was lethargic, *Cycle* magazine in June 1967 putting their test machine through a standing-start quarter-mile in 16.1 seconds at 84.9mph (136km/h).

While various prototypes had appeared throughout 1965 and 1966, only 30 production V7s were built in the latter year, plus 52 V7 USAs. Regular production began in 1967, these differing in several details to the prototypes. There was now a round taillight, new passenger grab rails, new silencers, and rear shock absorbers with exposed springs. Colours were no longer silver but burgundy with chrome tank panels.

**BELOW** The V7 was
superseded by the
757cc V750 Special
from 1968.

The delay in putting the V7 into production was undoubtedly due to the instability facing the company during 1965. At the time of the V7's conception, Carlo Guzzi had retired from the company and died at Mandello on 3 November 1964, before he could see the V7 come to fruition. Enrico Parodi was totally in control during this period but had completely underestimated the significance of the Fiat 500 in the Italian market for mass transportation. Whereas during the 1950s people were clambering for Cardellinos, Zigolos and Gallettos, they were not enthusiasts and when prosperity arrived in the mid-1960s they deserted these basic motorcycles for cars. Parodi put his faith in the Dingo but this was misguided.

There were also other problems facing the company. Much of the plant and machinery was out of date, as was the management and marketing. Enrico Parodi dramatically sacked Dott Rag Bonelli in the early 1960s, signifying the beginning of the company's decline. On top of these problems the Parodis were running out of money and on 25 February 1966 the company went into receivership.

Under the control of the IMI (*Istituto Mobiliare Italiano*), a group of creditors, a provisional board chaired by Arnaldo Marcantonio was installed. The day before receivership the entire workforce was sacked, with instructions to report for re-hiring the following day. This was too much for the proud Carcano who expected to be asked back to the factory. In a move that showed little appreciation for his technological and racing achievements, Carcano was not asked to return. This left the V7 design unfinished, and much sadness within the company. Later, many of the workers were laid off, Cantoni being another casualty. Following the unfortunate circumstances that saw Carcano leave Moto Guzzi, he left motorcycles and became a world class yacht designer.

One year later, on 1 February 1967, a new company, SEIMM (*Società Esercizio Industrie Moto Meccaniche*), was formed. Although still owned by IMI, SEIMM initially rented the Moto Guzzi plant and equipment for three years, with an option to buy. SEIMM eventually bought the plant after two years. New directors were installed, Luciano Francolini as chairman and Romolo De Stefani as manager. In 1968 Donato Cattaneo replaced Francolini as chairman, and remained for the next five years. De Stefani came from Bianchi, bringing Lino Tonti along with him as chief engineer, and Luciano Gazzola as tester.

Tonti had a long and illustrious career in the Italian motorcycle industry. Hailing from the country's engineering heart, Emilia Romangna, since the war he had been associated with Benelli, Aermacchi, Mondial and Gilera, as well as Bianchi. Like Carcano, Tonti also had strong racing connections, also being involved with the Paton and Linto racing machines that bore his name. Gazzola had been a leading racer in smaller-capacity Italian Championships during the 1960s and would prove invaluable as a development rider for the V7 and later V7 Sport.

During 1967, the V7 was produced in modest numbers (1,031), and it continued into 1968 with a few changes to the specification. There was a new starter motor and seat, along with the rectangular taillight of the prototypes. The Dell'Orto SS 1 carburettors were replaced with a VHB 29 square-slide type. Colours were white with red pin-striping and production totalled 1,844 for the year. Although it was eventually

replaced by its larger siblings, the V7 with its 703cc engine, remained in production in limited numbers until 1976. These were mainly police bikes, the later V7 Special proving considerably more popular for civilian use.

# THE V7 SPECIAL/ AMBASSADOR

As soon as he joined the company, Tonti continued work on the V7. At that time the United States was the largest market for the bike, but Berliner, the US importer, wanted a larger-capacity motorcycle. To get this capacity quickly these first Ambassadors of 1968 were created simply by increasing the bore of the V7 to 83mm (still with the 70mm stroke), to give 757.486cc. Thus 1968 Ambassadors had smaller V7 valves, as well as all other V7 features.

It was not long however, before the 757cc bike was further developed into the V7 Special for Europe, and as the Ambassador for the United States. Now there were many other changes apart from the larger bore. Valve sizes went up to 41mm inlet and 36mm exhaust with dual valve springs and new valve guides, now

retained by a circlip. Although they still had four rings, the pistons no longer featured the second oil scraper ring under the gudgeon pin. There were also new camshaft timing gears with a coarser pitch and an uprated oil pump, along with new crankcases and crankshaft. A four-speed gearbox was retained but the V7 Special now had a higher ratio final drive (8/35). While shifting was still on the right for the V7 Special, US Ambassadors featured left-side gearshifting.

In response to demands from the USA, the frame was lengthened, and strengthened around the steering head resulting in a longer wheelbase of 1,470mm (58in). A larger fuel tank with unique, left (main) and right (reserve) fuel taps, was also fitted, with police versions having footboards. The 757cc models also opened the door to the lucrative American police

market and in March 1969, ten Ambassadors were supplied to the Los Angeles Police Department for testing, 85 eventually being ordered. Other US police departments also eventually added the Ambassador to their motorcycle fleets.

With the 757cc engine, power went up to 60 horsepower at 6,500rpm and the reduction in claimed weight to 228kg (503lb), saw the top speed increase to 185km/h (115mph). The improved performance was reflected in *Cycle*'s test of an Ambassador in October 1969. Their test bike went through the standing quarter-mile as fast as many lighter British 650s in 14.36 seconds at 93.16mph (150km/h).

Production of the first 757cc Ambassador began towards the end of 1968, 286 being built. Taking over from the V7, 1,361 second-series V7 Specials and Ambassadors were manufactured during 1969. That

LEFT One of the highly
modified V7 world record
bikes of 1969.
Ivar de Gier

BELOW With two specially prepared V7s, a team
of four riders successfully attempted a series of
world speed records at Monza in June 1969.
Moto Guzzi

year also saw Moto Guzzi return to world record speed attempts. The V7 may have seemed an unlikely basis for such a challenge but Lino Tonti managed to create two remarkably light and powerful machines for these attempts at Monza on 26 June 1969. A 757cc engine was used for the 1,000cc class, and a slightly smaller, 739.35cc (83 x 70mm) engine for 750cc records. Compression was increased to 9.6:1

and with two 38mm Dell'Orto SS carburettors the power for both engines was similar at 68 horsepower at 6,500rpm. More significant was the reduction in weight to 158kg (348lb). These bikes still used standard V7 Special frames, swingarm, wheels and forks, but featured a 29-litre alloy fuel tank and an alloy dolphin racing-style fairing. Top speed was around 230km/h (143mph).

With chief test rider Gazzola out with a broken leg, four other riders were chosen for the June attempt: Remo Venturi, Vittoria Brambilla, Guido Mandracci and Angelo Tenconi. This first attempt was very successful in the 750cc category, where three records were broken: the 100-kilometre, 1,000-kilometre, and the hour. Although they had suffered tyre problems, this success prompted Moto Guzzi to go for further records a few months later, in October.

On 30 and 31 October 1969 a larger team of riders went to Monza, this time to attempt both solo and sidecar classes. The sidecar was the same unit used by Cavanna on the Supercharged 250 in 1948. Gazzola was still injured and the 750 class riders were Silvano Bertarelli, Brambilla and Alberto Pagani. Pagani was joined by Mandracci, Franco Trabalzini, and racing journalist Roberto Patrignani in the 1,000cc category.

The sidecar records were attempted by Brambilla, Giuseppe Dal Toè, and George Auerbacher. Nineteen new records were set, including the 1,000cc 100 and 1,000-kilometre and hour solo records. The 100 kilometres was completed at 218.426km/h (136mph), and the 1,000 kilometres at 205.932km/h (128mph).

The hour record was taken at 217.040km/h (135mph). The 739cc special Guzzi also completed 12 hours at 179.553km/h (111mph).

It was not only speed attempts that the V7 was adapted for. As unlikely as it may seem, V7s were also entered in occasional production races, more for testing than for race success, mostly ridden by Gazzola. In 1970, the V7 was entered for the 500-kilometre race at Monza, but Luciano Rossi crashed.

Another significant racing Guzzi was the ZDS racer of 1970. Sponsored by ZDS, the US West Coast distributor, this bike was essentially an insurance write-off 1969 Ambassador and was prepared specifically for the Daytona 200. Created by Bob Blair and George Kerker, it was planned to take on Harley-Davidson, but the AMA conspired to alter the regulations and the Guzzi was excluded when the protruding cylinder heads failed to pass a new test rig. As the USA was Guzzi's most important export market at that time, Kerker managed to obtain many of the engine parts of the 1969 world record bikes. He visited Mandello where he tested one of the record bikes, leaving considerably impressed.

LEFT Although not really a sporting motorcycle, the factory did race the V7 on occasion. This is Luciano Rossi on the V7 Special in the 1970 Monza 500-km race. Ivar de Gier

With Tonti's assistance the ZDS bike was considerably developed with Norris camshafts, 10:1 Mondial pistons, and cylinder head porting by C. R. Axtell. Carburetion was still by square-slide Dell'Orto VHB 29 carburettors, although it was also planned to fit fuel injection. The starter motor, battery and dynamo were removed and the frame altered considerably to get the weight down to 150kg (331lb). Rickman forks with a single Lockheed front disc brake were fitted but unfortunately, it did not get the opportunity to prove itself except in non-AMA races, mostly in California and later, Texas. The ZDS bike did prove however, that the big V7 could be an effective racing motorcycle.

In 1970, production of the V7 Special and Ambassador increased dramatically to 4,806 units. There was a new instrument layout (for civilian models) that included a speedometer and tachometer, and a return to the heel/toe gearshift, but generally the specification was unchanged. When the French Moto Guzzi importer, Charles Krajka, entered one of the 1969 world record bikes in the 1970 Bol'Dor at Montlhéry it gave Guzzi the incentive to develop their own sporting version of the V7. This would be one of Moto Guzzi's finest sporting models, the V7 Sport.

BELOW The US specification V7 Special was called the Ambassador. Moto Guzzi

Sharing the V7 Sport with Raimondo
Riva in its debut, Piazzalunga took the V7
Sport to third place in the 500-kilometre
race at Monza in June 1971.
Moto Guzzi

# 8 V7 SPORT:
## THE FIRST AND THE BEST?

While the V7 had surprised many with its performance in setting many world speed records at Monza in 1969, Lino Tonti had other ideas for Carcano's V-twin engine. He envisaged a lithe high-performance sporting motorcycle that could also be raced in endurance events. The V7 Sport that appeared in 1971 was not only a magnificent sporting motorcycle, but heralded a long and distinguished range of performance Moto Guzzis.

The transformation of the V7 into the V7 Sport showed Tonti's genius at its best. The V7 and the V7 Special may have been magnificent touring motorcycles, but they were not performance machines. The engine was not designed with that intention and considerably more than weight removal was required to enable the large V-twin to be used in a more sporting chassis.

During the world record sessions of October 1969 Tonti, with managing director Romolo De Stefani and FIM president Dore Letto, discussed building a street bike suitable both for production and production-based racing. De Stefani's outline for such a machine was that it needed to be capable of 200km/h (124mph), weigh less than 200kg (441lb), and have a five-speed gearbox. Thus the V7 Sport was born. Unfortunately, 1970 was a year beset by strikes and the development of the V7 Sport was delayed. Tonti, with the help of two former Aermacchi colleagues, Francesco Botta and Alcide Biotti, built the prototype frames in his own workshop.

When Tonti unveiled his creation in June 1971 at the Monza 500-kilometre race for 750cc production machines, the Italian motorcycle world was stunned. Not only did the new Sport look purposeful, but unlike any other sporting motorcycle it had shaft drive. To ensure the bike was competitive, prior to the race Mike Hailwood had tested it at Monza, afterwards proclaiming the V7 Sport was the best handling street bike he had ridden. Two bikes were entered in the event, Brambilla and Mandracci sharing one and Raimondo Riva and Piazzalunga the other. Riva and Piazzalunga finished third after being second for much of the race. It had been a brilliant debut and the design of the V7 Sport was immediately vindicated.

A few months later, at the end of September, a prototype 844cc V7 Sport was entered in the Bol d'Or at Le Mans, raced by Guido Mandracci and Vittorio

Brambilla, and Riva and Sciaresa. Again it was an impressive showing, Guzzis eventually finishing third and sixth. The V7 Sport was entered in the other rounds of the 500-kilometre Italian series at Modena and Vallelunga. However, victory eluded them, although Brambilla and Cavalli finished second at Vallelunga.

The FIM required at least 100 bikes to be manufactured to homologate the V7 Sport for production racing and 104 were built in 1971. There was initially some doubt as to whether production would even take place. Production manager Alberici was not convinced and this almost led to Tonti's resignation. Fortunately Alberici agreed to their production but as there was no room on the production line they had to be built in the racing department. This first production series continued briefly into 1972; these were the 'Telaio Rosso' (red frame) models, 150 being constructed (from frame number VK 11111 to VK 11261) according to the parts book. There is some confusion as to the actual number as the 'Telaio Rosso' continued to be built to special order during 1972. An

Italian owners' register puts the number at 153 (finishing at frame number VK 11263) but Lino Tonti has said that 204 were manufactured. The confusion appears because the racing department continued to build the 'Telaio Rosso' until the regular V7 Sport production line was completed. Even then they would occasionally manufacture specific racing or test bikes that were also technically 'Telaio Rossi'.

The chrome-molybdenum frame was lighter than that on later V7 Sports, and the early models were hand assembled with different internal parts, notably the primary drive and five-speed gearbox. The cylinder heads and rocker covers on the 'Telaio Rosso' also carried different numbers. The first version was also distinguished by a non-reinforced gearbox case (smooth exterior), similar to that of the V7 and V7 Special.

To enable the engine to fit a lower frame, Tonti started by reducing the height. The belt-driven Marelli 300-watt generator was replaced with a much smaller 180-watt Bosch alternator mounted on the front of the crankshaft. Other changes to the engine included new crankcase and sump castings (evident by more external ribbing), and a slight reduction in capacity to 748cc. Pistons were now 82.5mm, still using four rings, and the compression ratio was increased to 9.8:1. As with other Guzzis chrome bores were used but as there was no air filtration the cylinders and pistons were prone to premature wear. Valve sizes were the same as the V7 Special at 41mm inlet and 36mm exhaust, but the V7 Sport received a new camshaft with both more valve lift and increased duration. The inlet valve now opened 40° before top dead centre, closing 70° after bottom dead centre, and the exhaust valve opened 63° before top dead centre closing at 29° after bottom dead centre. Valve lift for both valves was 6.9 mm and this camshaft was used on all 750 Sports until 1974. Camshaft drive was by helical gear.

The forged one-piece crankshaft and two-piece con-rods were polished on the early V7 Sport, and Dell'Orto VHB 30 carburettors with accelerator pumps fitted. A five-speed gearbox was also used and the V7 Sport fitted with a new ignition system. This featured a Marelli distributor with twin points and coils. There was also a significantly lighter flywheel with different ignition timing marks, increasing ignition advance to a total of 39°. The first V7 Sport featured a gearbox with a unique set of ratios. The primary drive was that of the V7 and V7 Special, 16/22 (1.375:1) and other ratios

were: first 15/27, second 19/24, third 22/21, fourth 24/19 and fifth 25/24. The higher-ratio Ambassador final drive (8/35) was always used on the V7 Sport although two other ratios were available as a factory option: an even higher 9/37 and a Sport 8/37.

In order to save even more weight the starter motor was changed to a much smaller Bosch centrifugally-engaged type. Only 0.4 horsepower, this lacked a solenoid and would be one of the least reliable features of the new Sport. With 70 horsepower at 7,000rpm produced at the crankshaft (52 horsepower at 6,300rpm at the rear wheel), the V7 Sport was one of the most powerful motorcycles available in 1971.

While these engine modifications were significant, it was the design of the red frame that really set the V7 Sport apart. With more space between the cylinders, Tonti designed a long low frame with the backbone between the cylinders. Together with the unique feature of fully detachable lower frame rails to facilitate access to the engine, the double-cradle frame consisted of nearly straight tubes and would eventually feature on the entire range of large twins. The result

was an extremely compact motorcycle with a seat height of only 750mm. To accentuate this lowness, 18in wheels were fitted front and rear. This was the same as the V7 but was a pioneering feature for sporting bikes when 19in was the norm, especially on the front. The WM2 and WM3 alloy Borrani rims were shod with the latest-generation Michelin tyres, a ribbed 3.25 on the front and an 3.50 S41 on the rear. Brakes were a 220mm double sided twin leading shoe on the front with a 220mm twin leading shoe on the rear.

The 35mm front forks with polished alloy fork legs were manufactured by Moto Guzzi and included sealed internal dampers. Although they were a highly innovative design, cartridge-type forks becoming the standard from the mid-1980s, these forks were not particularly sophisticated or effective. They were much narrower than those of the V7 Special and Eldorado at 180mm, and were probably the weakest component in the Sport's chassis specification.

The V7 Sport abounded with quality components, such as 320mm Koni rear suspension units, a hydraulic

steering damper, and clip-on handlebars that could be adjusted both fore and aft, and up and down. The petrol taps were solenoid operated and the rear stainless-steel guard hinged to allow the rear wheel to be removed. Neat touches were in evidence and there was even a courtesy light that operated when the seat was opened. These early models were however, real production racers and came without turn signal indicators. Finishing off the V7 Sport was a wonderfully sculptured lime-green fuel tank and surprisingly quiet, chromed Silentium mufflers.

The V7 Sport represented a remarkable transformation from the V7, but it still was not exceptionally light despite its compact dimensions. Only through excellent design was the weight of 206kg (454lb) well disguised. However, when it came to performance the V7 Sport lived up to its expectations with a claimed top speed of 206km/h (128mph). In 1971 and 1972 the V7 Sport was the fastest production motorcycle available. In a superbike comparison test in September 1972, *Motociclismo* managed a top speed of 201.117km/h (125mph) from their 'Telaio Rosso', faster than any of the other 750s including the Honda CB750 and Kawasaki H2 750. At Monza, the V7 Sport lapped significantly faster than any of the other bikes in the test which included the Ducati GT 750 and Laverda SF 750. Weighing 212.5kg (468½lb), the standing-start 400 metres time was 13.44 seconds at 148.76km/h (92mph).

The first production version of the V7 Sport was announced to the press in September and displayed at the Milan Show in November 1971. At the show it was a sensation, the display bike differing in small details from the eventual 'Telaio Rosso' version, notably in its more rounded Lafranconi mufflers. Demand for the V7 Sport was so strong that it soon went into regular production, there being several changes made during 1972. The next European series had a black-painted

frame with the same green tank and black decals but were still without turn signal indicators. In all other respects the V7 Sport was as before, but no longer featured as many hand-finished internal engine components. For this reason the early 'Telaio Rosso' models are the most sought after, fetching premium prices over later examples. Producing special first editions was not unique to Moto Guzzi; both Ducati and Laverda also indulging in this practice in the early 1970s, with their 750 Super Sport and SFC respectively.

Regular production of the V7 Sport coincided with that of the 850 GT and Eldorado, so specific US versions were also produced. The gearbox casing now featured external strengthening ribs and revised internal ratios. The primary drive was raised slightly to 17/21 (1.235:1) and all the other ratios lowered to compensate. First gear became 14/28, second was 18/25, third 21/22, fourth 23/20 and fifth was 24/18. US Sports had a silver frame with red paint and a larger taillight, turn signal indicators, and reflectors. As the engine specifications were unchanged, though, so was the performance. Nevertheless, production levels increased significantly with 2,152 produced in 1972.

The racing programme continued during 1972. April saw the inaugural Imola 200 race, and special V7 Sports were prepared and tested at Monza prior to the event. One of the testers was Mike Hailwood who soon was lapping as fast as Gazzola. (He was offered a ride in the Imola 200, but Guzzi could not meet his salary demand.) When the racing bikes lined up at Imola the drum brakes of the prototype had been replaced by triple Lockheed discs, and also featured shorter exhaust pipes. Three bikes were ridden by Brambilla, Jack Findlay and Mandracci, finishing eighth, tenth, and eleventh respectively, the Guzzis being overshadowed by Ducati on this occasion. There were also further entries in endurance events that year, but as before these were 844cc prototypes and are covered in Chapter 10. Two V7 Sports were entered in the 1972

**BELOW** An early 1973 V7 Sport; still similar to the 'Telaio Rosso' and not yet affected by De Tomaso's economic rationalisation.

**BOTTOM** Dual front disc brakes were available as a bolt-on kit for the V7 Sport, but a rear disc was only available as a factory-fitted option.

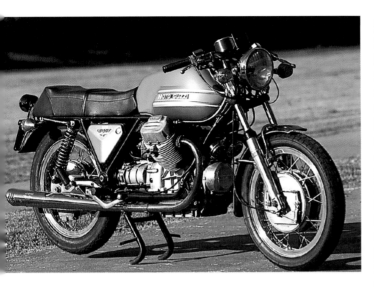

**BELOW** An early 1973 V7 Sport; still similar to the 'Telaio Rosso' and not yet affected by De Tomaso's economic rationalisation.

Monza 500-kilometre race, Ernesto and Vittorio Brambilla finishing third, with Luciano Gazzola and Carena fifth. The Brambilla's bike was one of the Imola racers while the Gazzola/Carena machine was a stock 'Telaio Rosso.'

The following year, 1973, was the beginning of the De Tomaso era for Moto Guzzi. By 1972 SEIMM had been looking for a buyer for the company, and, in December, after negotiations also with Berliner, they

formed an agreement with Alejandro De Tomaso. Born in July 1928 in Argentina, De Tomaso initially raced Maseratis, then after he moved to Italy in 1955, OSCAs, which were made by a small racing car manufacturer set up by the Maserati brothers after they had sold the company that bears their name. During 1957 and 1958 De Tomaso achieved some notable results, but it was his marriage to a wealthy American, Elizabeth Haskell, that gave him the finance to develop and construct his own sports cars in Turin. Elizabeth changed her name to Isabelle but continued to maintain ties with her family. The Rowan Controller Corporation, with Isabelle's brother Amory as chairman, was involved in the purchase of the Ghia coachworks and would continue to figure prominently in the history of the De Tomaso's business for many years to come.

De Tomaso and Rowan eventually sold their interests in De Tomaso Automobili and Ghia to Ford in 1970 and 1972. This provided the capital to invest in motorcycle manufacture, DTI (De Tomaso Industries, based in New York) purchasing 85 per cent of the ailing Benelli company at Pesaro in 1971, and leading him to Mandello del Lario the following year. There was much apprehension about the De Tomaso take-over, much of it justified. Yet De Tomaso

possessed a strong belief in Italian motorcycles, and a dislike of Japanese motorcycle industry practice, even though he obviously liked their designs. His influence on existing Moto Guzzi models was initially very limited, and the V7 (both sport and touring) remained unscathed for a short time. However, it soon became apparent that De Tomaso did not really see any future for the big twin and was committed to multi-cylinders.

Soon after taking control of the company he was reported to have strolled through the V7 assembly lines brandishing an engraved Arab sword, exclaiming 'no more stupid twins'. The immediate result was to restrict research and development, and 1973 was the beginning of a long period of limited model evolution. Many of the new motorcycles were simply re-badged Benellis and the larger Moto Guzzi twins continued with irritating design faults for many years.

Fortunately there were few changes to the V7 Sport for 1973. All bikes now came fitted with turn signal indicators and had black-painted frames. Colours were generally green, with the same decals as the US models had for 1972. In late 1972 the V7 Sport's replacement was displayed, the 844cc Le Mans, but as 1973 was a year of transition towards total De Tomaso influence it would be several years before production of the Le Mans came to fruition. Though a modified V7 Sport, this prototype represented the beginning of a new series and is also covered in Chapter 10.

The regular V7 Sport continued in production, but by late 1973 De Tomaso's influence began to take affect. Although the sporting ethos of the motorcycle continued and performance was unchanged, economic rationalisation began to play a part. From engine No. 33448 the helical gear camshaft and oil pump drive were replaced by a timing chain and sprockets, detracting from the purity of the original design. The rear brake and gearshift arrangement was also revised, the new system of rods being less satisfactory than the earlier type. The two-ball-joint connection for the earlier right-side gearshift and cable rear brake were replaced by a system of rods. A splined rod underneath the swingarm could now be adapted for either right or left-side gearshift and rear brake. The ball joints disappeared for a sloppier and simpler system of a clevis pin and right-angle connection. Compared with the earlier arrangement it was cheap and crude.

Most export versions now had the gearshift on the left, but as it was the right side reversed, the shifting pattern with a one-up and four-down arrangement was

opposite that of other left-side patterns. The rod-operated rear brake too was inferior to the earlier cable type, being far less progressive. It was obviously a quick solution because the rear brake plate still had the casting for the cable attachment. On these later V7 Sports there was also a new, bent, clutch arm that now cleared the back of the gearbox case. Earlier ones with the straight clutch arm were known to foul the case if not adjusted correctly.

There were also small cosmetic changes for late 1973. Metal tank badges replaced the decals and there was a wider range of colours, now including black, bronze and blue. Production too was reduced considerably, to 1,435 during 1973; 1974 model year V7 Sports were all manufactured during 1973, the 750 S taking over in 1974.

Also for 1974 was the option of a V7 Sport with a dual disc front brake. Similar to that of the prototype Le Mans displayed at the 'Premio Varrone' in 1972, which included twin 300mm discs and Brembo 08 caliper with a handlebar-mounted master cylinder, but retaining the 220mm double leading shoe rear brake. The twin 300mm discs certainly gave the V7 Sport impressive stopping power for its day, especially with twin opposed piston Brembo caliper. Most other large-capacity motorcycles generally used smaller diameter single disc brakes with floating calipers, placing the V7 Sport in an elite class. The twin disc kit was also offered by the factory for the V7 Sport and was very comprehensive, including replacement fork legs and front mudguard stays. Only 152 V7 Sports with front disc brakes were manufactured in 1973, as 1974 models, all going to the USA.

# THE 750 S

De Tomaso's intention was to double production at Mandello between 1975 and 1978 and the expensive V7 Sport did not fit into this scenario. The double-sided twin-leading shoe front brake was not only obsolete by 1974, it was more expensive than disc brakes, and the overall specification of the V7 Sport was considered too high to be profitable. As an interim model, Moto Guzzi released the 750 S for 1974, being homologated on 13 February. This was very similar to the disc-braked V7 Sport but for some cosmetic modifications. All 750 Ss had a left-side gearshift, still with the unusual one-up, four-down pattern. Most of

the changes were in the paintwork: black with diagonal stripes in either red, green or orange, new side covers, seat and a rather dubious combination of chrome exhaust pipes and matt black Lafranconi silencers. The seat was neither a single or dual, being a 1½ seater, again a rather unusual concept. The side covers came from the contemporary 850 T.

In all other respects the 750 S was a V7 Sport. It had the same multi-adjustable handlebars, instruments, solenoid operated fuel tap, CEV handlebar switches, and neat touches like the ignition key incorporated in the hydraulic steering damper. All engine and electrical specifications were also shared, the styling changes undoubtedly detracting from the original. There was no doubt that the 750 S was considered an interim model as only 948 were built.

## THE 750 S3

Although a final 100 drum-brake V7 Sports were manufactured in 1975, probably to use up spare parts, the 750 evolved into a final archetype that year. There was no disguising the existence of the 850 Le Mans that had been threatening to supersede the 750 since 1972. However, that model's delay gave the 750 a

one-year reprieve, the 750 S becoming the 750 S3. It may have looked superficially similar to the 750 S, but in nearly every respect the S3 was an inferior motorcycle. It was another victim of De Tomaso's rationalised production that meant that many components of different models were shared. This programme would eventually see the end of the Eldorado and 850 GT. Now the 750 S3 was very similar to the 850 T and T3, the S3 and T3, featuring triple disc brakes with a linked braking system. This had first featured on the Le Mans prototype of late 1972 (see Chapter 10).

The biggest problem with the S3 was its lack of performance. In an era where performance levels were increasing, it was ludicrous to offer a slower version of the 750 S. As it was really a sleeved-down 850 T3, the S3 used the 850 T3 camshaft that not only offered less valve lift, but also less duration. This camshaft worked well in the 844cc engines (like the Le Mans) but gave the S3 decidedly asthmatic performance, especially with the small Dell'Orto VHB 30C carburettors. The inlet valve opened 20° before top dead centre, closing 52° after bottom dead centre, and the exhaust valve opened 52° before bottom dead centre, closing 20° after top dead centre. Inlet and exhaust valve lift was 6.58mm. All other internal engine specifications were as before except for a heavier crankshaft, although some of the final S3s had the lighter flywheel of the Le Mans.

Later S3s also featured the T3 distributor with a revised advance curve, also contributing to a loss in performance. As the engine castings were shared with the T3, the exhaust manifolds were now bolted into the heads rather than screwed as before. Despite the milder cam, claimed power increased to 72 horsepower at 7,000rpm. One advantage that the S3 inherited from the T3 was the replaceable oil filter cartridge, this being housed in the sump and requiring oil pan removal for access. Although undoubtedly the oil filter was beneficial for engine life, the location inside the sump made replacement unnecessarily awkward and time consuming. It was also a design problem that Moto Guzzi refused to rectify under De Tomaso ownership.

Gearbox and primary drive were as for the 850 T3, the same as the 750 S except for a new fifth gear (28/21) giving the same ratio. The S3 also received the 850 T3 final drive (7/33) and wider, WM3 2.15in, Borrani alloy front wheel. It was really the braking system that set the S3 apart from the earlier versions. In addition to the twin 300mm front discs there was a 242mm rear disc. The right front disc was controlled by the handlebar-mounted 12.7mm master cylinder, and the left front and rear discs operated by the rear 15.875mm master cylinder. This braking set-up would

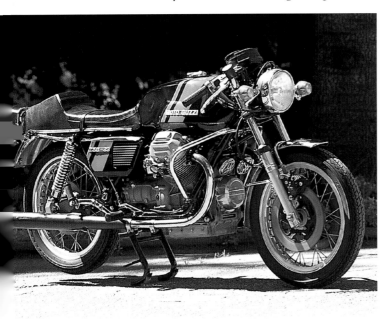

become another Guzzi trademark, and one that few other manufacturers have adopted. All S3s had a left-side gearshift and right-side brake.

Changes from the 750 S abounded. The multi-adjustable clip-on handlebars were discarded for non-adjustable forward offset clip-ons. These, along with footpegs mounted further forward, made the riding position very uncomfortable. There were new switches and an overall loss in detail quality. Side covers became those of the 850 T3, but colours mirrored that of the 750 S. While it was definitely built to a price, not all was inferior on the 750 S3. Finally, the Bosch starter motor gained a solenoid and was uprated at the same time. Now 0.6 horsepower, this was joined by a 280-watt Bosch alternator.

With an increase in dry weight to 208kg (459lb) and 230kg wet (507lb), the S3 suffered when compared with other sporting motorcycle of the period. Contemporary tests were rather unflattering about the S3's performance, and the very optimistic Veglia speedometer. One of the most memorable was *Moto Cycle Mechanics* in April 1976 describing the speedometer needle hovering at 140mph (220km/h), with a BMW R90S and Kawasaki Z900 disappearing into the distance. Actual timed top speeds reflected this disappointing performance. *Motor Cycle* of 17 July 1976 tested a 750 S3 and only managed a mean top speed of 114.2mph (184km/h). The very high final drive gearing also hurt the acceleration with a standing-start quarter-mile time of around 14.2 seconds at 169km/h (105mph). Only comparatively few 750 S3s were manufactured before it was replaced by the 850 Le Mans, total production being 950.

Obviously by 1975, the performance of the 750 S3 was no longer comparable with other sports bikes that were gradually growing in capacity. The Ducati 750 Super Sport had become a 900 SS and the BMW and Kawasaki 900s were about to become 1,000cc. Moto Guzzi's answer was to draw even more on the 850 T3 to create the Le Mans for 1976. Certainly there were performance gains to be had from the 844cc engine, as well as braking, lubrication and electrical improvements. Yet as a pure uncompromised sportster the larger machine offered little over the original 'Telaio Rosso' V7 Sport. The V7 Sport was built as the embodiment of an engineer's ideal, and not compromised by economics, fashion or marketing. As such they are the greatest sporting Moto Guzzis of the modern era.

Created specifically for the US
market, the Eldorado differed only
in details from the 850 GT. Most
noticeable, was the retention of the
weak twin-leading shoe front brake.

# 9 BIG TOURERS AND CRUISERS

Even though the V7 Sport stole the show at Milan in November 1971, almost as significant was a replacement for the V7 Special and Ambassador. This saw many of the engine and gearbox improvements of the V7 Sport, plus, largely as a result of influence from the United States importer Berliner, another increase in engine capacity, to 844cc. Throughout this period the demands of the United States market, including police departments, had a considerable influence on the design of the big twins as the USA accounted for about half the production.

As an evolutionary redesign, the 850 GT, and its US variant the Eldorado, would last through until 1974. The 850 was also offered as the California, primarily a police bike, but also available to civilians. This was the first of a long line of California cruisers that would eventually become the backbone of production at Mandello. Initially all these 850s used the larger loop-type frame, but after 1974 the 850 engine would be used in the Tonti-designed Sport chassis.

## THE 850 GT/ELDORADO/ CALIFORNIA

Despite looking superficially similar to the final 1971 V7 Special, the 850 GT, or Eldorado, featured a number of significant developments. The new engine gained its capacity through a stroke increase to 78mm for a capacity of 844.06cc. Although 83mm pistons were retained, these now had three, rather than four, piston rings and gave a 9.2:1 compression ratio. The stroke was longer, but the lower end of the engine was largely unchanged, the con-rod length remaining at 140mm. This gave the 844cc engine a stroke-bore ratio of 1.79:1. Crankshaft horsepower went up to 64.5 at 6,500rpm.

The engine crankcase castings now featured the internal and external webbing of the V7 Sport, as did the gearbox housing that accommodated a five-speed gearbox. The reinforced gearbox housing was also shared with the regular production V7 Sport of 1972, as were the primary and gearbox ratios. Another significant development was a larger and stronger rear

LEFT The gradual
evolution of the V7
resulted in the 850 GT
of 1972.

RIGHT For 1974, the 850 GT California
received a Brembo front disc brake. The
California also included touring equipment.
Moto Guzzi

towards the end of 1971. The next year saw the 850 become Moto Guzzi's premier model, with 2,412 Eldorados and 2,626 850 GTs produced.

Although the California had also been displayed at the Milan Show of 1971, it was not until 1972 that this went into production. The first California models were built for the American market as a civilian version of the police bikes, initially as 750 then 850cc. They were called the 'Police Special' before becoming the California. Deviations from the specification of the 850 GT included even higher handlebars, footboards, a thickly padded white and black solo seat, crash bars, and a windscreen. Like the 850 GT, the California also featured a four leading shoe front brake, this too eventually being fitted to the Eldorado during 1973.

The additional power and weight had increasingly taxed the double leading shoe front brake and it had come under criticism in the US press. The same year also saw new Lafranconi silencers, shaped more like those of the 750 S, these appearing on both the California and 850 GT. As with the V7 Sport, the helical timing gears were also replaced by a cheaper timing chain (from engine No. 58532). While only 835 Californias were built in 1972, production increased to 1,335 in 1973.

There were a few more alterations to the specification of the 850 GT and Eldorado for 1974. Some of the final variants were fitted with Spanish Amal 930 carburettors because of strikes at Dell'Orto. As with the V7 Sport, the front four leading shoe drum brake was also replaced on the 850 GT, Eldorado and California for 1974. Whereas the Sport received a dual disc set-up, the touring models now featured a single 300mm Brembo disc. Although 300mm was quite large for a disc brake in 1974 it was not much stronger than the drum it replaced. They were fitted with a 15mm handlebar master cylinder that was intended for dual discs. With the front disc came new fork legs, now in aluminium.

Only 350 850 Eldorados were built with the front disc brake, and 164 850 GTs for Italy, before this model was superseded by the 850 T. More Californias featured the disc (1,590) and with the disc came cartridge-type forks that had been pioneered on the V7 Sport. By 1974, De Tomaso's production rationalisation for Moto Guzzi would see the end of the large loop-frame models, all big Guzzis sharing Tonti's lighter and more compact Sport frame.

drive casting, with a return to the lower (8/37) ratio of the first V7. The rear hub featured a finned sludge trap, an increased oil capacity, and a six-bolt sump in place of the earlier single 10mm plug.

An improvement over the V7 Special was a Bosch starter motor instead of the Marelli, but the 850 GT still shared the V7 Special's belt-driven Marelli dynamo rather than the alternator of the Sport. Also shared with the Special (and Ambassador) was the rod-operated rear brake enabling the gearshift and rear brake to be fitted either on the right or left side. While the US Eldorado still used the earlier double leading shoe brake, 850 GTs now had a four leading shoe brake similar to that of the V7 Sport. With the new engine came an increase in weight to 235kg (518lb) so the performance of the 850 GT was comparable with that of the V7 Special. *Cycle* magazine tested an 850 Eldorado in July 1972 managing a top speed of 116mph (187km/h), and a standing-start quarter-mile in 14.04 seconds at 94.65mph (152km/h). The 850 immediately superseded the V7 Special, 815 being produced

# THE 850 T (INTERCEPTOR)

While it may have made economic sense to create a touring bike out of the Sport, it also turned out to be an inspired idea. The resulting 850 T, also known as the Interceptor for the United States, was a sport-touring motorcycle that was a match for anything else on the market. So impressed was I by the 850 T when I tested it in 1974 that I immediately traded in an early Ducati 750 GT for one.

The 850 T was a bike that combined the best sporting elements of the Ducati with the shaft-drive and low maintenance of a BMW. In many ways the 850 T was a landmark motorcycle for Moto Guzzi. It showed that a Guzzi was more than a huge interstate tourer or uncompromised sportster, and could appeal to a wider market. In the process of transformation, the 844cc engine also received a number of upgrades to improve horsepower and reliability. The biggest problem with the 850 T was that the concept was so successful that it was used as a basis for all large touring Moto Guzzis for many years to come, limiting development and model evolution.

Although the 850 T engine shared its displacement with the GT and Eldorado, the 83mm pistons had thinner piston rings and the compression ratio was increased slightly to 9.5:1. Four piston rings were still used, three compression and one oil scraper. As usual at that time, the cylinder bores were chrome plated. The camshaft was new, being less sporting than that of the 750 S, and the same as used on the S3 of 1975 (see timing figures in Chapter 8), and first homologated in Italy on 3 November 1973.

For the 850 T the rocker arms were modified so the rockers were located further from the cylinder bores. Already it was apparent that there were plans to enlarge the engine further with bigger cylinders. The only change to the bottom end was a small increase in crankpin diameter (to 44.008–44.020mm). There was yet another flywheel for the 850 T, with different timing marks. The V7 Sport dual-point distributor was still used but maximum ignition advance reduced to 34°. The five-speed gearbox and 18/37 final drive were as for the 850 GT. Carburettor size also increased to that of the V7 Sport, the twin Dell'Orto VHB 30Cs unfortunately without any air filtration, and claimed power was 68.5 horsepower at 6,300rpm (53 horsepower at the rear wheel).

In many respects the 850 T engine was an improvement on both the V7 Sport and 850 GT. The Tonti frame required a lower engine so that necessitated an alternator, initially 180 watts (13-amp) but later increased to 280 watts (20-amp) during 1975. The starter motor was a Bosch 0.7 horsepower, now with a solenoid located above the starter motor. This was a much more reliable system and would serve the big twins well until 1988. The few final 850 Ts produced during 1975 also featured the replaceable oil filter cartridge in the sump that would become standard that year.

The cycle parts were new for the 850 T, and excellent quality. Mudguards were stainless steel and a 220mm twin leading shoe drum brake fitted on the

rear. Inside the rear wheel was now a rubber
cush-drive that almost eliminated driveshaft spline
wear. Rims were alloy Borrani WM3 front and rear
(although the 1973 prototype was fitted with steel
rims), with 3.50 x 18in and 4.10 x 18in tyres. The
single front 300mm Brembo disc was identical to that
used on the 1974 850 GT and California and lacked
feel and stopping power due to the 15mm master
cylinder. The instruments came from the V7 Sport,
but there was new switchgear.

Because the 850 T owed more to the V7 Sport, it
was much lighter and handled better than the 850
GT. With only 35mm fork tubes, the cartridge-type
front forks were still less rigid than other types, this
being accentuated by the wide spacing of the fork legs
at 195mm (25½in). However, the balance of the
motorcycle was superb and if anything detracted
from the 850 T's quality it was the insipid colour
scheme of green, red or the pure 1970s brown,
accentuated by gold tape. Underneath this blandness
however there lurked a true Grand Tourer that was
the equal of any on the market. Sales reinforced this,
and production was 5,086 in 1974, with a further
214 in 1975. These production figures were at least
double that of some of the competition, in particular
Ducati's 750 GT. Performance too was stronger than
the comparable Ducati. *Cycle World*, in August 1974,
managed a standing-start quarter-mile in 13.78
seconds at 98.03mph (158km/h) and a top speed of
123mph (198km/h). Weight was 506lb (230kg).
Although considerably lighter than the 850 GT, the
850 T was still no featherweight.

## THE 850 T3/T3 CALIFORNIA

The next year one of the 850 T's main shortcomings
was addressed: the poor braking, especially at the
front. The single Brembo had always been lacking in
outright power so 1975 saw the implementation of the
linked braking system that had featured on the Le
Mans prototype back in 1972 at the 'Premio Varrone'.
The resulting 850 T3 would form the basis of most
Guzzis through until the mid-1980s.

With the 850 T3 there were also a few improvements
to the engine and drive train. All engines now had the
oil filter in the sump, the 280-watt alternator, and the
larger U-joint and carrier bearing. The exhaust headers
were bolted to the cylinder heads rather than screwed
as before. Finally, the carburettors received a paper air
filter, although surprisingly, the square-slide Dell'Ortos
remained when they had been effectively replaced by
the newer PHF type on other motorcycles.

To reduce emissions the T3 also received a new
Marelli distributor with a modified advance curve.
This distributor provided more advance at lower revs
and a maximum of 33°. Together with a new flywheel,
this distributor would be used on lower-performance
engines in the future. The T3 also featured a new fifth
gear (28/21), still with the same ratio, and a lower final
drive (7/33).

It was primarily the braking system that set the T3
(and S3) apart from all other motorcycles. Designed by
Tonti to enhance safety by both limiting front wheel
lockup in an emergency and the rider's reliance on the

**BELOW** The 850 T3
California of 1975 had
linked disc brakes.
Moto Guzzi

**BOTTOM** In 1979, cast alloy FPS wheels
replaced the Borrani wire type and there
were also a number of styling updates.
Moto Guzzi

rear brake, this linked the rear 242mm disc and left-side front 300mm disc through a master cylinder under the right-side cover and was operated by a foot pedal. On the early versions of the integrated braking system the hydraulic lines were joined at a simple four-way manifold without a proportioning valve. Weight transfer generally resulted in a proportion of around 70 per cent to the front and 30 per cent to the rear brake. The right-side front disc was worked by a handlebar master cylinder as before, but with a smaller, 12.7mm diameter. Wheel lockup was virtually eliminated and again this system showed Moto Guzzi's capacity for innovation. Interestingly enough, although Moto Guzzi has persevered successfully with the integrated braking it has not been widely adopted by other manufacturers.

There were other small changes to the specification of the T3. Handlebars were taller and the clutch cable incorporated a cut-out switch. With the T3 also came the return of the California, an amalgam of the 1974 California and T3. Like the earlier California, there were footboards, a Plexiglas screen, thick seat and panniers. As tested by *Bike* magazine in August 1975, the T3 California managed a top speed of 97.4mph (157km/h) and weighed in at 576lb (261kg). Underneath the California was the T3, and it would prove to be exceptionally successful, both in civilian and police guise, over its eight-year lifespan. In the USA the T3 was also offered as the

850 T3 FB (footboard), a combination of the California and T3 with footboards and high handlebars.

The 850 T3 continued virtually unchanged until 1979 when the Borrani alloy wheels were replaced by the cast-alloy FPS that were used on several other models (notably Le Mans and SP 1000). There were also other detail touches in line with these other models, including the taillight, switches, seat, headlight, locking fuel cap, and a plastic cover for the alternator. Up until this time the alternator covers had been polished aluminium, and while it may have seemed another cost-cutting measure the plastic cover was also designed to cool the alternator by directing air in and out. Production of the 850 T3 and T3 California continued on a limited scale until 1982.

# THE V 1000 I-CONVERT

The direction of Moto Guzzi under De Tomaso took a significant turn during 1975. De Tomaso saw Guzzi's future with their big twin away from sporting bikes and he wanted a more luxurious touring bike. He also wanted more automotive influence in motorcycles and nothing represented this more than the V1000 I-Convert with automatic transmission. The Convert was conceived for the Italian 'Servizio Scorta', for escorting convoys, which required a motorcycle that could be ridden at walking pace. Later it became available as a civilian version, but was unpopular. Again, De Tomaso completely misread the motorcycle market, yet the Convert was an interesting technological exercise.

The Convert's heart was a bored version of the 844cc engine, 88mm pistons taking the capacity to 949cc. These pistons gave a compression ratio of 9.2:1 and no longer used the chrome bores, featuring instead, cast-iron cylinder liners. A more usual arrangement of three piston rings was also used. The top end of the Convert engine was as with the other 850s, including the Dell'Orto VHB 30C carburettors. As the 949cc engine still used the 78mm stroke, 140mm con-rods were maintained. Although the claimed crankshaft power was up to 71 horsepower at 6,500rpm, the larger engine was required to offset drive-train power loss through the torque converter.

In a move that not only astonished the motorcycling world, but also seemed totally unnecessary, the regular clutch and five-speed gearbox were replaced by a torque converter, dry multi-plate clutch, and manual two-speed gearbox. As it was really a semi-automatic transmission it was neither manual nor fully automatic. Called the I-Convert after the torque converter (Idro-Convert), this unit was supplied by Fichtel & Sachs.

The torque converter sat behind the engine where an impeller was driven by the crankshaft, pumping fluid through a turbine fixed to the gearbox input shaft. To help cool the fluid there was a trocoidal pump mounted at the front of the engine, above the alternator, pumping automatic transmission fluid to a tank under the left-side cover, and a cooling radiator mounted on the front downtubes. This pump was known to fail on early Converts but was later improved. Unfortunately, pump failure was catastrophic, leading to overheating, ultimately torque converter failure, and an expensive repair bill. Unlike automotive torque converters the Convert also required an additional overdrive ratio. Although the drive range of 1.6:1 to 1:1 was sufficiently wide for a motorcycle a two-speed gearbox was also fitted, with a clutch to enable the selection

of either gear. This clutch was different to the usual twin-plate automotive-style Guzzi clutch being a dry multi-plate type (seven friction and five driven plates) located between the torque converter and the gearbox. Primary drive was by straight cut gears (19/22) and the two gearbox ratios were 18/24 and 22/22. In concert with the torque converter there was considerable overlap between the maximum range in normal and the minimum in overdrive, effectively meaning that the Convert could be treated as an automatic. In the low gear it could run to nearly 130km/h (80mph) and while the owners' manual warned against it, it was possible to shift into overdrive before around 65km/h (40mph). The Convert had a 9/34 final drive and the driveshaft U-joint and transmission U-joint had 20 splines instead of the manual versions' ten.

In keeping with its luxury status, the Convert featured a number of amenities, most of which were also of doubtful usefulness. The large instrument panel included only a speedometer (but no tachometer) together with an array of ten warning lights. There was an electronic fuel tap and fuel gauge, and rear disc parking brake and an ignition cut-out operated by the side stand. Other features specific to the Convert were the air spoilers mounted on the crash bars, and an adjustable steering damper. Apart from the standard screen and panniers, the rest of the Convert was 850 T3, the chassis being identical except that most Converts had footboards. It was also produced in a police version but this was never as popular as the 850 T3 California.

The I-Convert won the 1975 Italian design award, the 'Premio Varrone', but this did not translate into sales success. *Cycle* magazine tested one in March 1976 and found the performance and complexity difficult to justify. The curb weight was 272.6kg (601lb) and a standing-start quarter-mile was covered in only 16.432 seconds at 80.71mph (130km/h). *Bike* magazine, in September 1978, achieved a top speed of 108.7mph (175km/h) after removing the screen.

Early Converts had a lighter flywheel that was prone to failure and these were later recalled and changed to a heavier type. Generally, the Convert was a reliable, if somewhat slow, motorcycle. In 1979, the Convert received the same updates as the 850 T3: FPS cast wheels, new taillight and switchgear. Other alterations were a locking fuel cap, fork-mounted ignition switch, and for the USA, PHF 30 Dell'Orto carburettors with accelerator pumps.

The Convert soldiered on in production until 1984, after which the torque converter survived briefly in the California II Auto. The Convert has come in for a lot of criticism but for what it was endeavouring to do it was a groundbreaking concept. The handling and braking were of a very high standard for such a large motorcycle, but unfortunately it was a victim of poor timing and a general misreading of the market. Always an expensive machine, concerns about drive-train reliability, and the complicated electrical system, really sealed its fate.

## THE SP 1000 (SPADA) AND NT

Together with the Convert, one of De Tomaso's plans for the Guzzi V-twin engine was a sport touring motorcycle to compete with BMW. This called for a revised riding position, effective fairing and full instrumentation. For Moto Guzzi, it was also surprisingly simple to create as most of the components were from existing models. The frame and footpegs were from the Le Mans, and the engine from the Convert. The result, especially with the unique fairing, was a superb all-round sport-touring motorcycle, and one that fitted nicely in between the sporting Le Mans and touring Convert and T3. First displayed at the Milan Show in November 1977, the SP 1000 went into production during 1978. For the UK it was termed the Spada (Sword).

The top-end of the engine was identical to that of the Convert, and even though 88mm pistons (still with cast-iron liners) were used the valve sizes (41mm and 36mm) and camshaft remained unchanged from the 850 T3. A 9.2:1 compression ratio, Dell'Orto VHB 30C carburettors and the distributor were also as for the Convert but the SP 1000 lacked the power-sapping torque converter so that more of the power was usable. Still, the 949cc engine with the small square-slide Dell'Ortos was working hard on the SP 1000. The exhaust system, with the upswept pipes was similar to the Le Mans.

The five-speed gearbox and 7/33 final drive were from the T3 but the FPS cast-aluminium wheels from the Le Mans. These had identical rim sizes of 2.15 inches and were fitted with 100/90H18 and 110/90H18 Pirelli MT18 Gordon tyres. The 35mm forks were fitted with new cartridge dampers and provided another 25mm of fork travel. On the SP 1000 the integrated braking

system was further refined through the use of a larger 09 rear brake caliper and four-way proportioning valve with regulator instead of a simple manifold. The larger caliper (with 48mm pistons) resulted in a stronger rear brake and the proportioning valve transferred pressure to the front caliper as more brake was applied. No parking brake was fitted to the SP 1000, but the Convert's rear brake bracket with park brake attachment was used, as it was also on the T3 and Le Mans.

The SP 1000's most original feature was the fairing. By re-commissioning the wind tunnel that had stood idle since 1957, except for scientific purposes, a unique fairing was designed for the SP 1000. All the testing had to be done at night because the wind tunnel consumed so much power that the production lines were unable to operate at the same time. Unlike most other designs, the fairing comprised three glassfibre parts, the top section turning with the handlebars and the two side panels were mounted on the frame. These incorporated angled airfoils to increase downthrust at speed. With this new fairing

came a redesigned instrument panel (in 1970s-style pseudo alligator skin), new CEV switches and throttle, and a metal cover over the fuel cap. The steering damper was now an adjustable friction type rather than hydraulic as before. Colours were silver, gold, or silver/blue, with an abundance of matt black paint.

Unfortunately the SP 1000 was let down by its engine performance. In April 1979 *Cycle* achieved a standing-start quarter-mile in 14.29 seconds at 91mph (146km/h). The wet weight of 251.2kg (554lb) undoubtedly blunted the performance and the wind tunnel-designed fairing also restricted the top speed. *Bike* in September 1978, managed a maximum speed of 113.72mph (183km/h), well down on the 850 Le Mans.

Gradual development saw the SP 1000 evolve into the NT 80 of 1980. Changes included Nigusil cylinder bores (from engine No. 215000), new and more restrictive silencers that were no longer upswept (from the T4), a thicker G5 seat, different colours, and new turn signal indicators. The frame now had a more durable gloss, reflecting a general improvement in finish.

LEFT The most significant feature of the 1000 SP was the wind tunnel-designed three-piece fairing. Produced to compete with the BMW R100RS, the 1000 SP remained available from 1978 until this final version of 1983.

BELOW The expanding range of the early 1980s saw the introduction of the 850 T4, which was essentially an 850 T3 with the top part of the 1000 SP fairing. Moto Guzzi

The final year for the SP 1000 was 1983, by which stage it received red and white (or white and red) paintwork and a number of subtle changes. The fairing lowers were now splayed further outwards to suit taller riders, and the footpegs were lower, more forward and non-folding; these were from the T3. US versions now had Dell'Orto PHF carburettors, while for everywhere else the stiff square-slide VHBs continued. While it may not have fulfilled its role as a BMW-beater in performance or in the marketplace, the SP 1000 was a formidable opponent. Offering more character and a substantially lower price tag, for the first time an Italian motorcycle could be considered a viable alternative in the world of long-distance interstate and intercontinental sport-touring.

## THE V1000 G5

Continuing with the concept of expanding the line-up through amalgamation of models was the V1000 G5 (G5 indicating a five-speed gearbox). Essentially a V1000 with a five-speed gearbox, this was offered alongside the SP 1000 during 1978. The G5 was underrated, as it offered the performance advantages of the 1000cc engine, without the power-sapping torque converter. Thus it was not only lighter than the Convert, with a claimed weight of 220kg (485lb), but it also had a top speed of around 190km/h (118mph).

Most of its features came from the Convert, the same instrument panel now including a tachometer, as well as featuring the wide array of warning lights. While the Convert side stand was maintained, the G5 also received the revised braking system of the SP 1000 with the larger, 09 rear Brembo brake caliper and four-way proportioning valve. Other chassis parts were more Convert than SP. The wheels were still alloy Borrani and the front Brembo brake calipers were forward mounted. While most Converts came with footboards, the G5 had normal footpegs, lower and more forward than those on the SP 1000 and T3. In 1979, the G5 received the updates of the similar Convert, in particular cast wheels and a new taillight, switches and US versions had Dell'Orto PHF carburettors. By 1980, all engines had Nigusil-plated cylinders, and the final G5 featured a more normal instrument panel with side-by-side speedometer and tachometer.

## THE 850 T4

With the NT 80 of 1980, there was also an addition to the 850cc range, the T4. The 850 T3 continued as before, the T4 filling the gap between it and the SP 1000. From the SP 1000 came the upper fairing, and forks with rear-mounted brake calipers, like the later 850 T3, although the T4 used a longer fork damper and dual spring. The braking system with proportioning valve and regulator also came from the SP 1000, and the T4 had the new, lower mufflers. The 850cc engine was unchanged from the T3 except for Nigusil-plated cylinders. Claimed power was 68.5 horsepower at 7,000rpm, giving the 215kg (474lb) T4 a top speed around 190km/h (118mph). Not available in the USA, the 850 T4 was primarily sold as a police model.

## THE CALIFORNIA II/ AUTOMATIC/850 G

While the 850 T3 California continued in production until 1982, and the SP 1000 into 1983, the days of the round-finned engine were clearly numbered. The Le Mans III had made its debut in late 1980, and a replacement California with a new square-fin engine appeared in 1981. This new model, the California II, harked back to the big loop-frame 850 GT and Eldorado, last seen in 1974. It may have used the Tonti frame as a basis but with the California II came a model

delineation similar to that which existed in the early 1970s, a specific big tourer in addition to the more sporting models.

There was much more to the California II than simply a restyled engine and 850 California styling. Apart from the finning, the engine was almost identical to the final SP 1000 NT, so it was now 949cc, featured the Nigusil cylinders, new silencers, and a proper air filtration system. It also had the small valve cylinder head (41mm and 36mm valves), 9.2:1 compression ration, and Dell'Orto VHB 30C carburettors. Later versions were fitted with round-slide Dell'Orto PHF 30 carburettors.

The emphasis was on torque rather than peak power with the larger engine, with a claimed 77Nm at 5,200rpm. As with all square-fin engines there was also a sump spacer, and the entire unit was quieter. In 1987 (from engine No. 18786), the Bosch alternator was replaced by a Spanish Saprisa, and from engine No. 21100 the engine oil breathing was improved with vent tubes from the cylinder heads.

There were even more changes to the frame for the California II. Not only was the swingarm longer than that of the Le Mans III, but it was of a much heavier construction. The steering head was also longer at 212mm with an extra gusset to the frame backbone tube. The result was a motorcycle considerably larger than its predecessor, and quite similar in size to the earlier 850 GT. Bodywork too mirrored the 1974 California: deeply valanced guards, black and white seat, crash bars, screen and panniers were standard equipment.

Together with longer and wider, 195mm forks with 35mm fork tubes and air-assisted dampers, there were new cast alloy wheels for the California II, still only 2.15 x 18in. On these were mounted Pirelli Gordon MT18 120/90 x 18in tyres, which were really too large for the rims. At the rear, slightly longer inverted air-assisted Paioli shock absorbers (330mm) also contributed to a larger-feeling motorcycle. The integrated braking system with three Brembo 08 brake calipers (the front mounted in front of the fork legs) were carried over from the 850 T4 rather than the SP 1000. From frame No. VT 17500 (1985) the California II received a longer seat, seat lock and different footboards. The crash bars too were wider on later models. The overall result was a large touring motorcycle that weighed a claimed 250kg (551lb) dry.

In 1985, some California IIs were manufactured with the Convert automatic gearbox and these were the final Moto Guzzis with the torque converter. Released specifically for the large German market in 1986 was the 850G. Essentially a California II with an 850 T engine this was only available for the one year.

Although really designed for the American market, the California II was a consistently good seller between 1981 and 1987, with numbers rivalling the Le Mans. The peak years were 1982 (2,338 units) and 1983 (2,341). While it was not intended as a performance motorcycle, the California II offered equivalent performance to other vehicles of its type. *Motorrad*, in June 1982, managed a respectable top speed of 159km/h (99mph). So successful has the California idea been for Moto Guzzi that it later became the California III, and today, the EV dominates production.

# THE 850 T5

Even before fashion dictated the form of the Le Mans,
it begin to infiltrate to the 850 T line. Along with
fashionable trends, another of De Tomaso's beliefs was
that automobile design should influence that of
motorcycles and he had his Modena styling studio
rework the T4. The resulting 850 T5 of 1983 was a
much more integrated design, but not an entirely
successful one. The concept was also a little too radical
for the conservative Moto Guzzi clientele and,
combined with very negative press reports, the 850 T5
was a sales disaster. As with Giugiaro's Ducati 860 GT
of 1974, it again proved that motorcycles cannot be
treated as two-wheeled cars when it come to styling.

The engine of the T5 was similar to that of the T4,
but for the square finning. Thus it continued with the
small valves, carburettors and lower performance
distributor. Power was 67 horsepower at 7,000rpm and
just about everything else was new on the T5. The first
(1983) series featured a frame with the shorter, 165mm
(6½in) steering head, but from 1985 the frame was the
longer steering head type of the California II, with the
extra gusset between the steering head and backbone
tube. All T5s had a swingarm that was the same length
as the Le Mans III (410mm/16in), but reinforced as
with the California II and wider, to allow for the larger
rear tyre.

The biggest changes concerned the use of 16in
wheels front and rear and new front suspension. For
the first time a Moto Guzzi featured forks with larger
fork tubes than 35mm, the T5's being 38mm. With
linked air-adjustable dampers, these forks initially had
dual springs but this was later changed to a single
spring, and finally, to a longer and shorter two-spring
combination. The fork width was the narrow, 180mm
(7in) of the Le Mans I rather than the wider, 195mm
(7⅔in) of all the other T series, and the forks featured
an integral fork brace. Rear shock absorbers were
air-assisted 320mm Paioli. The combination of these
normal length shock absorbers and the 16in wheels
meant the T5 suffered from a severe lack of ground
clearance.

Although the 16in wheels were chosen more for their
fashion than function, there was one benefit over all
other Moto Guzzi wheels. The rim width was increased
to 2.50in on the front and 3.00in on the rear. This
enabled larger MT29 and MT28 Pirelli Phantom tyres

to be fitted, a 110/90H16 and a 130/90H16. While
the patented Guzzi integrated braking system with
four-way manifold was retained, there were several
changes to the T5 brakes. Because of the smaller
diameter wheel, the front disc brake rotors were
reduced to 270mm (one-piece and drilled), and there
was now a matching 270mm disc on the rear. With
the strengthened frame in 1985 the integrated braking
system was also upgraded to incorporate a four-way
proportioning valve.

The styling, too, was a significant departure from
the earlier T3 and T4. A small fairing incorporated the
rectangular headlight and instrument panel, and there
were new switches. Integrating the side covers with
the fuel tank, seat, and mudguards was not only
unlike other Moto Guzzis but was also a styling trend
shared with some Ducatis of that era. With the
moderate power of the small-valve engine the T5 was
not a particularly strong performer. *Motociclismo*, in
March 1984, managed a top speed of 196.5km/h
(122mph) from their 225kg (496lb) machine.

In 1984, a few styling changes were made to the T5,
and in response to criticism, particularly regarding
stability and handling, there were more developments
for 1985. In addition to the frame and fork
alterations, the biggest change on the 850 T5 NT was
the substitution of the 16in rear wheel for a 3.00 x
18in. Tyres were now Michelin A/M48, the rear being
a 120/90V18. Koni shock absorbers also replaced the
Paiolis, and the fairing had a taller screen. This final
series also featured dark grey anodised Dell'Orto PHF
30C carburettors, and from engine No. 13400 the
revised engine oil breather system of other models.
The claimed power was the same but there was a
slight reduction in performance. *Motociclismo*, in
February 1986, achieved a top speed of 191.3km/h
(119mph) from their lighter, 221kg (487lb) 850 T5
NT.

Produced until 1989, by this stage the T5 had been
transformed into the more acceptable Mille GT. The
Mille GT proved that the T5 could have been far more
successful if it had not originally been such a victim of
fashion. Underneath those 16in wheels and integrated
bodywork was an excellent motorcycle waiting to be
unleashed. While the 850 T5 was subsequently
replaced in the civilian line-up by 1,000cc variants, it
continued as the basis for police models through until
1998. These had 18in wheels front and rear, and all
the engine improvements of the later models.

BELOW Another confused model was
the Mille GT, Moto Guzzi's first attempt
at a retro-look. Wire-spoked wheels were
standard, while cast wheels were an option.

# SP II

Complementing the T5 in late 1984 was the similar 1000 SPII that replaced the SP 1000 NT. This was very much an amalgam of the 1985 850 T5 and the California II. The 949cc square-finned engine was shared with the California II, the running gear with the T5, and it was really more a 1000cc T5 with an SP fairing. Continual development of the small valve 949cc engine now saw 67 horsepower at 6,700rpm, and while European specification models still used the Dell'Orto VHB 30 C carburettors US versions had Dell'Orto PHF 30s.

Later examples featured a Saprisa rather than Bosch alternator which was generally more reliable, and also the revised engine breather system. The frame came from the California II, with the longer steering head and extra gusset, but with the 850 T5 swingarm. Also from the T5 were the 38mm forks, 16in and 18in wheels, and 270mm one-piece disc brakes. The 337mm Koni shock absorbers were also shared with the California II. Unlike the early SP 1000, however, only a four-way manifold was used for the integrated braking system.

While the fuel tank, seat and side covers were from the T5, the fairing was the familiar SP 1000 NT item with two rigidly mounted side panels incorporating a spoiler and a handlebar-mounted centre section. In the same way that the T5 failed, the SP II still did not fulfil expectations. The performance was particularly disappointing and in November 1984, *Motorrad* could only manage a top speed of 177km/h (110mph) from the SP II.

# THE MILLE GT

The ultimate development of the T series was undoubtedly the Mille GT. While in some respects it was regressive, market forces in Germany required the return of a standard motorcycle. With the Mille GT the days of the 850 T were recalled, with 18in spoked wheels and no fairing. In many ways the Mille GT was almost a reaction to the smooth, integrated look of the T5, and Moto Guzzi's first effort at a retro look.

The engine of the Mille GT was the small-valve 1,000cc unit (41mm and 36mm valves) with Dell'Orto PHF 30mm carburettors providing 67 horsepower at 6,700rpm. The first batch was individually numbered,

differing in slight details to later versions. In 1989 (from No. VT 024596), the clutch was modified to minimise spline wear on the input transmission hub and included a new clutch plate and input hub. After No. VT 024724 a spring-loaded self-adjusting camchain tensioner was fitted and from engine No. VT 024876 the Mille GT was fitted with a Motoplat electronic ignition. From 1991, some Mille GTs were fitted with larger valve engines (44mm and 37mm) and 36mm carburettors, producing 71 horsepower at 6,800rpm with a corresponding increase in performance. These, from No. VT 25277, also featured a new oil pump. As with most large Moto Guzzis except the Le Mans, a 50 horsepower version was produced for Germany.

While much of the running gear was shared with the SP II, in particular the frame and medium-length swingarm, a retrogressive step was a return to spindly, 35mm forks with the air-assisted damping of the California II. As the front disc brakes increased in size to 300mm and alloy wheel rims were fitted, the skinny forks seemed incongruous on such a heavy machine, which could otherwise have been a competent handler. Cast alloy wheels were an option, these having wider rims (2.50 x 18in and 3.00 x 18in). Like the T5, the integrated braking system used a four-way proportioning valve. The Mille GT featured many new components, in particular, the improved switchgear off the Le Mans V, and a new instrument panel from the smaller Custom models.

The performance of the small-valve versions was similar to the SP II. *Cycle* magazine, in September 1989 managed a standing quarter-mile in 13.51 seconds at 96.46mph (155km/h) from their 252.5kg (557lb) (wet) Mille GT. *Moto Sprint*, testing a Mille GT in 1987, achieved a top speed of 189.7km/h (118mph). These figures are really only put into perspective when compared with the performance of the 850 T back in 1974. Fifteen years of development and a capacity increase had certainly not translated into a faster, or even-better-handling, machine.

# THE CALIFORNIA III/ C.I./CLASSIC

A more significant machine for Moto Guzzi was the California III, also released in 1987. This offered

considerable improvements in many areas over the California II, and such was its success that it would be the most popular big twin through until 1993. Initially the engine was the small-valve (41mm and 36mm) 67 horsepower unit with 30mm carburettors of the Mille GT, and this was developed over time. In 1989, a clutch modification was made which that included a new plate and input hub (from engine No. VT 032542), and from number VT 032698 a spring-loaded self-adjusting camchain tensioner was fitted.

When introduced, the ignition was the usual Marelli dual-point distributor, but from 1990 (engine No. VT 032931) a Motoplat ignition with an electronic ignition advance was used. Saprisa alternators were fitted to the California III, and most also had an improved French-made Valeo starter motor. In 1991 (from VT 34474 and I.E. VY 11307) there was a new, higher-capacity, oil pump with 16mm instead of 14mm gears.

Many variants of the California III were produced. In 1989, a fuel-injected version was introduced with a Weber Marelli system very similar to that used on the Daytona. This early variant of the Marelli EFI used a P7 processor. The following year also saw the introduction of the Classic, a more basic California

without bags or windshield, with slightly lower handlebars and an optional catalytic converter. While the latter was an option on all models, it was standard on the California i.e. catalizzatore, also with fuel injection.

Both the California III and Classic were available in carburettor and fuel-injected forms, and an 'Edizione Limitate' was produced at the end of 1991 with the 71 horsepower SP III engine with 44mm and 37mm valves and 36mm carburettors. This engine was then fitted to all European California IIIs during 1992, but US Californias continued with the small-valve engine until 1993. That year all 1,000cc twins were fitted with the SP III engine, now with a Digiplex ignition that adjusted ignition timing for engine speed and load. These engines also used a Ducati Energia alternator, an improvement on the low-output Saprisa. Injected versions now featured an upgraded P8 CPU.

Inconsistencies abounded with the California III over its seven-year lifespan and many versions were offered. To use supplies of engines that had difficulty meeting emission requirements some California IIIs in 1991 and 1992 were fitted with big-valve Le Mans V units. These also had the Le Mans V performance camshaft, Bosch alternator and Marelli dual-point performance distributor. The first batch of California IIIs also featured a lower final drive ratio (6/32), with a fine, 20-tooth spline, but this was soon changed to 7/33.

While the engines fitted to the California III were familiar, if inconsistent, the bodywork came in for serious restyling over the California II. The seat was much lower than before at 800mm (31½in), and the overall style more cruiser orientated. The frame and long swingarm were carried over from the California II, but the instrument panel was shared with the Mille GT. With the exception of US models, a windshield and pannier bags were fitted as standard. Initially the panniers were colour-matched to the bike but were later replaced by regular Givi bags.

A big advance over the California II was the change to 40mm forks, still with the wide fork spacing of 195mm 7⅔in). Later versions shared their forks with the California 1100, which looked similar externally but were quite new, offering improved action due to anti-friction bushes. The shock absorbers were 337mm Konis, while the front brake disc size remained at 300mm (but with floating rotors), as did the integral braking, but the 270mm rear disc of the 850 T5 was fitted. Until 1993, the four-way manifold was used (except on German Californias), this being replaced by the four-way proportioning valve in 1992. As with the Mille GT, the wheels on the California III were either cast or spoked, generally the latter, with the spoked rims narrower than the cast.

A special anniversary edition, the California Anniversary, was created in 1992 to celebrate 70 years of Moto Guzzi. Typically this came one year late, but made up for it with a leather saddle, engraved plate and certificate signed by De Tomaso. Later, to add to the confusion surrounding the various models of the California III, was the LAPD, also in carburettor and fuel-injected forms. These appeared in 1993 with panniers and windshield and featured the SP III engine.

**LEFT** The Carenatura Integrale, or C.I., offered full touring equipment. This 1988 example has carburettors and colour-coordinated luggage. Moto Guzzi

**BELOW** Offering improved suspension and engine performance over the SP II, the SP III was underrated as a sport tourer. Two Wheels

Another version of the California III was the Carenatura Integrale, or C.I., introduced in 1988. This offered even more touring equipment than the California III, and only came with the small-valve engine, initially with 30mm carburettors, and in 1989, an option of fuel injection. In the style of the larger BMWs, there was now a full fairing (with rectangular headlight), and a rear top box that incorporated a passenger backrest. As with the California III, both spoked (CIRR) or cast wheels (CIR) were available, and all C.I.s featured the integrated braking system with four-way proportioning valve. This model did not prove especially popular, particularly the injected version with only a few being produced each year.

## THE SP III

The final expression of the SP idea was the SP III of 1988. Taking the touring Moto Guzzi concept beyond that of the California C.I. and into sport-touring BMW territory, it was a clever amalgam of bodywork on a California III, but with a higher-performance engine. The engine was the most significant feature of the SP III in that it combined improved performance with reduced emissions. The cylinder head and valves sizes (44mm and 37mm) now came from the 850 Le Mans, as did the Dell'Orto PHF 36C carburettors.

The pistons featured a higher dome than the earlier small-valve 1,000cc engine but were lower than those of the Le Mans IV and V. The camshaft used on these medium valve engines was the same as that of the

earlier small-valve engine. Contributing to the improved emissions was the Motoplat ignition, which was soon changed for a Digiplex; power was 71 horsepower at 6,800rpm.

The chassis was a combination of the California III and SP II. From the California came the 40mm forks, 300mm floating front and 270mm rear discs, and 18in cast wheels. These were fitted with large-section 110/90V18 and 120/90V18 MT28 Pirelli Phantom tyres. The frame was that of the SP II, as was the medium-length swingarm. A completely new fairing and integrated tank, seat and side covers graced the SP III. The fairing was totally frame mounted, and huge, contributing to the feeling of a massive motorcycle.

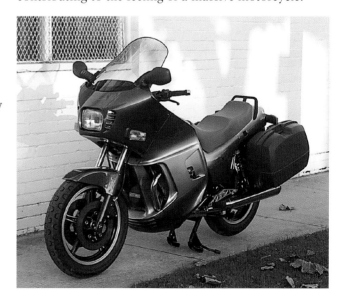

Although the SP III had a more powerful engine than earlier examples, the weight conspired against performance. *Moto Sprint*, in 1989, could only achieve a top speed of 188.1km/h (117mph) from their 268.8kg (593lb) (wet) machine. It was undoubtedly the finest example of the SP line, but suffered from uncertain styling, poor market perception, and limited performance. After the confused SP II, the SP III was a definite improvement, but needed more refinement and power to be a true BMW beater, and was discontinued in 1992.

## THE QUOTA

Another unusual Moto Guzzi of this period was the Quota 1000. It was almost as if Moto Guzzi wanted to cover every aspect of the marketplace with the venerable big-twin, so a dual-purpose street-trail bike was created in 1989. While the result was hardly a state-of-the-art off-road machine, creating it forced Guzzi to incorporate many up-to-date features in the design. So many new characteristics were featured that production of the Quota was delayed, it finally making it into production during 1992.

When first displayed, the engine of the Quota was the same as the SP III, but when it finally made the production line the 36mm carburettors had been replaced by Weber Marelli electronic fuel injection. Unlike the California III I.E., the Quota used a single-injector body with the P8 CPU. All other engine and drive train parts were shared with the California III, including the long driveshaft and ten-spline pinion.

With the frame of the Quota, Moto Guzzi came up with a completely new solution to house the V-twin engine. Two box-section steel spars connected the swingarm with Marzocchi monoshock suspension to the steering head, the engine was supported by a detachable duplex cradle. This did not feature the parallelogram set-up of the Daytona or the rival BMW GS. Wheels, tyres, brakes and forks, however, were as expected for a large-capacity trail bike. Spoked 1.85 x 21in front and 2.75 x 17in rear wheels were shod with Pirelli MT 50 90/90 x 21 and 130/80 x 17 tyres. The brakes were all new for the Quota: twin 280mm discs on the front with Brembo four-piston calipers (28mm pistons), and a 260mm disc on the rear with a twin-piston caliper. There was no integration between the front and rear brakes, and Marzocchi 41.7mm leading axle forks completed the chassis layout.

The downside of the Quota as an off-road motorcycle was its overall size. The wheelbase was 1,620mm (63⅔in) and the seat height a massive 880mm (34⅔in). This was no bike for short-legged riders, and when tested by *Moto Sprint* in 1992 the wet weight was a considerable 258.1kg (646lb). Although not intended as a performance motorcycle, it still managed a top speed of 191.1km/h (119mph). With production peaking at 349 in 1992 the 1,000cc Quota was only built in limited numbers, primarily for the Italian market, remaining in production until 1997. It was replaced the following year by the Quota 1100 ES, detailed in Chapter 13.

## THE STRADA 1000

Representing the ultimate development of the standard big-twin Moto Guzzi was the Strada 1000 of 1993. Taking the underrated SP III, removing the fairing but keeping the fuel tank, seat and the side-cover bodywork, created one of Moto Guzzi's most successful attempts at the standard motorcycle. Mille GT instruments and headlight were used and in every respect the Strada was an improvement over that model. The engine, initially with Motoplat ignition, was the higher-performance SP III unit. Always with carburettors, the Strada was the final version of this engine and featured Digiplex ignition and a Ducati alternator.

The chassis too was from the SP III including the 40mm forks, frame and medium-length swingarm, and fully floating 300mm brake discs. Shared with the Mille GT was the option of cast or spoked 18in wheels. As tested by *In Moto* in May 1993, the 241.1kg (532lb)

Strada achieved a top speed of 201.7km/h (125mph).

Unfortunately, the Strada 1000, while an undoubted improvement over the Mille GT, came too late to save the no-frills standard Moto Guzzi. Situated in the middle of the marketplace, neither cruiser nor sportster, the Strada lacked direction in a world demanding motorcycles with a more specific focus and sophistication. While twin-shock absorber rear suspension and 71 horsepower may have been acceptable for a cruiser, a standard type of motorcycle needed to be more powerful and offer an alternative style. The future would rely on more specialised machines with sporting varieties offering improved engine and chassis performance. Guzzi now looked at widening the gap between the cruiser and sporting lines.

The early production Le Mans
had a 1½ seat and the
taillight was incorporated in
the rear mudguard.

# 10 LE MANS

The 1971 Bol d'Or 24-hour race at Le Mans had seen the debut of the 844cc racing bikes. A modified 'Telaio Rosso' of Mandracci and Brambilla had led for more than ten hours before being delayed by a broken rocker. This was followed by a crash by Mandracci, and finally, a rear wheel puncture half an hour from the end of the race. They eventually finished third, behind Ray Pickrell and Percy Tait on a BSA and the Laverda SFC of Augusto Brettoni and Bruno Cretti. Riva and Abbondio Sciaresa, on another 844, finished sixth. These promising results on a debut performance saw the Le Mans designation used when the first 850 sporting prototype was displayed at the 'Premio Varrone', the Italian design award, towards the end of 1972.

Although still based on the V7 Sport, this first Le Mans had a half fairing and solo seat. With Dell'Orto PHM 40mm carburettors, power from the 83 x 78mm engine was 82 horsepower at 7,500rpm. The claimed top speed was 225km/h (140mph), with a standing 400 metres in 12.25 seconds. While the weight of 206kg (454lb) was unchanged from the V7 Sport, the Le Mans featured triple disc brakes and Borrani alloy wheels fitted with larger Michelin tyres; a 3.50 x 18 on the front and a 4.25 x 18 on the rear.

The brakes were twin 300mm discs on the front and a 240mm on the rear, with new Brembo calipers, the first time the later ubiquitous Brembo 08 caliper had been seen. Perhaps the most significant feature of the brakes was the linked hydraulic system, the left-foot pedal operating both the rear brake and right front disc. The left front disc was operated by a handlebar master cylinder. Unfortunately for the Le Mans prototype, its announcement coincided with the De Tomaso take-over of the company and it was a bike that De Tomaso was not particularly interested in producing. Eventually the engineers and marketing department got their way but it would be three more years before the Le Mans made it into production, by which time there were a number of changes to the specification.

During 1972, the 844 was again raced in Endurance events. At the Bol d'Or 24-hour race on 16 and 17 September, Riva and Mandracci finished fourth at an average speed of 115.59km/h (71.78mph) after leading for 18 hours. Riva and Carena also rode in the 24 Hours of Liège at Zolder in August.

In 1973, De Tomaso gained control of the company and the scale of the official racing programme was immediately reduced. There were only a few entries in major events during that year, in particular the Barcelona 24-hour race in July. Here, an 844cc

endurance racer ridden by Riva and Luciano Gazzola finished fifth, completing 683 laps. Again, the Guzzi was overshadowed by Ducati, their 864cc prototype winning the event at record speed.

After 1973 the only Guzzis raced were by privateers or distributors, often with factory assistance, and even the production Le Mans looked doomed. De Tomaso saw Guzzi either without twins altogether or as a touring or sport-touring motorcycle like the 850 T and later SP 1000 and was more committed to producing the Benelli 750 Sei, which he hoped would become Italy's premier sporting motorcycle. As he wanted this to also be sold as a Moto Guzzi, just as the smaller 350 and 400 GTS were, De Tomaso could see no sense in pursuing the path begun with the V7 Sport.

Fortunately, Lino Tonti and his engineering department persuaded him that there was life in the V-twin as a sporting motorcycle, and they were allowed to proceed with the development of the production 844cc Le Mans during 1975. With a production span of 19 years, the Le Mans would eventually become as symbolic of the marque as the earlier Falcone.

# THE LE MANS

Now considered not only one of the classic modern Moto Guzzis, but also representative of the archetypal street sportster, the Le Mans came at a time when the Italian motorcycle industry was setting the sporting standard for others to follow. In the late 1970s the Italians undoubtedly produced the best handling and braking motorcycles available. As the Japanese street competition at that time shared little with their racing cousins, and with the British industry virtually extinct, it was really only the Italians who built motorcycles with true race-bred chassis.

However, while the 750 S and S3 provided excellent handling, by 1975 their engine performance (particularly the S3) was not competitive. Ducati's 750 SS had grown into an 860, and Laverda's 1,000cc triple had supplanted their 750. The 844cc Le Mans gave Guzzi a true complement to these, concluding a magnificent Italian sporting triumvirate.

First displayed at the Milan Show of November 1975, the Le Mans not only offered more performance than any of the earlier 750 Sports, but was also one of the styling miracles of the 1970s. As Ducati also managed with their first 900 Super Sport of 1975, the elegant purity of the 750 was transformed into a remarkably aggressive and attractive motorcycle. The interesting thing about both the Le Mans and 900 SS was that underneath they were surprisingly similar to their smaller brethren. The parallels did not end there as both larger versions, while offering higher performance, were also less exotic in their components, and were produced in larger numbers.

While the engine had fewer special internal parts than imagined (even the camshaft was the same as the T3), the changes translated into significant performance gains. In the cylinder head the combustion chamber was reshaped to incorporate larger valves, 44mm inlet and 37mm exhaust. To obtain a compression ratio of 10.2:1, the 83mm pistons had a much higher dome, and unlike the 850 T with its chrome-plated cylinders, the Le Mans featured cast-iron liners. Although the thinner piston rings of the 850 T were used on the Le Mans, there were now only three rings, two compression and one oil scraper. Lighter pushrods were also used.

Unlike the T3 (and later S3), the distributor was that of the earlier 750 Sport, providing 34° of full advance.

The Le Mans also had a thinner and lighter flywheel (reduced from 12mm to 8mm), and new clutch plates. These would now feature on all big twins through until 1993, but smaller valve twins received the lighter flywheel with different timing marks for their 'touring' distributor.

Complementing the higher compression and bigger valves were Dell'Orto PHF 36B carburettors, with bell-mouths and no air filtration, mounted on rubber manifolds as the 1950s Grand Prix racer's had been. The 36mm carburettors also featured accelerator pumps and, together with the single-walled 40mm exhaust system, undoubtedly contributed to the claimed 80 horsepower at 7,300rpm (at the crankshaft). The standard Le Mans gearing was as for the S3, with the 17/21 primary and 7/33 final drive, although some Le Mans came fitted from the factory with a straight-cut racing gearbox.

As with the engine, there were remarkably few changes to the chassis from the 750 Sport. The frame was painted satin black, and similar 35mm cartridge forks used, still with a 180mm (7in) fork width. The forks featured thinner-walled fork tubes as a weight-saving measure. These were unique to the Le Mans, and also included a different threaded fork nut, which was round with an Allen bolt rather than

BOTTOM Although no longer competitive, a group of stalwart
enthusiasts continued to race the Le Mans in endurance racing.
This is Thierry Esnault in the 1977 Bol d'Or on a 1,000cc version.
Ivar de Gier

BELOW The Le Mans
for 1977 had a new
dual seat and taillight
assembly.

hexagonal nut. LIPSA shock absorbers replaced the
earlier Konis but still 320mm.

The biggest change was to the wheels. Following
fashion trends the functional and light alloy Borrani
rims made way for heavier cast alloy FPS wheels, but
still with the same WM3 rim sizes (2.15 x 18in). Tyres
were originally Metzeler, an unusual combination of a
Rille 10 3.50H18 on the front and a C7 Block Racing
4.10V18 on the rear. These tyres were known for
transmitting a greasy and insecure feeling and some Le
Mans were fitted with Michelin or Pirelli tyres.

The Le Mans also featured the integrated braking
system of the 750 S3 with the same four-way manifold.
Three Brembo 08 brake calipers were used, with two
300mm front discs and one 242mm rear disc. To save
on unsprung weight, the front cast-iron discs featured
aluminium carriers. All discs were drilled. Styling
considerations saw a new seat, partly covering the fuel
tank, small fairing with orange Day-Glo front section,
and lighter mudguards and side covers. Weight-saving
measures extended to the use of a smaller, 20Ah
battery. Most Le Mans were red but they could also be
ordered in metallic blue, and later white.

For 1977, the Le Mans remained virtually
unchanged but for a proper dual seat and the angular

taillight of the SP 1000 although US versions featured a
more protruding headlight. Production was initially
modest, with 219 being built in 1975, but by 1978 the
Le Mans had been the most important model in Moto
Guzzi's line-up. As demand for the T3 and California
dwindled the Le Mans increased in popularity, with
2,532 manufactured in 1976, 2,548 in 1977, and a
further 1,737 in 1978.

**BELOW** Stephane Heltal teamed with D'Angelo in the 1977 Bol d'Or, finishing 14th on the Krajka Le Mans. Ivar de Gier

An optional racing uprating kit was also available for the Le Mans. This included two sets of straight-cut close-ratio gears (one with a higher first and second gear) and a choice of two primary ratios (16 and 17 teeth). Also available were four different final drive ratios (6/32, 7/33, 8/33, 9/34), creating an amazing selection of alternative overall gear ratios. Other items in the racing kit included Dell'Orto PHM 40 carburettors, a higher lift camshaft, megaphone exhaust system, and a 24-litre aluminium fuel tank. The camshaft gave 7.2mm of intake valve lift, up from 6.8mm.

Contemporary road tests confirmed that the Le Mans was a significantly faster machine than any of the earlier 750 Sports, particularly the S3. *Bike* magazine, in August 1976, achieved a maximum speed of 132.15mph (213km/h). The extra capacity and tuning also translated into far better acceleration despite a dry weight of 210kg (463lb). *Motociclismo*, in May 1976, saw a standing-start 400 metres in 12.314 seconds at 173.04km/h (108mph).

As well as offering similar performance to other large capacity sportsters, the Le Mans provided a more civilised and compact package. Even though the handlebar switches were not too reliable, electric start and shaft drive placed the Le Mans in a different category altogether from many other Italian motorcycles. My own experience confirmed the Le Mans had considerably more mid-range power than the 750 S, being an overall more muscular machine.

Tonti's magnificent frame was more than up to the task of handling the extra power and the Le Mans was still one of the best-handling motorcycles available. All the improvements made to the electrical system over the previous few years meant it was also an easy bike to live with for a sports bike. Functionally, it was only really compromised by the heavy cast-alloy wheels, 35mm forks and slippery seat. Combined with its aggressive styling and compact dimensions, it was undoubtedly one of the great sporting motorcycles of the 1970s, and together with the V7 Sport, a classic modern Guzzi. In the world of motorcycles the Le Mans was a masterpiece.

While not officially raced by the factory, in the hands of distributors and privateers the Le Mans had a moderately successful racing career. Much of this was due to the financial contribution of Luciano Gazzola and the support of Tonti and factory mechanic Bruno Scola. Their work in developing the Le Mans as a private team led to many modifications carried through to the production line and the official factory racing kit.

In 1976, there was a return to the world of endurance racing with entries in the Montjuich 24-hour race and the Bol d'Or. Riva and Gazzola finished ninth at Montjuich, while Guzzi filled 15th and 16th places at the Bol d'Or. Results were not much better in 1977, Perez Rubio and Morante coming 12th at Barcelona and Heltal and D'Angelo finishing 14th at the Bol d'Or. The results were slightly improved in 1978 with Michel Biver and E. Guchet achieving tenth place in the Liège 24-hour, and A. Rusconi and Giovanni Pretto finishing eighth at Misano on a 1,000cc Le Mans.

While outclassed in the Coupe d'Endurance, in the world of production racing, the Le Mans was surprisingly competitive. Roy Armstrong won the British 1977 Avon Roadrunner Production Series, while in the USA, Mike Baldwin raced an 850 Le Mans during 1976 and 1977. Sponsored by the US importer Berliner, and tuned by Reno Leoni, Baldwin had some considerable success in the AMA Superbike Championship. He won at Loudon in 1976, and also at Charlotte in 1977, proving that the 850 Le Mans was a very competitive racing machine. Only moderately modified, the Leoni-tuned Le Mans had 40mm Dell'Orto carburettors, a 10.8:1 compression ratio and a swingarm altered to accommodate a WM5 rim. Estimated power was 90 horsepower and the bike was timed at 143mph (230km/h) at Daytona.

# THE LE MANS II

The success of the Le Mans proved to De Tomaso that there was definitely life left in the V-twin and undoubtedly ensured its survival. However, it has often been a failing of Italian companies to unnecessarily alter a winning formula, and that is exactly what Moto Guzzi did in 1978 to the Le Mans. By incorporating many features of the SP 1000 they created the Le Mans II, unfortunately destroying some of the appeal of the original. Functionally, the Le Mans II was similar to the earlier bike, but the SP 1000-inspired fairing and instruments detracted from the original's sporting purity.

Initially, there were no changes to the engine specifications on the Le Mans II. The 844cc engine had earned a reputation for exceptional robustness, as well as strong performance, which was particularly evident in a 25,000km (15,500-mile) test undertaken by the German magazine *Motorrad* in 1981. No serious problems were encountered and compression and overall performance actually increased over time. Nigusil-plated cylinders replaced the cast-iron type in 1980 (from engine No. 80390).

The Le Mans II saw a return to the normal, thicker, 35mm fork tubes and with the normal hexagonal spring retaining nut, these forks had 25mm longer dampers, providing additional fork travel. The fork width was increased to that of the 850 T series and SP 1000, at 195mm. Springs were now dual rate and in 1980, air-adjustable dampers were incorporated with individual valves for each fork leg (from frame No. VE 22636). The 08 Brembo front brake calipers were now mounted behind the fork legs. Rear suspension units on the Le Mans II were either FUTA, LIMS, orLISPA. Other features continued as before, notably the integrated braking system and FPS wheels, although the tyres were now generally a much more satisfactory Pirelli Gordon MT 18.

It was the fairing and instrument panel that set the Le Mans II apart from the earlier bike. The fairing was similar to that of the SP 1000 with two rigidly mounted side panels and a front section that turned with the handlebars. Also similar to the SP 1000 was the instrument panel that incorporated a voltmeter and a clock as well as a friction steering damper under the fuel tank. The fuel tank cap was now covered by a locking panel. As with the Le Mans, a full racing uprating kit was available.

Unfortunately the extra equipment saw the dry weight of the Le Mans II rise to 228kg (503lb) (as tested by *Motociclismo*), which was considerably more than the factory's optimistic claim of 196kg (432lb). Performance however, did not seem to suffer and, in February 1979 *Motociclismo* achieved a top speed of 203.6km/h (126.5mph), with a standing-start 400 metres in 12.198 seconds at 173.127km/h (107.6mph). The lower top speed than the Le Mans was undoubtedly due to the larger fairing.

However, even while the Le Mans II may not have had the raw appeal of its predecessor, it was still a magnificent sporting motorcycle. My experience of a Le Mans II in 1979 was that it gave away nothing functionally to the earlier model but suffered from the styling compromises. The plastic instrument panel and square headlight only detracted from the sporting ideal, and the lack of air filtration limited the Le Mans II's usefulness as a long-distance machine. Because it has been perceived as being less sporting than the Le Mans, many Le Mans IIs have been converted to the earlier specification and these days a Le Mans II in original condition is surprisingly rare.

RIGHT To increase sales, a black and gold Le Mans II was offered in the UK during 1980.
Ivar de Gier

Despite this, the Le Mans II was produced in similar numbers to the classic Le Mans. Although only 560 were manufactured in 1978 as it usurped the Le Mans, production increased to 2,980 in 1979 and 2,786 in 1980. Even though it was effectively replaced by the new-generation Le Mans III in 1981, 1,009 Le Mans IIs were constructed that year. In 1980 many Le Mans IIs were painted black and gold by the British importer Coburn & Hughes to move unsold stock.

## THE CX 100

With the high-compression 850cc engine no longer meeting emission requirements in the United States, 281 hybrid CX 100s were manufactured for that market in 1979. A further 72 were also built in 1981 while the Le Mans II was being replaced. The CX 100 was a surprisingly successful concept that somehow did not get accepted, being an amalgam of the Le Mans II chassis and the SP 1000 engine. Thus the engine had the air filters and Dell'Orto VHB 30C carburettors, together with the smaller valves and lower performance distributor advance of the SP. Theoretically this should have indicated a 9 horsepower deficit but the real-world performance of the CX 100 did not sustain this.

*Cycle* magazine, in July 1980, found their test bike performed only slightly slower than the Le Mans with a standing-start quarter-mile covered in 13.50 seconds at 98.46mph (158km/h). Where the CX 100 really suffered was in the increase of weight, with a wet weight of 240.4kg (530lb), compared with the 232.7kg (513lb) of the Le Mans. The few 1981 CX 100s featured Nigusil-plated cylinders and round-slide Dell'Orto PHF 30 carburettors.

## THE LE MANS III

While it seemed that the Le Mans II had been marking time, its replacement in 1981 restored the faith of the Guzzi enthusiast. In what looked initially to be simply a restyle of the earlier bikes, the Le Mans III included 44 significant modifications and improvements. Even the angular styling was a success and the Le Mans III again showed that the engineers and designers at Moto Guzzi could still achieve aesthetic miracles.

The engine too was restyled, with angular cylinder heads and cylinders, but internally there were few changes. Capacity remained at 844cc, and the valve sizes at 44mm and 37mm, the cylinders being Nigusil-plated as they were on the later Le Mans II. There was a new cylinder head gasket, and even by lowering the compression ratio only slightly, to 9.8:1, Guzzi engineers managed to redesign the cylinder head sufficiently to enable the Le Mans III to pass the more stringent US emission standards. This was so successful that the Le Mans III was no slower than a Le Mans or Le Mans II and claimed power was 76 horsepower at 7,700rpm.

Other changes included a spacer between the oil pan and engine, which was also incorporated in later versions of the Le Mans II racing kit. This was as a result of racing practice that found there were considerable benefits with the oil sump further away from the spinning crankshaft. Carburetion was still by Dell'Orto PHF 36B carburettors, but these were re-jetted as there was now an effective air filter. The Le Mans III also featured a completely new, chromed exhaust system with larger-diameter exhaust headers, much larger capacity mufflers, and no front exhaust balance pipe as this was now under the gearbox.

**LEFT** Although the styling was angular to complement the square-finned engine, the Le Mans III was a styling success.

**BELOW LEFT** One of the most impressive aspects of the Le Mans III was the new instrument panel, dominated by the white-faced Veglia tachometer. The air-assisted forks were linked.

While it looked similar to before, the Le Mans III also had a new frame, incorporating an engine crankcase breather in the top frame tube. However, one of the most significant changes was a 20mm longer swingarm, which increased the wheelbase to 1,505mm (59in). The 35mm front forks were longer, at 141mm (5½in), and provided 20mm more travel. These were also narrower than the Le Mans II, reverting to the 180mm (7in) of the Le Mans, and featured linked air-adjustable dampers and fork legs painted the colour of the bodywork. A linked air pressure system was also fitted to the softer Paioli rear shock absorbers. The wheels and integrated brakes were as before, and tyres were excellent Pirelli Phantoms (100/90V18 and 110/90V18). Surprisingly, however, there were no changes to the ignition or electrical systems apart from a larger, 24Ah, battery.

There were many alterations to the cycle parts on the Le Mans III. A new frame-mounted fairing combined the best aspects of both the Le Mans and Le Mans II's fairings, and there was a new, larger, 25-litre fuel tank, footpeg mounts and an instrument panel dominated by a 100mm white-faced Veglia tachometer. If anything summed up the styling success of the Le Mans III it was the purposeful instrument panel. The main colours were either red/black, white/black, or metallic grey/black.

The smaller fairing saw a slight reduction in claimed weight from the Le Mans II, to 206kg (454lb), but the wet weight was 240.9kg (531lb) as tested by *Cycle* magazine in September 1983. Performance was increased over all the earlier Le Mans, *Motociclismo* in November 1981 managing a top speed of 210.120km/h (130mph) with a standing 400-metre time of 11.950 seconds at 175.600km/h (109mph). With production beginning at the end of 1980 (180 manufactured), the Le Mans III would become the most successful of all the Le Mans bikes and also had the longest production run. Even when superseded by the larger, 1,000cc version, the Le Mans III continued for a short time with 2,296 built in 1981, 3,288 in 1982, 2,609 in 1983, 1,625 in 1984, and a further 58 in 1985. In many ways it represents the epitome of the Le Mans concept by offering a balance between performance and practicality. It also retained the compact dimensions of the earlier bikes and a clear bloodline with the V7 Sport. Unfortunately, that was about to change with its replacement.

A change in fortune came for Moto Guzzi in 1982 with the highly competitive Endurance World Championship. In the opening round at Imola, Francesco Giumbini, Alfio Micheli, and Francesco Tamburini

**BELOW** The Le Mans
1000 appeared for 1984.
The dimensions were
increased and there was
a 16in front wheel.

finished fourth, with the German entry of Mattias
Meyer and Klaus Hoffman eighth. These teams
followed this with a fifth and ninth respectively at the
Liège 24-hours. This was the final racing Le Mans
prepared by Luciano Gazzola and today, Micheli works
as a test rider at Moto Guzzi.

# THE LE MANS IV

De Tomaso was always a strong follower of fashion
and nothing epitomised this more than the Le Mans IV
of 1984. In nearly every respect this was a lesser
motorcycle than the earlier 850cc Le Mans, but it
should have been superior. After the excellent Le Mans
III, the sporting Moto Guzzi concept was brutally
attacked with the extremely disappointing Le Mans IV.
The mid-1980s obsession with 'bigger is better' was
not only confined to Moto Guzzi, but the first 1,000cc
Le Mans was one of the worst examples of this dubious
philosophy. Unfortunately, production of the Le Mans
IV coincided with one where quality and assembly
standards were also very mediocre, contributing to the
bike's poor reputation.

There were many changes from all the earlier models
so it was effectively a completely new version. The
valve sizes were increased on the 850 Le Mans to
47mm for the inlet, and 40mm for the exhaust.
However, with little room left for an effective squish
band, very high piston crowns were needed to get the

10:1 compression ratio. Thus many of the emission
problems encountered with the early Le Mans and Le
Mans II were repeated with the Le Mans IV. This
engine would have a limited life in those countries with
strict emission requirements.

To further boost performance there was a new
camshaft for the Le Mans IV, which was the same as
was available previously in the earlier Le Mans racing
kit. Providing more valve lift (7.2mm) for both inlet
and exhaust valves, the valve timing was also much
more sporting. The inlet opened at 29° before top dead
centre, closing 60° after bottom dead centre, while the
exhaust opened 58° before bottom dead centre, closing
at 31° after top dead centre. Completing the
performance package was a set of Dell'Orto PHM 40N
carburettors. Unfortunately, these had extremely strong
slide return springs, which detracted from aggressive
sporting riding. However, the result was a healthy
power increase to 81 horsepower at 7,000rpm. The
exhaust system was black chrome and featured a large
crossover under the gearbox.

While the 1000 Le Mans exhibited many signs of
following fashionable trends, in many respects it
continued with Moto Guzzi tradition. Ignition was still
by dual points, the distributor being the
high-performance type of the other Le Mans machines.
Another problem that Moto Guzzi refused to solve on
the larger twins was the clutch. With the Le Mans IV
came a new clutch plate but still with no solution to the
problem of spline wear on the transmission input hub.

**LEFT** The Dr John Le Mans 1000 won the 1985 AMA/CSS US Endurance Road Race Series; riders Greg Smrz and Larry Shorts winning six races. Ivar de Gier

Other engine modifications were shared with the California II and SP II, including the modified engine breather with valve cover vents.

When it came to the chassis and styling the Le Mans IV moved away from the excellence of the earlier bikes. As a tribute to a particularly dubious fashion trend the front wheel was now a 16in, and this just did not suit the motorcycle. The frame and swingarm was shared with the later T5, with the longer steering head and extra frame gusset. Even though it retained the 410mm swingarm, the wheelbase was increased over that of the Le Mans III to 1,514mm (60in). The wheels, a 2.50 x 16 and 3.00 x 18, accommodated tubeless tyres, but the Michelin A/M48s fitted to most examples were not the most confidence inspiring.

One area that was an improvement over earlier bikes was the 40mm forks, still with the traditional cartridge damper and linked air assistance. Initially the dampers were Paioli, but these were soon changed to Sebac. As with the Le Mans I and III, the forks were the narrow, 180mm (7in) type. The brakes were shared with the 850 T5, but the 270mm rotors were now a superior two-piece floating type.

All the bodywork was new for the 1000 Le Mans, and styled similarly to the V65 Lario. Although the instrument panel was that of the Le Mans III, the switches were revised. Completing the styling-over-function idea was a belly pan under the sump; a feature of other Italian motorcycles of this period this served no useful purpose except for collecting road debris. Colours were red or white, with a red and white version with different decals also available during 1986.

Contributing to a much larger-feeling-motorcycle than any of its predecessors was the use of longer, twin 337mm Koni P7610 shock absorbers. No longer was the Le Mans a low and lean motorcycle in the style of

the V7 Sport. Surprisingly, considering the larger forks and stronger frame, the weight of the Le Mans 1000 was only slightly increased on that of the Le Mans II and III, to a claimed 215kg (474lb). The wet weight as tested by *Cycle* magazine in March 1986 was 245.2kg (541lb). However, they found the performance of the larger engine was remarkably similar to that of the 850 with a standing-start quarter-mile covered in 12.48 seconds at 109.46mph (176km/h). *Motociclismo*, in October 1985, also found the 1000 Le Mans offered few performance advantages over the 850, managing a top speed of 217km/h (135mph).

Almost immediately there were complaints about the stability of the Le Mans IV and in 1986 revised steel triple clamps with less offset were offered to increase trail from 90mm to 108mm. These also lowered the steering head, and during 1987, from frame No. VV 100165, an aluminium type was fitted as standard. The factory also offered other modifications to cure instability, including the replacement of the plastic handlebar end plugs with steel ones and the rubber mounting of the fork brace. Undoubtedly the best solution was to simply replace the offending 16in wheel with a normal 18in type. This too became a replacement kit and eventually the factory itself realised that the Le Mans worked better with an 18in front wheel.

Modifications continued for 1987 with Pirelli MP7R radial tyres replacing the Michelins and there was a lengthened front and wider rear mudguard. The fork dampers were changed to Bitubo, a significant improvement, and these were no longer air-assisted. Never as popular as the 850cc models, production of the Le Mans IV tapered off after a high of 1,766 in 1985. Although 1,179 were produced in 1986, only 754 were built in 1987, with a final 71 in 1988.

While it may have suffered a confused identity on the street, the 1000 Le Mans formed the basis of one of Dr John Wittner's successful racing Moto Guzzis. Wittner had campaigned an 850 Le Mans III in 1984, winning the middleweight class of the AMA/CCS US Endurance Road Race Series Championship with a 100 per cent finishing record. In 1985, the Dr John's Team Moto Guzzi took the endurance title outright with a 1000 Le Mans. With a very low budget and a traditional American hot-rod approach to engine tuning (hot cams, high compression and combustion chamber shape), Team Moto Guzzi won four events and proved the Le Mans could provide surprising

performance and reliability. By 1986, the team was struggling financially and early 1987 saw the Dr John Le Mans with a steel box-section spine frame and cantilever suspension (see Chapter 12).

## THE LE MANS IV SE

As a commemorative model to celebrate 20 years of the V7, a Special Edition Le Mans IV was released for 1987. All these were red/white and were differentiated

by a black engine and gearbox. The SE differed from the regular Le Mans IV in that they had a straight-cut close-ratio gearbox. This had a completely new set of ratios, different even from the earlier Le Mans race kit. The primary ratio was 18/23, with first gear, 17/28; second, 21/24; third, 32/21; fourth, 25/19; and fifth, 27/19. With fourth almost identical to the previous fifth gear this gearbox (with the standard 7/33 final drive) offered considerably higher and closer gearing than the regular Le Mans IV. As expected, such high gearing hurt drag strip acceleration, *Motorcyclist* magazine, in May 1988, achieving a standing-start quarter-mile in 13.59 seconds at 102.2mph (164km/h).

## THE LE MANS V

Fortunately, Moto Guzzi took heed of complaints about the Le Mans IV and designed a much improved version during 1987, this being homologated in January 1988. With the replacement Le Mans V the Le Mans concept had progressed, but it still did not offer any significant advances over the earlier 850s. The

LEFT Many variants of the Le Mans
V were produced, such as this one
in black with gold wheels.
Two Wheels

engine specifications were unchanged from the Le Mans IV, and this was the final version of the big-valve engine. Thus ignition remained with the dual-point higher-performance distributor rather than the electronic ignitions of other big twins, although the Le Mans V now featured a Spanish Saprisa alternator.

Improvements to the engine continued to filter through. In April 1989 there was yet another new clutch plate and input hub, which had deeper splines to prevent premature wear, but the new clutch plate still failed to rectify the problem of rivets loosening on the plate. These new clutch components were fitted from engine No. VV 016375, again demonstrating Moto Guzzi's reluctance to rectify a persistent problem. This was strange considering the smaller twins suffered none of the clutch problems of their bigger brothers. From No. VV 016418 a spring-loaded self-adjusting camchain tensioner was fitted, and some of the final examples were fitted with the straight-cut close-ratio gearbox of the Le Mans IV SE. The final Le Mans V (from No. VV 017817) had the higher capacity oil pump, also shared with other 1,000cc models.

Although the 40mm forks still featured the later Le Mans IV Bitubo dampers, these now featured externally adjustable damping and spring preload. The biggest improvement over the Le Mans IV however was the replacement of the 16 inch front wheel with an 18in. The rim sizes remained at 2.50in and 3.00in, with smaller section tyres fitted to the Le Mans V. These were generally Pirelli Phantom MT29/28 tube type, a 100/90V18 on the front and 120/90V18 on the rear. Unfortunately, the small, 270mm discs remained, limiting braking power, but the Le Mans V finally received the four-way brake proportioning valve that had first appeared on the SP 1000. There was also an improved front brake master cylinder.

Contributing to the better stability at higher speed the fairing was frame-mounted, rather than handlebar-mounted, although the ugly belly pan remained. Early versions had the instrument panel mounted on the top triple clamp, but later this was changed to a fairing mount. The Le Mans V had much improved switchgear and later versions did not feature the integrated turn signal indicators in the fairing. Handling and stability were definitely improved over the Le Mans IV, the smaller section tyres contributing to this along with the frame-mounted fairing and 18in front wheel. As expected, performance was very similar to the Le Mans IV. *Moto Sprint*, in 1988, achieved 213.4km/h (133mph) from their 228.1kg (503lb) machine.

The Le Mans V soldiered on until 1993 with the only changes being the colour schemes. Black and red for 1988 and all black with white wheels for 1989. Production over its six-year lifespan was considerably less than earlier versions, with 724 produced in 1988, 720 in 1989 and 325 in 1990. After that the days of a twin rear shock absorber sporting motorcycle were clearly numbered and only 147 were produced in 1991, 143 in 1992, and a final 54 in 1993. The final 100 were listed as 'Ultima Edizione' models with a numbered plaque and signed certificate. While there was nothing especially inferior about the Le Mans V, it really should have been produced ten years earlier. By 1993 it was an anachronism and offered little improvement over its 850cc predecessors. Also, by this stage Dr John's four-valve Daytona had rendered the Le Mans obsolete.

# THE 1000 S/SE

Although not strictly a Le Mans, the ethos of the retro 1000 S was such that it deserves to be categorised with the sporting Guzzis rather than the tourers and cruisers. Introduced in 1989 the 1000 S replicated the style and the black and red paintwork of the 1974 and 1975 750 S and S3, but little was really shared with those earlier bikes. When it started life late in 1989 the 1000 S was an unfaired Le Mans V, with retro features such as spoked alloy-rimmed wheels and a simpler instrument panel and side covers, later versions having a revised instrument panel.

RIGHT The final Le Mans was the 'Ultima Edizione,' introduced at the Amsterdam Show at the end of October 1992.
Ivar de Gier

Most 1000 Ss used the large-valve engine (81 horsepower) of the 1,000cc Le Mans (also with the higher performance camshaft, Dell'Orto PHM 40 carburettors, and the twin point distributor). However, with the end of the Le Mans, and the difficulties faced getting the larger-valve engine through tightening emission requirements, the final 1000 Ss of 1992 and 1993 used the engine of the 1000 Strada and SP III. With 44mm and 37mm valves, this also featured the Digiplex electronic ignition with a lighter flywheel. This ignition also adjusted timing for both engine speed and load. Dell'Orto PHF36 carburettors were used, as was a new Ducati Energia alternator mounted on the crankshaft. Power was less than with the large-valve engine (71 horsepower at 6,800rpm), but the engine was compatible with unleaded fuel. From No. VV 50625 these engines also featured the higher capacity oil pump.

Although much was shared with the Mille GT, the 1000 S was a considerably higher-specification motorcycle. The forks featured the 40mm fork tubes and Bitubo dampers of the Le Mans V, also with external damping and preload adjustment. These were still the narrow type (180mm), and surprisingly the 1000 S continued to use the 270mm floating discs of the Le Mans V rather then the 300mm type of the less powerful Mille GT. Two versions of the 1000 S were produced, one with cast wheels and the other with spoked. These also required different forks and the spoked wheels had narrower rims, a 2.15 x 18in and a 2.50 x 18in.

Despite the more powerful Le Mans V engine, the 1000 S only offered similar performance to the older 750 S. *Moto Sprint*, in 1990, achieved a top speed of 206.3km/h (128mph), the wet weight of 229.1kg (505lb) undoubtedly blunting performance,

1000 Ss with the smaller valve engine provided even less performance, but it wasn't this alone that determined its fate. The market just was not ready for a retro Moto Guzzi and thus very few were produced. After a high of 524 in 1990, 401 were manufactured in 1991, only 196 in 1992, and a final 84 in 1993. In addition to the S styled along the lines of the 750 S3, the British market was treated to the 1000 SE during 1991. These were red with a small Le Mans-style fairing, but in all other respects were identical to the 1000 S.

BELOW A final attempt at the retro look was the 1000 S of 1989. This also came with the option of wire-spoked wheels but was a disappointing attempt at re-creating the earlier 750 S.

A sporting variant of the V50,
the Monza, appeared in 1979.
Looking like a miniature Le Mans
the Monza was attractive, but
underpowered.

# 11 SMALLER TWINS

During the mid-1970s, many Italian motorcycle manufacturers were looking towards expanding their middleweight range. Moto Guzzi was no exception, but where they differed was in the utilisation of their traditional layout, a 90° V-twin with shaft final drive. While they still marketed the re-badged Benellis, the continued success of the larger V-twins finally persuaded De Tomaso to sanction a smaller version. He was determined, not only to increase production of Moto Guzzis, but he was also committed to reducing manufacturing costs.

After building a small-block prototype in 1972, Lino Tonti was authorised by De Tomaso to design the V35 and V50. Apart from horizontally split crankcases, the eventual design was quite similar to that early prototype. Tonti went to some trouble to reduce production costs, but also managed to create a brilliantly compact motorcycle. Although the 90° V-twin closely followed the layout of the larger bikes with its chain-driven central camshaft and pushrod-operated valves, in many other respects the design was highly innovative, incorporating several technical advances over the larger twins.

Unfortunately, the quest for cheaper manufacturing compromised the ultimate performance potential of the engine design and consequently, the smaller twins initially suffered in comparison with competitive products from other manufacturers. Combined with production and quality problems that persisted for many years, the smaller twins never achieved the development and accolades they deserved. That aside, they have had an extremely long production run, have been subject to a myriad of modifications, and been produced in an extraordinary number of varieties.

## THE V35 AND V50/V50 II

In many respects the new design solved some of the problems that had never been tackled on the V7, in particular the clutch and accessibility of the oil filter. The crankcases were horizontally split, and the oil filter replaced without removing the sump. The one-piece steel crankshaft used split shell main bearings with a 32.9mm journal on the timing end of

15° after top dead centre. Although there were several modifications to camshafts on small V-twins over the next few years the timing remained unaltered.

Further effort at reducing costs was evident in the use of cast-iron valve guides instead of bronze as with the larger twins. Bores on the first models were chrome plated and carburetion on both the V35 and V50 by Dell'Orto VHBZ 24F carburettors. For the first time on a Guzzi, Bosch electronic ignition was fitted and the claimed power of the V35 was 33.6 horsepower at 8,100rpm, and the V50, 45 horsepower at 7,500rpm. Other electrical equipment followed that of the larger twins, including a Bosch 280-watt alternator and 0.7kW starter motor.

There were several other changes to the overall design of the smaller engine and drive train. As it was always designed to be produced in a variety of engine displacements, the helical primary gears lived in an intermediate housing between the engine and gearbox. This enabled the easy fitting of different primary gear ratios, and on the 350 this was 13/24 and the 500, 14/23. Ultimately there would be a vastly confusing array of primary drive gears fitted to the range of small V-twins. Instead of the engine output shaft running directly into the clutch and on to the gearbox as with the larger twins, a smaller gear on the output shaft engaged a larger gear on the gearbox mainshaft. Thus the gearbox centreline was below that of the engine. The five-speed gearbox also differed in that the gears were straight-cut and the overall design less sophisticated so as to reduce production costs.

The 410mm alloy swingarm pivoted on the rear of the five-speed gearbox in a manner similar to that of the 500cc V8 racer. To facilitate rear wheel removal the rear drive incorporated the 235mm rear disc and there was also provision for an optional kick-starter. This was a standard fitting on military versions. All small twins used a 8/31 final drive ratio.

In most respects the rest of the motorcycle was a downsized version of the larger Tonti-framed twins. The frame followed a similar layout, with a detachable lower section, and extremely skinny air-assisted (springs only, not damping) 32mm forks and shorter, 305mm (12in) shock absorbers. The forks also featured a narrow width, 160mm (6⅓in). The cast alloy wheels were also smaller in section, a 1.85 x 18 on the front and a 2.15 x 18 on the rear. Triple integrated disc brakes were also fitted (twin cast-iron 260mm on the front) with small Brembo 05 calipers. The brake proportioning was also

the crankshaft and 40mm on the drive end. There were two-piece connecting rods as before, these having a length of 106.5mm with a 15mm gudgeon and 35mm big-end. The dry clutch too was improved through the use of one friction plate and a diaphragm spring in place of multiple coil springs. This clutch design gave far fewer problems than that of the larger twins, with minimal spline wear and a smoother action.

Another variation from the larger engines was the cylinder head design, utilising Heron heads with two parallel valves, the combustion chamber being incorporated in the piston crown. While this enabled high compression ratios (10.8:1), excellent fuel economy and simplified manufacturing, ultimate breathing was limited by the small valve sizes and sharply curved ports. The V35 (346cc) with its 66 x 50.6mm dimensions had valve sizes of 30.6mm and 27.6mm, while the V50 (490cc) with dimensions of 75 x 57mm had a slightly larger inlet valve of 32.6mm. The valve timing was inlet opening 18° before top dead centre, closing 50° after bottom dead centre, and exhaust opening 53° before bottom dead centre, closing

was in its weight and compact dimensions. The test weight was only 178kg (392½lb), which, together with the short, 1,395mm (55in) wheelbase and rigid frame ensured excellent handling.

Apart from the sedate performance, other problems faced the V35 and V50. They were not as inexpensive to produce as had been expected and the plant at Mandello was too small to cope with a massive increase in production. By 1979, engine production of the smaller twins had moved to the old Innocenti factory in Milan that De Tomaso had purchased. Not only were costs reduced, but also quality. The bikes were plagued with irritating problems such as gasket leaks, and the finish was often very poor. Thus the small twins have always struggled to maintain the tradition of reliability perpetrated by the V7 family.

## THE V35 IMOLA AND V50 MONZA

Not unexpectedly, sporting versions of both the V35 and V50 followed soon after their release. Styled along the lines of the Le Mans, with small fairing clip-on handlebars and rear-set footpegs, the first to appear was the V35 Imola in 1979, named after the race track where Guzzi had triumphed so often during the 1950s. Although there were few changes to the engine, the claimed power was 36 horsepower at 8,200rpm. Valve sizes remained the same as on the V35, but while the compression ratio was reduced slightly to 10.5:1, carburettors were now two Dell'Orto VHB 26F. As with the V50II, cylinder bores were Nicasil. The electronic ignition reverted to the twin points, said to provide an improved ignition advance, but possibly to reduce costs. This new ignition was actually inferior, and contributed to off-idle sluggishness by providing no advance until 2,000rpm.

The angular styling of the Imola predated the Le Mans III, and most of the running gear was shared with the V35. The same 32mm Guzzi forks and Sebac 305mm rear shock absorbers, but the twin 260mm front discs were drilled (as was the 235mm rear) and the front Brembo 05 brake calipers were situated behind the fork legs. The front master cylinder was now mounted on the handlebar rather than on the top frame tube in front of the fuel tank.

Soon after the release of the V35 Imola a 500cc

by a 'V' three-way manifold. Not everything about the new design represented an improvement and a couple of poor features were the cable-operated front master cylinder, and the ball steering head bearings which were especially prone to wear.

The angular styling and engine finning would eventually influence the larger twins and the overall result was a remarkably light and compact motorcycle. Unfortunately it was not without problems, and consequently there were continual updates.

The first variation was the V50 II of 1979. Essentially identical to the V50 but for stripes on the tank and side covers, the chrome cylinder bores were replaced by Nicasil bores as used on other European motorcycles of that period. Also for the V50II came a deeper sump, increasing oil capacity to 2 litres. While the early V35 and V50 were initially primarily for the Italian market, the V50 II was exported and performance was disappointing. *Cycle World*, in September 1980, achieved a standing-start quarter-mile in 15.93 seconds at 85.1mph (137km/h), barely faster than a Falcone. Where the V50 II succeeded, however,

version was announced. Called the Monza, after the race track near Milan, this was first shown at the Bologna Show at the end of 1980. Looking essentially identical to the Imola, the Monza had a considerably uprated engine over the V50 II. Although the compression ratio was slightly reduced as with the Imola (to 10.4:1), there were larger valves and wider spacing of the ports. Valve sizes were 34.6mm inlet and 30.6mm exhaust and, together with the dual ignition points of the V35 Imola, the single-chain camshaft drive became a duplex. The plated cylinders were now Guzzi's own Nigusil and incorporated an additional stud next to the pushrod tubes.

While the crankshaft was similar to before, it featured a larger timing side journal at 35mm, and revised oil ways. The con-rods, also 106.5mm in length, now used a 3mm larger gudgeon pin (18mm), but the 35mm big-end was retained. These modifications also found their way to the V35 and the V50 III. With Dell'Orto PHBH 28B carburettors the power was increased to 48 horsepower at 7,600rpm and the primary drive was raised to 15/22.

The gearbox ratios were unchanged, but the sizes of the shafts, gears and bearings were increased, with a 12-tooth (instead of ten-tooth) transmission U-joint spline. Three versions of gearbox were fitted to the Monza, Imola, and the later V50 III and V35 II. These only affected shifting forks and fourth gear on the layshaft but reflected the continual refinement of the design.

The chassis was shared with the V35 Imola, but with 310mm air-assisted Paioli shock absorbers and forks with air-assisted dampers rather than springs, as with the larger twins. While the V50 Monza provided

significantly improved performance over the V50II, it was still no match for the other sporting 500s appearing at that time, in particular Ducati's new 500 Pantah. *Motociclismo*, in September 1981, achieved a top speed of 172.9km/h (107mph), with a standing 400 metres in 14.118 seconds at 148.76km/h (92mph). The Monza was the lightest in its class with a test weight of 171.5kg (378lb), but already it was outclassed and in need of more horsepower.

# THE V35 II AND V50 III

Making its appearance with the V35 Imola at the end of 1979, the V35 II was an amalgam of the V35 Imola engine in a V50 II chassis. Claimed power was slightly less than the V35 Imola, at 35 horsepower at 8,100rpm. Production of the V35 II commenced early in 1980 and, as had occurred with the Imola, the smaller versions incorporated developments sooner than their larger brothers. Moto Guzzi was well aware of the problems with the V50 II but it was not until 1981 that many of the features of the V35 II filtered through to the new V50 III.

The V50 III shared its engine with the V50 Monza (larger valves and carburettors, dual-point ignition, duplex timing chain, and gearbox), but still used the 14/23 primary drive. As with the V35 II, the claimed power was also slightly less than the Monza at 47 horsepower at 7,500rpm. Other changes that had appeared on the V35 Imola also made their way to the V35 II and V50 III. The front master cylinder was now handlebar mounted, enabling the fuel tank cap to be neatly hidden by a steel cover. There were new silencers

and drilled steel brake discs rather then the previous cast-iron while a number of cosmetic alterations differentiated the V50 III from its predecessors and the V35 II. The mudguards were altered, the taillight now being incorporated with the rear guard. From 1982, on both the V35 (after engine No. 29135) and V50 (after engine No. 31344), the single timing chain of the V65 was used.

All these developments undoubtedly contributed to the V50 III being more successful than the earlier V50s, particularly outside Italy. With much assembly of the small V-twins being undertaken at the Benelli plant at Pesaro, production could not only be increased but there were also significant price reductions in many export markets. However, the V50 III continued to struggle to find the balance between production quality and performance. Quality was continually elusive, but Moto Guzzi hoped performance would come from a capacity increase.

## THE V65 AND V65 SP

While the V50 III was more successful than its predecessors, it still only offered moderate performance for a 500cc twin. This led to the V65, first shown at the Milan Show in November 1981. Production commenced in 1982, not at Mandello but at the Benelli works at Pesaro. The engines continued to be built by Innocenti, with the frames by Maserati at Modena, and there was considerably more to the V65 than extra capacity.

The engine was not only bored and stroked (80 x 64mm) to give 643.4cc, but the entire bottom end was

strengthened, obviously with the intention of enlarging the engine to an eventual 750cc. The con-rods were lengthened to 120mm (4¾in), with a 40mm big-end and 20mm gudgeon. On the crankshaft the journals were increased to 40mm on the timing side and 43mm on the drive side, and the duplex timing chain that had been introduced on the V35 II and V50 III reverted to a single chain.

Where the V65 was obviously at a disadvantage compared with other 650s, however, was in the cylinder heads and small valves, still shared with the V50 III. Thus, even with larger Dell'Orto PHBH 30B carburettors with a revised air filter box, and a 10:1 compression ratio, the power was only 52 horsepower at 7,050rpm. The entire clutch and gearbox was also new for the V65. Apart from third gear all the internal gearbox ratios were also altered, giving a slightly closer ratio spread. The 15/22 primary drive gears came from the Monza, along with the 12-tooth U-joint spline.

The gearbox was strengthened for the larger engine, and the clutch redesigned, but as with the V35 and V50, the gearbox was subject to several revisions. Over the next few years there were three versions of layshaft, new shifting fork locating dowels, and improved internal lubrication. In 1983 the V65 received almost a totally revised gearbox in an endeavour to reduce noise. Further updates also included stronger replacement ring and pinion rear gear sets and bearings. Despite all these developments ignition was still by dual points, but total advance was reduced to 33°.

Although the frame was similar to the V50, to create more room for a passenger, the swingarm was lengthened to 435.5mm (17in). Other chassis parts too were upgraded for the larger bike. Finally the flimsy

32mm forks were replaced with 35mm units, 180mm wide, similar to those of the Le Mans, but fitted with extremely strong fork springs. The inverted Paioli shock absorbers, with linked air pressure valves, were slightly longer than on the V50 III at 320mm. Much of the rest of the chassis, however, was shared with the V50 III. The narrow-rimmed wheels and integrated brakes were unchanged but tyre sizes increased to 100/90H18 and 110/90H18.

For a 650cc twin the V65 was still a remarkably light and compact motorcycle. As tested by *Motorrad* in March 1985 the wet weight was only 199kg (439lb). The top speed was a respectable, but hardly earth-shattering, 176km/h (109mph). In addition to the V65 there was the V65 SP, a diminutive of the SP 1000. The V65 SP had identical specifications to the V65 but for the three-piece fairing with handlebar-mounted centre section.

The V65 SP generally had a Lucas, rather than Bosch, starter motor. Weight was marginally increased, and while the handling was impeccable, both 650s suffered through offering only sedate performance. This was largely overcome with a new cylinder head design, both the V65 and V65 SP were discontinued in 1987, replaced by the equally sedate Sessantacinque, and more sporting Lario.

# THE V35/V50/V65 CUSTOM AND V35/65 FLORIDA

While many of the smaller V-twins were excellent motorcycles, it was unfortunate that Moto Guzzi decided to expand the line-up with a series of poorly executed customs, epitomising the crisis period of the 1980s. Starting with the V35 and V50 Custom in 1982, the V65 Custom joined them in 1983. The engines on all the Customs were identical to those of the respective touring models but for the exhaust systems. Thus they all featured different primary ratios: 13/24 for the V35, 14/23 for the V50, and 15/22 (together with the 650 gearbox) for the V65. On all three Customs, the 35mm forks, headlight and instruments were shared with the V65, while the handlebars came from the California II.

The front wheel was increased in size to 2.15 x 18in, with a 100/90H18 tyre, and the rear wheel became a 2.5 x 16in with a 130/90H16 tyre. This required the swingarm to be lengthened to 458mm (18in). To compensate for the lower wheel, 330mm inverted Paioli shock absorbers were fitted. However, these chassis modifications were not sufficient to allay the handling and stability problems that afflicted the Custom, particularly the V50 and V65. This was especially prevalent when they were fitted with the windshield or panniers that were sometimes supplied as standard equipment. The Custom was slightly restyled in 1984, the seat incorporating a passenger backrest, and the 350 and 650 remained in production until 1988.

Responding to criticism of the Custom, in 1986 Moto Guzzi released the more radical V35 and V65 Florida, which by 1988 these had replaced the Custom. As well as offering a more extreme chopper-like styling, overall quality was improved, evident in ancillary components such as instruments and footpegs. On the 350 the engine was also redesigned with a different bore and stroke, so that cylinders and heads were shared with the V50. The bore was the V50's 74mm, with a shorter, 40.6mm stroke giving 349.2cc. Compression was 10.3:1 and carburetion by twin Dell'Orto PHBH 28 carburettors. While the V35 Florida used identical gearing to the V35 Custom, the V65 Florida shared its 16/21 primary drive with the Lario. The ignition on the Florida was also Motoplat electronic, and from 1988 Saprisa alternators were fitted.

The chassis on the Florida was quite different to that of the Custom. Longer front forks, with 38mm fork tubes, elevated the front and 332mm Sebac shock absorbers replaced the 330mm Paiolis. The V65 also included a standard windshield and panniers, again contributing to instability at higher speeds. Final versions featured spoked wheels, with the rear disc moved to the left as on the TT. While obviously never intended as performance machines *Motorrad* tested a V65 Florida in November 1986 and achieved a respectable 161km/h (100mph) from their 197kg (434lb) machine. Although effectively replaced by the Nevada from 1991, the 650 Florida remained in limited production until 1994.

## THE V35 AND V65 TT

In a further bid to expand the line-up, in 1984 a dual-purpose trail bike was created out of the 350 and

650. Called the TT, these were not really effective off-road motorcycles, but did offer the convenience of electric start and shaft drive, which was unusual for this type of motorcycle. Engines were shared with the V35/65 Custom (and V35 II/V65) but with different gearing. The V35 TT had 12/24 primary gears and gearbox with the earlier V35 ratios, later V35 TTs having an even lower 12/25 primary drive. The V65 TT used the V50 III primary gears (14/23) with the regular 650 gearbox.

While the frame was the stronger Lario design with tapered-roller steering head bearings, and the swingarm also the longer 458mm Custom type, all-new suspension graced the TT. It was fitted with non-cartridge-style Marzocchi leading-axle 38mm forks, with 180mm spacing, and 360mm Marzocchi remote-reservoir shock absorbers. Non-integrated braking was by a single Brembo 05 caliper with a 260mm disc, with the rear a 260mm disc located opposite the rear drive. Spoked wheels with Akront alloy rims were 1.60 x 21in and 2.15 x 18in, mounted with dual-purpose tyres, but it was not really enough to create a truly functional off-road vehicle. With the V65 Baja, first shown at the Milan Show of 1985, Moto Guzzi created a much more serious off-road motorcycle, but it failed to get into production.

## THE V35 IMOLA II, V40 CAPRI, V50 MONZA II AND V65 LARIO

A more significant development in the small V-twin line-up occurred in 1984 with the introduction of a four-valve cylinder head. It was indicative of Moto Guzzi during this period that this improvement took so long to occur, but it was worth the wait. The four-valve engine was reserved for the more sporting models, the V35 Imola II (and corresponding Japanese market V40 Capri), V50 Monza II, and a new 650, the Lario.

Bore and stroke, crankshaft and con-rods were unchanged from the two-valve versions, as was the camshaft timing and compression ratio, except for an increase in compression for the Lario to 10.3:1. A single pushrod operated a forked rocker with the four valves now organised in a pent-roof, Cosworth style.

Valve sizes were 24mm inlet and 21.5mm exhaust for the 350, with the 500 and 650 sharing 27mm and 24mm valves. The 350 used Dell'Orto PHBH 28B carburettors, and the 500 and 650 larger Dell'Orto PHBH 30Bs. All three sporting variants now shared the closer ratio V65 gearbox, but with the expected different primary gears. To compensate for the 16in rear wheel the V35 Imola II had a 13/23 primary drive, and the V50 Monza II 15/22 primary gears. The higher performance V65 Lario had an even higher primary ratio (16/21).

Not all was evolutionary with the four-valve engine. Ignition was still by twin points, but now with a modified points plate allowing easier individual timing of the cylinders. As expected from the better-breathing cylinder heads, power was significantly increased over the two-valve versions, but still less than competitive offerings from other manufacturers. The 350 produced 40 horsepower at 8,800rpm, the 500 50 horsepower at 7,800rpm, and the 650 60 horsepower at 7,800rpm.

With the four-valve engine, finally, came a frame with tapered roller steering head bearings. The 458mm

swingarm of the Custom lengthened the wheelbase, and, following the fashionable trend of the mid-1980s, 16in wheels were fitted front and rear. These had wider rims than the earlier V65 — 2.15 on the front and 2.50 on the rear — allowing for 100/90 and 120/90 tyres. To compensate for the smaller wheels, all had longer (330mm) air-assisted Paioli shock absorbers, although later versions were fitted with Konis. Up front were the usual air-adjustable 35mm Guzzi forks, and the size of the front disc brake rotors was increased to 270mm (shared with the T5).

The styling (fairing and seat) and many ancillary components, such as instruments and poorly-designed switches, followed the example of the contemporary Le Mans 1000, but the overall result was probably more successful. Exhausts were black chrome, and the somewhat dubious bellypan also featured. The 16in wheels also suited the smaller bike better than the 16in and 18in combination of the Le Mans: steering and handling being less idiosyncratic. As expected, the performance, particularly of the Lario, was up on the two-valve versions. *Cycle* magazine, in April 1988,

managed a standing-start quarter-mile in 13.40 seconds at 98.2mph (158km/h) from their 196.4kg (433lb) (wet) V65 Lario. The Lario also proved to have a higher top speed than other small twins. *In Moto* achieved 191.1km/h (119mph) in 1987, faster than many of the 1,000cc Guzzis. Although production lasted through until 1989, the Lario was only moderately successful. By 1989 16 inch wheels were unfashionable and 650cc inadequate. The demise of the Imola and Monza II followed in its wake.

# THE V35III AND V75

The continual evolution of the small V-twin continued in 1985 with the V75, and very similar V35 III. The biggest difference between these two models was the engine, the V35 III still utilising the 35 horsepower two-valve 346cc engine, while the V75 featured a development of the 650cc Lario four-valve engine. In other respects these two models somehow managed to combine many of the least satisfactory features of Moto Guzzis of the mid-1980s, notably a 16in front wheel and the ugly integrated fairing and instruments of the T5.

Stroking the 650 engine to 74mm created 743.9cc, but the four-valve cylinder head of the V75 was the

same as the V65 Lario. With the new crankshaft came correspondingly longer con-rods (130mm) with a slightly larger gudgeon at 22mm. The V75 had an even deeper oil sump with a spacer as with the larger square-finned engines. This did not increase sump capacity but moved the oil further from the spinning crankshaft. There was also a larger capacity oil filter. Carburetion was the same as the Lario, with twin Dell'Orto PHBH 30B carburettors. An improvement that featured on both the V35 III and V75 was an electronic Motoplat ignition that provided more advance (41° on the 350 and 38° on the 750).

Overall however, the V75 was a disappointing performer, the extra capacity translating into more torque but little extra horsepower. Maximum power was only 65 horsepower at 7,200rpm. The V75 gearbox and primary drive were as with the V65, with the lower 15/22 primary gears. The V35 III, still with the 66 x 50.6mm engine, reverted to the earlier V35 II gearbox rather than the 650 type of the Imola II, with 12/24 primary gears.

Both the V35 III and V75 were standard-type motorcycles in the style of the 850T5 rather than sporting vehicles, so the styling, with a small handlebar fairing followed the larger bike's example. Stronger Guzzi air-assisted 38mm forks, 180mm wide, were used, along with 320mm Koni shock absorbers.

The frame was similar to that of the Lario with tapered roller steering head bearings and a 458mm swingarm. The integrated braking was carried over

from the Lario, and these were twin front 270mm discs and a 235mm rear with Brembo 05 calipers. Contributing to the odd looks were a 2.15 x 16 inch front and 2.50 x 18in rear wheel. Another dubious feature was the vacuum operated fuel tap that was leaky and unreliable. In 1986, this was replaced by two separate manual taps.

While the wet weight of 191.1kg (421lb) for the V75 and 181.3kg (400lb) for the V35 III was extremely moderate, the performance of both was disappointing. *Moto Sprint*, in 1987, achieved a top speed of 188.7km/h (117mph) from the V75 and 158.3km/h (98mph) from the V35 III.

The reality was that these models were a lost opportunity for Moto Guzzi. If the V75 had been less compromised in its design the four-valve cylinder head may have survived longer. Consequently, the V75 was the only 750 with a four-valve head.

# THE 350/650/750 NTX

While the V35 and V65 TT had provided a taste of how the small V-twin could be adapted to an off-road motorcycle, a considerably more effective version became available in 1986, the NTX. Styling now followed that initiated by Paris–Dakar racing bikes, but the NTX was still a long way removed from those purpose-built machines. Initially only available as a 350 and 650, the 350 used the new short-stroke (74 x 40.6mm) engine of the V35 Florida. Early 350 NTXs had the V350 III gearbox and 12/24 primary drive, but later, after No. 12137, used lower, 12/25 primary gears. From 1988 there was also a 750 NTX, with a two-valve engine. This 743.9cc engine had a slightly lower compression ratio of 9.7:1 and produced 46 horsepower at 6,600rpm. All NTXs had the Motoplat electronic ignition, and from 1988 the Saprisa alternator.

The rest of the NTX was considerably upgraded over the TT for off-road use. A more practical addition was a centre-stand, and a less-exposed exhaust system, while the Marzocchi forks were strengthened with 40mm fork legs. Rear suspension now featured twin 370mm upside-down Marzocchi shock absorbers, while the 260mm brakes and 21in and 18in wheels were carried over from the TT. Completely new was the 32 litre plastic fuel tank, integrated with a small fairing and painted in bright colours: white, yellow and black for the 350, and white, blue and red on the 650.

With the 750 NTX came quite different bodywork. The fuel tank was incorporated within a full fairing, there was a low front mudguard, hand guards, and the front disc had a plastic cover. The front brake caliper was a four-piston Grimeca and colours were red and white; in 1989 came new colours of blue and light blue.

In the highly competitive world of enduro motorcycles the NTX did not offer sophisticated enough suspension, however, and it was also extremely heavy. *Moto Sprint* tested all three varieties, the 350 and 650 weighing 191.3kg (422lb) and 191.9kg (423lb)

respectively with the 750 NTX slightly heavier at 195.8kg (432lb). The performance too, particularly the 650 and 750, was very strong for this type of motorcycle. The 650 managed 164.7km/h (102.3mph) and the 750 164.8km/h (102.4mph). Despite this, the NTX was not very successful and was discontinued in 1990.

# THE TRENTACINQUE GT AND SESSANTACINQUE GT

A further development of the V35 III and V65 appeared in 1987 as the Trentacinque (350)and Sessantacinque (650) GTs, primarily for the Italian market. The 350 GT was effectively the V35 III restyled along the lines of the Mille GT, the 650 GT looking virtually identical. These rather unremarkable motorcycles offered little advance over the earlier V35 III and V65, except for improvements that affected all smaller twins, including the Saprisa alternator and a revised rear drive housing to overcome premature pinion bearing wear. The Trentacinque GT, with the long-stroke (66 x 50.6mm) V35 III engine, now had the Imola II (650-type) gearbox and 13/23 primary gears. The Sessantacinque GT shared the same gearbox, but with 15/22 primary gears.

Although the GT was based on the V75/V35 III, the swingarm was the shorter 435.5mm item of the V65. In 1995, at the end of the production run, the longer, 458mm swingarm of the V75 was fitted. Earlier GTs had air-assisted Paioli shock absorbers but models with the longer swingarm had 330mm Koni rear shock absorbers. In other respects, the GT was, like the V35 III/V75, fitted with air-assisted 38mm Guzzi forks (longer than the V65), and the usual integrated braking set-up. Front discs were 270mm and the wheels on the 350 GT the same 16in front and 18in rear. Fortunately with the 650 GT the 16in front wheel was replaced by a normal 1.85 x 18in V65 type. However, the substitution of V65 wheels for V35 III type also saw a

reduction in the rear rim width to 2.15 x 18in. Details like this indicated Moto Guzzi's inconsistency in product development during the 1980s.

As a basic no-frills standard motorcycle the 350/650GT was adequate, but really provided no improvement over the original V35/V65. With its elevated front end it even looked less satisfactory than the earlier model, and the styling of the instruments and headlight was over done. When it came to performance the 650 GT, with its larger frontal area, offered even less than the V65: *Moto Sprint* managing 168.7km/h (105mph) from their 178.9kg (394lb) Sessantacinque GT.

# THE 750 TARGA, SP AND STRADA

The ultimate expression of the more-sporting smaller V-twin was the 750 Targa of 1989. Although it seemed to be an extension of the 650 Lario idea, the use of a two-valve engine and a return to 18in wheels saw its roots back in the first V50 Monza. The styling followed that of the Lario and the 750 Targa was very much a smaller Le Mans V. It could have been a brilliant recipe, but unfortunately the Targa was fitted with an underpowered 750cc engine.

This engine was essentially the two-valve unit of the NTX, so it still had the Heron cylinder heads with small parallel valves. The gearbox and primary drive were from the Lario but from 1990 there were revised first and fifth gears. As with other Moto Guzzis of this period a French Valeo starter motor replaced the Bosch unit. Even though it displaced 744cc the performance of

RIGHT Although it was a finely balanced machine with excellent handling, the two-valve 750 Targa was the slowest sporting 750 available in the early 1990s. Moto Guzzi

BELOW The 750 SP of 1990 included a larger fairing and panniers. Moto Guzzi

the Targa was noticeably inferior to its smaller predecessor, with a claimed power of 46 horsepower at 6,600rpm. The styling mirrored the development of the Le Mans V over the Le Mans IV. There was still the rather unfortunate belly pan but the small fairing was now frame-mounted as with the larger bike. The attractive instrument panel, with the large, white-faced Veglia tachometer was carried over from the Lario.

There was little new in the chassis department. As with the Lario, the frame used a 458mm swingarm, but there were now air-assisted 38mm forks along with 330mm Koni shock absorbers. The integrated braking system with twin 270mm front discs was also carried over from the Lario. One improvement was an increase in wheel rim width to 2.50 x 18 and 2.75 x 18in, but still fitted with obsolete Pirelli Phantom MT29/28 tyres in 100/90V18 and 120/90V18. Probably the most disappointing aspect of the Targa was its performance; even compared with other Italian twins it struggled. *In Moto*, in October 1991, pitted a Targa against a Ducati 750 Supersport. The tall and skinny 195.6kg (401lb) Targa was not only heavier but considerably slower with a top speed of only 183.8km/h (114mph).

The Targa was a confused effort. Not only was engine performance poor, but chassis design was progressing by 1989, and 18in wheels were becoming obsolete on a sporting motorcycle. Yet it could have been so much more. The Targa offered a non-extreme sports bike with a unique combination of comfort and rideability, but needed more development. Unfortunately this did not happen and the Targa was the final sporting small V-twin. For the U.K. a standard version was also available, called the 750 T and styled like a V50.

In 1990, the 750 SP joined the Targa in the style of

the 1000 SP, but with a one-piece fairing and optional Givi panniers. The fairing and panniers were dropped in 1993 and the 750 SP continued with a few minor changes such as fully floating front brake discs before becoming known as the Strada 750. This now featured the Marelli Digiplex ignition which adjusted timing for engine speed and load and it was styled along the lines of the Strada 1000. Tested by *In Moto* in May 1993, the 190.8kg (421lb) Strada 750 had a top speed of 179.1km/h (111mph).

# THE V35/75 NEVADA

As the sporting and touring models struggled to find their niche, it was the development of the unremarkable American-style Custom that would see the final form of the small V-twin. Introduced in 1989, the Nevada did

not go into general production until 1991, and took the development of the Custom even further down the 'chopper' route than the Florida. Unlike the V350 Florida, the 350 Nevada saw the return of the 66 x 50.6mm engine with the closer-ratio gearbox of the V35 Imola II, but with a lower (13/24) primary gear. The two-valve 750 Nevada shared its gearbox and primary drive with the Lario.

Over the succeeding years there were continual updates to the 350 and 750cc engines. Marelli Digiplex ignition replaced the Motoplat from 1993 and from the

following year, all small V-twins received new, stronger crankcases with longer outside cylinder head studs. These also featured a higher-capacity oil pump. The compression ratio on the 750 was 9.6:1, and on the 350 10.6:1 with carburetion as before: twin Dell'Orto PHBH 30 carburettors on the 750 and PHBH 28s on the 350. Power for the 750 was 48 horsepower at 6,200rpm, with 30 horsepower at 8,200rpm produced by the 350.

The swingarm length on the Nevada was the now-uniform 458mm, and forks were 38mm. The first series used 375mm Biturbo shock absorbers, but these later

LEFT Continuing the line of the Custom
and Florida was the 750 Nevada. Still a
cruiser-style, the Nevada was also offered
with a full range of touring accessories.

became 387mm. As with the earlier Florida, 18in and 16in wheels were fitted, but all Nevadas had spoked wheels. The floating 270mm front discs and left-side-mounted rear 235mm disc were also unchanged from the final Florida, but the braking system was no longer integrated. All the ancillary equipment, such as windshield, panniers and crash bars, was no longer offered as standard equipment, but was still available as an option. There was also considerable variation in specification and styling from year to year, the biggest changes being for the Nevada Club of 1998. This included a wider handlebar, adjustable rear shock absorbers, and electric fuel taps and fuel gauge. The Nevada Club was designed as an interim model before the production of the Ippogrifo, which had originally been intended for 1997. Originally there was to be no Nevada offered for 1999, but the surprising end to the Ippogrifo project during 1998 saw it continue.

## THE IPPOGRIFO

Back in 1991 Umberto Todero had designed a replacement V75 engine, the V75 Hie. First used in the Israeli Air Force Hunter twin-engined aerial spy planes, it was decided to modify it in 1996 for a motorcycle application. Noted for exceptional reliability, the engine passed strenuous tests at the US Naval Air Warfare Centre in New Jersey and official homologation in Tel Aviv. This involved 200 hours at 7,000rpm and 196 hours with a temperature varying from −32° to +55°C.

The layout followed that of the earlier V75, a 90° longitudinal V-twin with a centrally located camshaft operating two valves by pushrods and rockers. Where the new engine differed was the cylinder head design which now featured a hemispherical combustion chamber. Valve sizes were 40.5mm inlet and 35.5mm exhaust, these having a relatively narrow 56° included angle. The aeronautical engine displaced 744cc (80 x 74mm), but when proposed for the Ippogrifo it had new dimensions of 82 x 71mm, giving 749.9cc. Weber-Marelli electronic fuel injection was used on both the aeronautical and land versions, the throttle diameter being 36mm. With a 9.5:1 compression ratio, the power of the Ippogrifo was 58 horsepower at 7,500rpm. Other improvements over earlier small twins included a 32-amp alternator and a six-speed gearbox with twin secondary shafts reducing the distance between the bearings to only 106mm (4¼in).

Following the example of the larger Centauro, the Ippogrifo took its name from the Hippogryph, a mythical winged beast, half horse, half eagle. The prototype was also quite an innovative model, being neither cruiser nor sportster. A completely new chassis featured a single White Power shock absorber under the seat operated by a linkage from the swingarm to help shorten the wheelbase. To minimise shaft drive reaction a Magni-inspired parallelogram rear fork was employed. A tubular steel removable cradle frame was still used but the running gear was far superior to that of any earlier small twin. Marzocchi 45mm forks similar to those on the California EV were fitted, as were BBS spoked wheels that allowed the use of 110/90 x 18 and 150/70 x 17 tubeless tyres. Non-integrated braking was by a single 320mm front disc with four-piston Brembo caliper, and a 276mm rear disc.

Superior quality was evident throughout. From the Centauro instruments, and hydraulic clutch, the Ippogrifo promised a fresh interpretation of the traditional Moto Guzzi formula. It may have looked like a flat tracker but with a weight of only 180kg (397lb) and compact dimensions the Ippogrifo was eagerly awaited. Announced at the Milan Show at the end of 1996, it was originally intended to go into production during 1998. That was eventually delayed until April 1999, but the company restructure of late 1998 saw the project abandoned. It was another case of Guzzi disappointing enthusiasts by displaying the motorcycle and failing to deliver. The Ippogrifo not only promised to replace the unremarkable Nevada, but was to be joined by a trail bike version, and then a custom.

## POLICE MODELS

Police motorcycles have always played an important role in Moto Guzzi production, and it was no different with the smaller twins. Police versions of the V35, V50, and 350 and 750 Nevada were produced, together with specific 750s, the V75 PA NTX, based on the NTX, and the V75 PA, a modified 750 SP. While only a few hundred were produced each year these have always been significant, with the V75 models being the most successful. The various Italian forces accounted for 70 per cent of production but the bike's future was in the balance when Moto Guzzi lost the contract to BMW early in 1998.

Dr John Wittner with the
AMA/CCS US Endurance
Road Race Series-winning
Le Mans of 1985.
Cycle World

# 12 DR JOHN AND THE DAYTONA

During the mid-1980s there was no official factory racing programme but in the United States, former dentist Dr John Wittner entered a modified Le Mans in endurance races with astonishing success. In 1984 and 1985 Dr John's Team Moto Guzzi won AMA/CCS U.S. Endurance Road Race Series Championships, proving there was life left in the venerable Moto Guzzi V-twin. After these two successful seasons working out of his shop in Dowington, Pennsylvania, Wittner looked forward to more victories in 1986 but was plagued with bad luck.

Although he had limited sponsorship from Moto Guzzi North America and the American-based Moto Guzzi National Owners Club, a debacle at the Isle of Man when the bike did not arrive, followed by a rained-out Daytona race saw Wittner withdraw from endurance racing. He had plans for a new frame and approached Moto Guzzi North America with the proposal to build a sprint racer for the Battle of the Twins series. Shortly afterwards, in December 1986, De Tomaso flew Wittner to Italy, as he was interested in a new chassis for the Moto Guzzi twin and was impressed with Wittner's chassis ideas. Thus Wittner returned to America with enough funds to allow him to build the new frame and swingarm with floating final drive.

The new frame was heavily influenced by a Tony Foale design for Dick Wood of Motomecca, itself inspired by the later Aermacchi Ala d'Oro. Instead of Foale's round spine, Dr John used a strong 50 x 75mm rectangular-section backbone running between the 'V' of the cylinders. Rigidity was ensured by connecting the steering head axis perpendicular to the backbone tube. The backbone, which was also part of the engine breathing system, connected the steering head to a 63mm round steel tube mounted transversely across the swingarm pivot. This tube bolted to 13mm plates cut from aluminium sheet on each side that also located the swingarm and gearbox.

The swingarm employed cantilever rear suspension with a single Koni F1 shock absorber. Torque reaction was virtually eliminated with a floating final drive unit pivoting on the axle. Thus the driveshaft was no longer incorporated in the swingarm and featured an extra, exposed, U-joint. To transfer torque reaction from the floating final drive case to a fixed part of the frame was an arm running parallel to the swingarm. This system

of a parallel arm working in compression was not unlike versions by Arturo Magni and Fritz Egli.

The two-valve engine acted as a stressed member and was bolted at the front by two triangulated steel tube structures which then bolted to the backbone tube. These triangulated structures used the upper engine mounts on the timing chest, the lower crankcase mounts being connected by a pair of aluminium plates. The engine was also offset 13mm to the right of the frame to allow for wider racing tyres. The fork rake was 26½° and the wheelbase 1,440mm (56⅔in). It was also important for a shaft drive to place the engine as high as practical, at the same time keeping the rider low, for maximum ground clearance. The spine frame achieved this perfectly with the crankshaft 380mm above the ground and the seat height only 770mm. Wheels and brakes were fairly standard racing issue of the period, utilising twin 300mm fully floating front discs with four-piston Brembo calipers and Marvic magnesium wheels. While the front was a 17in, an 18in rear was still employed. Forks were 41.7mm Marzocchi M1R.

For the 1987 series a modified two-valve Le Mans engine was installed in the new chassis. A 95.25 x 70mm engine displacing 992cc was developed, the engine using Pro Series power-jet flat slide carburettors and producing around 95 horsepower. The power and handling was immediately sufficient for Doug Brauneck to place sixth in the shortened 1987 Daytona Pro-Twins race. Further development and a set of Manfred Hecht ported cylinder heads saw the engine eventually produce 118 horsepower at 10,000rpm at the gearbox, and Brauneck went on to win the 1987 Pro-Twins Championship. Dr John's Guzzi was now the most successful racing Moto Guzzi since the 1950s. At the beginning of 1988, Wittner took the 1987 bike to Italy where it was analysed by factory mechanics with the possibility of installing a four-valve engine in the new chassis.

The four-valve engine was the brainchild of Umberto Todero. Having joined the company on 6 March 1939, he was a faithful pupil of Carcano and the final link with the great racing period of the 1950s. During 1986, the 63-year-old Todero designed a four-valve double overhead camshaft engine, but it was considered too tall

LEFT The first version of the Dr John spine frame as it appeared at Daytona in March 1987. This was the basic layout that continued through to the production Daytona and Centauro.
Two Wheels

BELOW A formidable combination of power, handling and reliability. Dr John's highly developed 992cc two-valve racer went on to win the 1987 Pro-Twins Championship in the hands of Doug Brauneck.
Two Wheels

LEFT Dr John Wittner checks the piston crown colour of the four-valve racer after practice at Daytona 1988. The new bike finished third in its debut race.
Two Wheels

by De Tomaso. This was followed by a four-valve engine with the camshaft in the head, but not over the valves, and by 1987 this was being bench tested. Originally intended for a street machine, the 90 x 78mm 992 four-valve engine with a 10:1 compression ratio, and mufflers, produced 92 horsepower at 7,500rpm. However, Dr John's success in Pro-Twins saw a more immediate use for the design.

Still using the traditional air-cooled 90° V-twin layout with its longitudinal crankshaft, Todero's design eliminated the central camshaft and pushrods. Instead of the camshaft, there was a driveshaft for twin 19mm toothed belts, driving single overhead camshafts positioned in the sides of the cylinder heads. The usual chain and sprocket drive between the crankshaft,

camshaft, and oil pump were replaced by straight-cut gears. The valves were actuated by short tappets and long cylindrical rocker arms positioned perpendicular to the cams. This allowed the looks of the trademark Guzzi inlet and exhaust port layout to be maintained. The cylinder head design was Cosworth-inspired with a 44° included valve angle (22° inlet and 22° exhaust), and valve sizes 33.6mm for the inlet and 29.6mm for the exhaust. Considering the extra hardware, the new engine was only 7kg (15½lb) up on the earlier pushrod design, and merely 40mm (1⅔in) wider.

Although Wittner had expressed interest in the new engine early in 1987, it was not until early 1988 that the four-valve engine became available, the cylinder heads arriving from Italy, three days before the Pro-Twins final at Daytona. Using the 90 x 78mm engine dimensions, with a set of Crane camshafts and minimal preparation, Brauneck finished third, posting lap times similar to that of the previous year and a trap speed of 259km/h (161mph).

More development followed during 1988. Searching for increased revs, after Daytona, Wittner went back to the earlier short-stroke engine dimensions. A V7 Sport 70mm crankshaft with Carrillo con-rods and 95.25mm Ross 11.25:1 pistons were installed, together with 41.5mm flat-slide Mikuni carburettors. Valve sizes were increased to 34mm and 30mm, and later developments included testing even larger, 45.5mm carburettors and new camshaft profiles from Crane Cams in Florida. Ignition was electronic Dyna S/Raceco, running 31°–34° of advance, and total loss to save the weight of a charging system.

Other developments included Nicasil cylinders and more head work by Hecht. Twin megaphone exhausts were also used for faster circuits, with a two-into-one and short megaphone on shorter tracks. The single-plate clutch was a Swiss Transkontinental with a diaphragm spring and 3.5kg (7¾lb) aluminium flywheel, with a factory close-ratio gearbox. Power was 115 horsepower at 9,300rpm at the gearbox.

Also during 1988 a new chassis was produced by the factory. The frame was 5mm longer, with 1° less steering head angle. To allow for the use of a new, 17in radial Metzeler tyre and special Marvic wheel, the engine was also angled up 2° and the range of swingarm operation angled down 2°. Wittner made further changes to the chassis. The Marzocchi fork was gutted leaving only the springs inside the fork tubes, damping now controlled by another Koni F1 car shock absorber mounted externally in front of the steering head between a set of Kosman triple clamps. Another unusual feature was a further interpretation of Guzzi's integrated braking set-up, only this time all braking was controlled by the handlebar and there was no foot brake. To prevent rear wheel lock-up there was an adjustable brake proportioning valve. The weight of Dr John's 1988 racer with oil was an impressively light 158kg (348lb). However, the new engine proved to be less reliable than the 1987 two-valve and Dr John could not repeat the previous year's victory.

With increasing interest in Battle of the Twins racing in Europe, the factory decided to produce some two-valve Dr John Replicas in 1988. These were very similar to the 1987 Dr John bike, sharing the short-stroke 992cc engine but producing only 100 horsepower. The spine frame too was similar but for a longer swingarm, increasing wheelbase to 1,500mm (59in). The fork rake was 25½° with only 95mm (3¾in) of trail. While tyres were still Metzeler, the rear remained at 18in. Suspension was Marzocchi M1R forks with a Koni rear shock absorber and brakes the same Brembo 300mm twin front discs with four-piston calipers, and 230mm rear disc. The weight with oil was 167kg (368lb). Three of these machines were produced, one going to Germany and another to France.

Further development of Dr John's racer continued for 1989. The engine was redesigned from the cylinder base upwards in an effort to improve power and reliability. This included new Crane camshafts, flat-topped Wiseco pistons, modified combustion chambers, and reinforced and heat-treated rockers. The biggest change was the replacement of the carburettors by Weber-Marelli electronic fuel injection with 52mm throttles and a single injector. Because this required a fuel pump a small-twin Saprisa brushless alternator was installed on the front of the crankshaft, with the magnetic rpm pick-ups for the injection on a aluminium plate above the alternator.

The 1989 season started poorly when a cam belt broke two laps from the end of the Daytona Pro-Twins race while Brauneck was lying fourth, but the bike was faster through the speed trap than the previous year

(167mph; 269km/h). By the end of the season Wittner had managed to increase power to 128 horsepower at 8,500rpm at the gearbox, but still could not emulate the results of 1987. At that stage Wittner retired from racing to work in Italy full time on the production Daytona.

## THE DAYTONA

With De Tomaso's involvement in the Dr John project, it was inevitable that this development would eventually filter through to the production line. In 1988, Moto Guzzi production had slumped to less than 6,000 and the company needed something new. De Tomaso sold 70 per cent of Benelli, and despite rumours that Guzzi would also be sold, the company was merged with Benelli to create a new concern, GBM SpA. The Daytona was finally displayed at the 1989 Milan Show and by late 1989 the first prototype version of the Daytona appeared, with a promised 500 in 1990. However, in what was becoming typical of Moto Guzzi, production versions were some time in coming.

Despite a prototype being tested by the press in late 1989, it was not until 1991 that another solitary Daytona was built, with regular production beginning in 1992. It was an unfortunate delay and by the time the Daytona became generally available it was upstaged by the competition. In 1992, most potential buyers were tired of waiting and as such the Daytona never received the accolades it deserved, and remains one of Moto Guzzi's most underrated models.

The early prototype of late 1989 featured a number of variations from both later production versions and the Dr John racer. The engine was similar to Todero's 1986 design with dimensions of 90 x 78mm, and a 10:1 compression ratio. Valve timing was moderate and symmetrical. The 33.6mm inlet valves (with 8.7mm of lift) opened 22° before top dead centre, closing 57° after bottom dead centre. The 29.6mm exhaust valves (with 8.65mm of lift) opened 57° before bottom dead centre, closing 22° after top dead centre. The flywheel and ring gear were much lighter than that on the regular two-valve 1,000cc twins (2kg; 4½lb), and the clutch also used ten, rather than eight, springs.

The five-speed straight-cut gearbox also had three engagement dogs on each gear rather than six, and featured all-new ratios. Primary gears were 17/23, with

an 8/33 final drive. Overall gearing was higher to allow for the lower profile rear tyre. The unusual stainless-steel exhaust system, with a large central collector, may have looked strange but was extremely effective, both for muffling and horsepower.

When first displayed it was intended to produce the Daytona in two versions, carburettor and fuel injection, but the prototype had twin Dell'Orto PHM 40 carburettors. There were also three airboxes, with a capacity of ten litres, two sat behind the intakes on each side, with the third in the tail section inhaling through a scoop in the seat cowl. The carburettor version produced 91 horsepower at 7,800rpm, with the injected version (with 50mm throttle bodies) providing 94 horsepower.

The chassis closely followed the lines of the racer. The spine frame and 400mm (15¾in) long swingarm were identical but the aluminium engine mounting plates were now castings, 15mm thick, incorporating internal webbing. Following developments during 1989, the fork rake was decreased to 25.9° with 103mm (4in) of trail, and the wheelbase lengthened to

1,470mm (58in). Front suspension was Marzocchi M1R, with a Koni rear shock absorber, and the white-painted wheels were 3.5 x 17in on the front and 4.5 x 18in on the rear. These were shod with Michelin 120/70 ZR17 TX11 and 160/60 ZR18 TX23 radial tyres.

Already there were signs that the wheel and tyre sizes were inadequate and obsolete. Brakes followed the example of the racing bikes and were non-integrated, with twin 300mm front discs with four-piston Brembo calipers, and a 280mm disc on the rear. Painted red and white to mimic the Dr John bike, the first Daytona weighed in at 205kg (452lb). Styled at Modena, it had a race shop, hand-crafted, appearance.

The main reason for the delay in production was the difficulty in adapting a pure racing design for the street. Lean air-fuel ratios and mufflers led to extreme cylinder head temperatures requiring special alloys. It must be remembered that the Daytona was one of the highest output air-cooled engines available. This ultimately delayed production by about a year and when the production Daytona was displayed at Milan

LEFT The prototype Daytona appeared in late 1989, with carburettors or fuel injection. This is the injected version.
Moto Guzzi

BELOW The frame of the Daytona closely followed that of the racer. This is the carburettor prototype of 1989.

at the end of 1991 it differed in a number of details from the earlier prototype. Still, it would be several months before the bike became available during 1992.

The bodywork, designed by Dr John in the wind tunnel, was all new, and painted red, although eventually black and silver versions were also available. The engine still closely followed Todero's original design with the crankcases now reinforced around the cylinder spigots. All production engines were fuel injected, and featured new camshafts with different valve timing. The inlet valve opened 23½° before top dead centre, closing 57½° after bottom dead centre, with the exhaust valve opening 49½° before bottom dead centre, closing 12½° after top dead centre.

The Weber-Marelli electronic fuel injection with single injectors per cylinder used a P7 CPU until 1993, while a few examples of the Daytona used the later P8 CPU in 1994. To meet the demands of fuel injection a higher-output 350-watt (25-amp) Ducati alternator was now used. This was upgraded again for 1995, but was still rated the same.

Three performance kits were also available for the Daytona. The 'A' kit consisted of a new exhaust system, computer chip and foam air filters. 'B' kits added Carrillo con-rods, lighter pistons, cylinders and crankshaft and the 'C' kit included more radical

camshafts, new tappets, a fuel regulator, and an EPROM chip.

The chassis followed that of the Dr John racer, a particularly poor feature being the exposed driveline universal joints with integral driveshaft. These were a constant source of problems, the exposed U-joints being subject to more wear than enclosed joints on other Guzzis. This was not only due to lack of lubrication but also because of the more extreme rear suspension angles. To overcome this problem, later bikes used a shorter shock absorber. The rear drive torque arm was 400mm (15¾in), this being lengthened after the introduction of the Sport 1100 to 406.3–407.8mm.

In 1994, the Daytona received a completely new driveshaft assembly (also shared with the Sport 1100), which now incorporated a grease nipple at each U-joint plus another at the sliding spline connection. The swingarm was also modified to allow access to the grease nipple. These early problems with the driveline indicated a lack of development that should have been rectified considering the delay in getting the Daytona into production.

Front brakes featured the newer-generation gold Brembo four-piston calipers with 34/30mm pistons, still with 300mm stainless-steel discs. Even though

fork legs, featured cartridge dampers but were considerably improved over earlier designs. After 1994 the forks were White Power and the fork legs painted to match the bodywork.

Initially there was still the Koni rear shock absorber but when the dual-seat version became available this was also changed to a White Power unit. White-painted 17in front and 18in rear wheels were the same as before but from 1993 these were also painted black. Probably due to cost there was no rubber cush-drive, although the wheel casting provided for it, and this was another area where the Daytona was deficient.

With the production Daytona came a new half fairing and seat unit, which was different from the prototype. The headlight was a unique shape but replaced by a more usual rectangular headlight for the USA, Britain, Australia and Japan. When it came to performance and handling the Daytona set completely new standards for a Moto Guzzi. The parallel arm locating the final drive was exceptionally successful at reducing shaft drive reaction and the four-valve engine, although only rated at 93 horsepower at 8,000rpm produced performance equivalent to Ducati's 851.

*Moto Sprint* managed a top speed of 231.2km/h (144mph) in 1992 from their 226.6kg (500lb) Daytona. The high gearing hurt performance on the dragstrip but the Daytona still set new standards for a Guzzi twin. *Cycle World*, in July 1993, managed a standing-start quarter-mile in 12.19 seconds at 113.63mph (183km/h). Yet despite the excellent performance the Daytona somehow failed to win acceptance in the hearts of Moto Guzzi enthusiasts. Production peaked at 486 in 1992, thereafter declining

they had stainless-steel brake lines, the small, 16mm master cylinder produced less than optimum braking feel. At the rear, the production Daytona featured a smaller, 260mm solid rear disc and an 05 brake caliper located by a torque-arm. The 41.7mm Marzocchi forks, with 195mm (7⅔in) fork leg spacing and red

to 283 in 1993, 155 in 1994 and 100 in 1995. Unquestionably the introduction of the cheaper and simpler 1100 Sport also hurt the Daytona, as did the earlier problems with premature driveline wear.

As a racing machine the Daytona followed in the footsteps of the Dr John racer, particularly in the British BEARS Series. In 1993 and 1994 the Amedeo Castellani-tuned Raceco Daytona finished second in the series and with Paul Lewis on board they went on to win in 1995. Now displacing 1,162cc (95 x 82mm), the Raceco bike, with 11.2:1 Omega pistons, 'C' kit camshafts, and 36 and 31mm valves produced 125 horsepower at 8,200rpm and weighed 175kg (386lb).

The exhaust system was a big-bore Termignoni and front suspension was White Power upside down forks. To accept a larger, 185-section rear tyre and 6.00in wheel rim, the final drive unit was re-engineered and offset by 18mm. The chassis was altered to reduce the wheelbase to 1,440mm (57in) and increase the steering head to 24°. For 1996, there were further developments to the engine, with a new crankshaft and lighter alternator. Power was increased to 130 horsepower.

The front end was strengthened with 43mm White Power forks and the total weight reduced to 170kg (375lb). Ian Cobby rode the bike in 1996, winning two races before a crash ended his season. Cobby rode the bike again in 1997, this time in the Sound of Thunder series, winning convincingly at Assen in June and August. Cobby's Raceco Daytona produced 139 horsepower and weighed 169kg (373lb).

# THE DAYTONA RACING

To save the Daytona from extinction in the wake of the 1100 Sport, the Daytona Racing was released in 1996. This was presumably to use up parts before the release of the new, and considerably improved, Daytona RS. Although initially the Daytona Racing was available without street equipment (no lights or indicators) and with a 'C' performance kit, the production Daytona Racing was a limited edition of 100 units, also with the 'C' performance kit, but with a street exhaust system. Each 1996 Daytona Racing

came with a numbered plaque on the top triple clamp.

The Daytona Racing featured a new Weber-Marelli P8 CPU. Other changes included a new flywheel (also shared with later Centauro and RS), but more importantly an updated driveshaft with an access hole in the swingarm for greasing. Finally the 18in rear wheel that made tyre choice awkward was replaced by a 17in Marchesini, now with a cush-drive. Tyres were Michelin Hi-Sport, a 120/70 ZR17, and 160/60 ZR 17. Although many of the improvements were welcome, especially the increased power, the Daytona Racing was very much an interim model, still incorporating many of the earlier Daytona's irritating design features.

## THE DAYTONA RS

Even while the Daytona Racing was being produced a much improved Daytona was announced, the Daytona RS. While it may have looked superficially similar, there were many refinements on the RS. As a result of some restructure within the company (see Chapter 13)

chief engineer Angelo Ferrari was able to implement many improvements. Introduced in April 1996, this was the Daytona that Guzzi should have built in 1990.

There were significant changes to the engine. The 'C' kit of the Daytona Racing was retained but with higher-compression 10.5:1 forged (rather than cast) pistons. Camshaft timing was inlet opening 22½° before top dead centre, closing 69½° after bottom dead centre, with the exhaust opening 63½° before bottom dead centre, closing 28½° after top dead centre. The crankshaft was lightened and polished with a larger, 45.5mm crankpin. Con-rods were now Carrillo and the flywheel and ring gear were also lightened. There were improvements to the Weber/Marelli injection system; a smaller, 16-megabyte CPU was used with the 50mm throttle body, without the troublesome pick-up above the flywheel. Air intakes were also revised and the pressurised airbox of the 1100 Sport fitted. The power of the engine was now 102 horsepower at 8,400rpm. For some countries with strict emission requirements (notably the USA and Switzerland), Daytona RSs were fitted with lower-output Centauro engines and an evaporative emission control system.

Together with all these changes came some serious modifications to the lubrication system. Not only was there a new oil pump incorporating a pressure regulation valve, but also an external thermostatically controlled oil cooler mounted in front of the sump. Arguably the biggest improvement, however, was the trap door in the bottom of the sump to allow access to the oil filter. It had taken more than 20 years, but finally Moto Guzzi was addressing some of the practical problems with the design. Early versions had the same straight-cut gearbox of the Daytona and Sport 1100, but from No. CL 011200 the gearbox had helical gears, still with three-dogs. For Switzerland the Daytona RS had the wider-ratio six-dog gearbox of the California 1100.

While the frame looked similar to the earlier Daytona there were a number of differences. The 63mm cross tube at the rear was narrower, and thus more rigid, with the ends now enclosed. As with the earlier Daytona, but unlike the Sport 1100, the front downtubes were still bolted on. The under gearbox mounts were now steel like the Sport and there was a new, more aesthetically pleasing, pressed-alloy support plate for the swingarm. The lighter and stiffer swingarm now featured oval-section tubing from the pivot to the rear wheel and was narrower at the pivot to fit the narrower frame.

The rest of the running gear was also upgraded. At the front, 40mm White Power upside-down forks were fitted, and at the rear, a White Power shock absorber. This was shorter than that on earlier Daytonas and all the suspension was fully adjustable for compression and rebound damping. Brakes were now Brembo fully floating cast-iron 320mm discs on the front, with a fixed stainless-steel 282mm disc on the rear. There were two types, the later type being shared with the Sport 1100 Corsa. New, lighter wheels came on the Daytona RS. In the same sizes as the Daytona Racing, these were a 3.50 x 17in on the front and a 4.50 x 17in on the rear, shod with Michelin TX15 120/70ZR17 and TX25 160/60ZR17 tyres.

Completing the upgrade was new styling, along the lines of the 1100 Sport, new switches, and an adjustable clutch lever. Quality touches extended to a sealed battery and waterproofed electrical system. At a claimed dry weight of 221kg (487lb) although the Daytona was large and heavy in a world where 1,000cc sporting motorcycles were becoming lighter and more compact. As such it did not receive universal acclaim.

However, the Daytona RS was a significant improvement on the earlier Daytona, not only was performance superior but the quality and execution put it into another league altogether. This was a great sporting motorcycle in the tradition of the earlier V7 Sport, but unfortunately, it came too late. The buying public also preferred the Sport 1100 and the Daytona RS was only produced in very limited numbers: 113, in 1996 and 195 in 1997. If Guzzi had produced the RS five years earlier it could well have achieved the success it deserved. Undoubtedly this will become one of the more sought-after Moto Guzzis in the future.

## THE V10 CENTAURO

To bridge the enormous gap in the range between the California and sporting models, the Centauro was created in 1995, being displayed at the Milan Show at the end of the year. Taking a Daytona engine and updated RS chassis and giving it swoopy bodywork created another unusual and individual Moto Guzzi. The name came from the Centaur, a mythological half-man, half-horse.

The Centauro engine was an amalgam of the regular Daytona and Daytona RS. The bottom end, with Carrillo con-rods and forged pistons was as with the RS, but with regular Daytona camshafts. The result was a reduction in horsepower to 95 horsepower at 8,200rpm. Primary and final drive were also shared with the Daytona, but the Centauro had a completely new gearbox. The gears were helical, the ratios reflecting the intended nature of the machine, being similar to the earlier Mille GT and not as closely spaced as the Daytona.

The chassis was similar to the Daytona RS with 40mm White Power upside-down forks, 17in Marchesini wheels, and 320mm stainless steel front discs. It was the styling however that set the Centauro apart from other Moto Guzzis. Rather than designed in-house, it was styled by industrial designer Luigi Marabese. It was undeniably different, but this probably contributed to the lukewarm reaction to the machine. Elsewhere there was evidence of quality construction: attractive white-faced Veglia instruments, adjustable handlebars, milled aluminium footpegs, Pirelli Dragon radial tyres, and braided steel brake and oil lines.

As expected, the Centauro was a very strong performer for this style of motorcycle. Although it weighed in at a considerable 244kg (538lb) in April 1997, *La Moto* managed 220.4km/h (137mph), with a standing-start 400 metres in 12.32 seconds at 179.2km/h (111mph). Yet despite its quality, style and performance, Centauro sales failed to meet expectations. Only 207 were built in 1996, with a further 1,265 in 1997. The first 25 Centauros were sold to Luxembourg as a limited-edition series, and in 1998 the model was replaced by two improved versions, the Centauro GT and Centauro Sport.

## THE CENTAURO SPORT/GT

Released in February 1998, the Centauro Sport and GT refined the concept, and instantly met with a more positive reception. These versions were cleverly designed as the only alterations to the original Centauro were cosmetic, although the wheels were changed to Brembos. The Sport came in two colours, red or British racing green, with white flashes to emulate the Mini Cooper S racing cars of the 1960s. Optional extras included a lower belly-pan, a small fairing along the lines of the original Le Mans, luggage rack, and Termignoni exhaust system. The Centauro GT came standard with adjustable handlebars, luggage rack, and larger seat, together with the option of a Plexiglas windshield, and luggage. *Motociclismo* tested a Centauro Sport in April 1998, managing a top speed of 221km/h (137mph) from their 234kg (516lb) machine. The standing 400 metres was covered in 12.094 seconds at 185.6km/h (115mph).

Although the Centauro was a brave attempt to mate the four-valve engine with a cruiser-style, even as a Sport or GT it was only moderately successful. However, the Centauro, particularly in its later incarnations, was an underrated machine. For a large motorcycle it provided Daytona performance and handling, with a less extreme riding position. Ultimately it was the traditional enthusiast's preference for two-valve cylinder heads that hurt both the Daytona and Centauro, even though these engines were more sophisticated and smoother running.

To commemorate 75
years of Moto Guzzi,
750 'Serie Anniversario'
1100 Californias were
produced in 1997.

# 13 NEW DIRECTIONS

The year 1993 was a crucial one for Moto Guzzi. Alejandro De Tomaso was not in the best of health and the company was operating at a loss. Turnover was down to 35 billion lire and the development of new models at a standstill. Despite this however, there were plans afoot at Mandello. A press release at the end of 1993 announced there would be a limited production run of 200 replicas of the 1957 350 Bialbero Grand Prix single. Each was to be individually certified and identical to the original. Unfortunately there were only two prospective buyers and this was yet another plan that came to nothing, but it did indicate that not all was lost with the company.

When De Tomaso Industries gave the Italian conglomerate Finprogetti the mandate to manage Moto Guzzi in 1994, it marked the beginning of a new era. Finprogetti was a group of Italian financiers organised through the Rowan Corporation. De Tomaso was still president, but Arnolfo Sacchi came in as managing director for the next three years. Thus DTI became the first Italian company to instigate TIM (Temporary Integrated Management) concentrating on turning around firms with a strong potential for recovery. Sacchi's mandate was to re-launch the company and immediately there were two welcome additions to the production line-up, the California and Sport 1100. Production was increased to 5,000 units and turnover went up to 45 billion lire, although the company was still running at a loss.

## THE CALIFORNIA 1100/1000

Spearheading the revival was a new, and significantly improved, California. Introduced in 1993, this was initially only in 1,100cc form, although in 1994 and 1995 it was also produced as a 1,000 (949cc). There was much more to the California 1100 than a 4mm bigger bore and 2mm longer stroke. The 92mm 9.5:1 pistons were forged rather than cast, and a lighter, 80mm crankshaft was used. Valve sizes were the same as the final California III, 44mm inlet and 37mm exhaust, and the California 1100 also received a new camshaft, with CAD-CAM-designed lobes to optimise separate inlet and exhaust profiles as well as minimising wear and noise. The inlet valve opened 20°

RIGHT Placing a hot-rod 1100 engine in a Daytona-style chassis was so successful that the Sport 1100 outsold its more exotic brother.

before top dead centre, closing 50° after bottom dead centre, with the exhaust opening 44° before bottom dead centre, closing 10° after top dead centre.

As with the final California III, the mixture was fed by Dell'Orto PHF 36 carburettors or Weber-Marelli IAW electronic fuel injection. This was further refined with a P8 CPU, this also now having 40mm injector bodies. Carburettor versions used Marelli Digiplex MED 550 electronic ignition. With both new induction systems came a larger airbox. The result of these improvements saw power increased by 15 per cent to 75 horsepower at 6,400rpm and torque 26 per cent to 9.7kgm at 6,400rpm.

Also with the 1100 came further developments of the engine. A higher capacity oil filter was introduced to increase service intervals. Although the gearbox was the same as the California III but for a new shock absorber, the 1100 was geared considerably higher with an 8/33 final drive. This was partly to compensate for the smaller 140/80 VB 17in rear tyre on a new, 3.50 x 17in wheel, which required a wider swingarm. The front wheel too was increased to 2.50 x 18in, with a 110/90 VB18 tyre. The tyres were now either modern Metzeler or Pirelli.

There were also several significant frame alterations for the 1100. The lower frame rails now included a cross-brace, and there was an additional brace across the top of the gearbox. Both suspension and brakes were upgraded. The 40mm front forks were redesigned with anti-friction bushings, and the longer (342mm) rear units were now Bitubos, which were prone to failure. Brakes were improved with an 11mm front master cylinder, although plated floating brake rotors remained at 300mm on the front and 270mm on the rear, with Brembo 08 calipers. Unlike the sporting models, the brakes were still integrated via a four-way proportioning valve.

It was the general improvement in the quality of finish and fittings that set the 1100 apart from its predecessor. Improved switches, fuel taps, seat latch and anti-vibration footboards were complemented by new paint for the engine and transmission and more durable plastic parts. Produced only as a stripped version with either carburettors or fuel injection, the California 1100 was available with a wide variety of factory options that included leather or plastic luggage and two sizes of windshield.

Although never offered as a performance motorcycle, the California 1100 offered superior handling and performance over others of its type. *In Moto*, testing a carburettor California 1100 in August 1994, saw 190km/h (118mph) from their 252.9kg (558lb) machine. The 1100 was immediately successful, superseding the California III in 1994. No carburettor 1100s were produced in 1995, 1,217 carburettor 1000s being manufactured instead. The carburettor 1100 returned in 1996 and 1997, although only a few were produced in comparison with the injected versions. With 1,045 in 1995 and a further 1,770 units in 1996, the 1100 IAW accounted for almost one third of total production. To celebrate the success of the California as Moto Guzzi's most important model, in 1997 750 75th anniversary 1100 Californias were produced. These were red and silver with a leather seat, aluminium alternator cover, new shock absorbers, and a limited edition serial number and silver medallion.

# THE SPORT 1100

By 1993, the 1,000cc Le Mans V was truly obsolete but still had a loyal following that was for some reason eschewing the Daytona. To recapture that market Moto Guzzi released the Sport 1100. This was a clever combination of the two-valve engine in a Daytona chassis, the origins being in the successful Dr John Pro-Twins racer of 1987. As the styling too was more successful than the Daytona, and the performance similar, the simpler and cheaper 1100 Sport was an instant success.

There was, however, considerably more to the Sport 1100 than simply taking a Daytona chassis and installing a tuned California 1100 engine. With Wittner's help the 92 x 80mm 1,064cc engine was uprated considerably with new 10.5:1 forged pistons, a lighter crankshaft, and camshafts developed by Crane in Florida. These were quite similar in timing to the mild cam of the earlier 850 Le Mans but featured much higher valve lift of 7.57mm (inlet and exhaust). The valve timing was: inlet opening 22° before top dead centre, closing 54° after bottom dead centre, with the exhaust opening 52° before bottom dead centre, closing 24° after top dead centre.

The valves too were reduced slightly from the Le Mans V to 46.5mm inlet and 39.5mm exhaust to allow for the increased valve lift. The squish band was also altered to improve combustion efficiency. The flywheel was even lighter than the Daytona and the Dell'Orto

PHM40 carburettors force-fed by a pressurised airbox. To overcome the problem of the excessively strong throttle springs of the earlier Le Mans V the throttle action was slowed down. This was successful but still not entirely satisfactory. Ignition was by Marelli-Digiplex and power was a muscular 90 horsepower at 7,800rpm. The straight-cut gearbox and ten-spring clutch were shared with the Daytona.

While the frame too was similar to the Daytona, there were some significant alterations for the 1100 Sport. The front frame downtubes were welded, not bolted, and the mounts under the gearbox were steel rather than aluminium. The driveshaft assembly was redesigned to include grease nipples at each U-joint, plus one at the sliding spline connection. Also to help reduce U-joint wear a shorter (White Power) shock absorber was used together with a longer rear drive torque-arm. Front suspension was 41.7mm Marzocchi, the fork legs initially painted to match the bodywork, then from 1995, the fork legs were painted silver. Braking was uprated over the Daytona with 320mm front discs, and a 260mm floating rear disc, although

this was no longer located with a brake torque-arm. The rear wheels remained at 17in front and 18in rear, still without a cush-drive.

With a restyled dual seat and fairing the Sport 1100 was immediately seen as better value than the Daytona. Performance too was comparable, *Cycle World*, in December 1995, achieving a standing-start quarter-mile in 11.91 seconds at 114.71mph (184km/h). *Motociclismo* found the 220.4kg (486lb) 1100 Sport not quite as fast as the Daytona, with a top speed of 218km/h (135mph). As with the Daytona there was a different fairing and larger rectangular headlight for the USA, Britain, Australia and Japan. Production immediately eclipsed the Daytona with 365 constructed from September 1994 and a further 1,191 during 1995. A final 215 carburettor 1100 Sports were manufactured in 1996 before it was replaced by the 1100 Sport Injection.

In 1995 had been seen the first positive result of Sacchi's management. Turnover was up to 63 billion lire, production up to 5,314 units, and for the first time since 1993 the company posted a profit. In January

BELOW Featuring all the improvements of the
Daytona RS, the 1100 Sport Injection also
offered comparable performance at less cost.
Unfortunately, it too was not a sales success,
and was discontinued after only one year.

RIGHT The final
1100 Sport was
the Corsa, a
limited edition
of 200 in 1998.

1996, GBM SpA changed to Moto Guzzi SpA and
paid-up capital increased from 2 to 5 billion lire when
Finprogetti purchased more shares in De Tomaso
Industries to become the major shareholder. On 22
August 1996, following the withdrawal of Alejandro
De Tomaso as company president, DTI became the
Trident Rowan Group Inc. (TRGI). The new president
was Mario Tozzi-Condivi, and that year saw
production increase to 6,027, with a turnover of 76
billion lire. The same year also marked the
introduction of the previously mentioned Daytona RS,
and the new 1100 Sport Injection.

# THE 1100 SPORT
# INJECTION CORSA

Alongside the announcement of the Daytona RS in
April 1996 was a Sport 1100 replacement, the 1100
Sport Injection. This took the Sport 1100 engine (the
same camshaft but with 9.5:1 pistons) with many of

the features of the Daytona RS. These including the
crankshaft with 45.5mm crankpin (without the
Carrillo con-rods), external oil cooler, and revised oil
filter arrangement. There was also yet another flywheel
and oil temperature transducer. As with the Daytona
RS, early examples used the straight-cut Sport 1100
gearbox, but later versions (from CF 011500) featured
helical gears. The Weber-Marelli injection system was
the same as the Daytona RS with a 16-megabyte CPU
but different (IW031) injectors and 45mm throttle
bodies.

The frame and running gear was shared with the
Daytona RS, the only differences being stainless-steel
320mm front brake discs and a higher-profile
160/70ZR 17in Pirelli Dragon rear tyre. Thus the 1100
Sport IE was significantly improved in most areas over
the preceding Sport 1100. Although it was still a heavy
motorcycle, many comparison tests with Ducati's 900
Supersport saw the 1100 Sport IE on top. Performance
too was up on the carburettor Sport 1100.

*Motociclismo*, in September 1996 achieved a top
speed of 223.3km/h (139mph) from their 227.2kg

The following month, Finprogetti, as the major share holder in TRGI, sold its shares to an American merchant bank, Tamarix. This led to two new Tamarix-nominated board members, Gianni Bulgari and Emmanuel Arbib. Later that year, in December, there was a further increase in paid-up capital to 25 billion lire. Although Tamarix was now the major shareholder, with 1.8 million shares, De Tomaso still controlled 0.7–0.8 million, and a private, unnamed American investor 0.7 million shares. This still gave De Tomaso a 14–16 per cent interest in the Moto Guzzi Corporation which also owned Moto America, Moto Guzzi France, and 25 per cent of MGI Germany.

## THE CALIFORNIA EV11/SPECIAL

As the sporting Moto Guzzis were being phased out, the California was entering a new, and highly successful phase. With 151 modifications over the previous California, the EV, introduced in April 1997, was hailed as the world's best cruiser. Changes to the 1,064cc engine were few, limited to stronger con-rods, and new, 40mm fuel injection bodies. The exhaust system was now chromed stainless-steel, but the rest of the EV was comprehensively updated. The instruments came from the Centauro and the fuel tank had a flush-mounted stainless-steel cap and electric fuel taps. Running gear consisted of a 45mm Marzocchi fork, White Power shock absorbers, and BBS tubeless spoked wheels.

The biggest changes were to the brakes which utilised twin 320mm stainless-steel front discs with four-piston Brembo calipers, and a 282mm rear disc with an advanced load-compensating integrated brake system that incorporated a Bosch proportioning and delay valve. The general finish was improved over the already high standards set by the previous 1100 and there was no shortage of chrome. Already on its way to becoming one of Guzzi's most successful models, the EV took the world by surprise when it was hailed as *Cycle World*'s best Ameri-cruiser in March 1998. From a class of 13, the EV was notable in that unlike other cruisers it had fully adjustable suspension, a fork brace, and even a steering damper. In the best Moto Guzzi tradition the 257kg (567lb) EV really handled. Performance was not too shabby either, with a top speed of 115mph (185km/h).

(501lb) test bike. Unfortunately, while the 1100 Sport IE was undoubtedly the finest of Moto Guzzi's sporting two-valve machines it also came too late. Although more popular than the Daytona RS it was discontinued during 1997.

A final 200 1100 Sports were released in March 1998 as the 1100 Sport Corsa Limited Edition. Featuring Carrillo con-rods and a black engine and wheels, these also came with a Termignoni carbon-fibre exhaust kit. This final series was seized upon immediately by collectors as the epitome of the 1100 Sport.

While quality and production levels were increasing at Mandello, the company experienced a further boost when shareholders increased the paid-up capital from 5 to 12 billion lire in February 1997. This was a result of TRGI announcing the private placement of 20 per cent of total shares in Moto Guzzi Corporation on the New York NASDAQ. Shortly afterwards, Arnolfo Sacchi's three-year term ended and Oscar Cecchinato, formerly with Aprilia, took over as managing director in April 1997.

Following on from the California EV was the California Special, released in July 1998. Essentially identical to the EV, the Special was designed to emulate the American 'Lowrider' style. Thus the Special had a lower seat (760mm; 30in), larger rear mudguard, wider handlebar, larger headlight and no footboards. Other changes included a smaller computer unit under the seat and Sachs-Boge adjustable shock absorbers.

# THE V11 SPORT/GT

With the four-valve line-up fading away, the two-valve line was further developed with the V11 Sport. First displayed at the Milan Show in September 1997, it would be almost two years before it went into production. Once again it showed Moto Guzzi's

capacity to expand the traditional line-up and create a unique machine. The V11 Sport cleverly combined sporting and nostalgic features, creating an individual style. With its green bodywork and red frame it harked back to the magnificent 'Telaio Rosso' of 1971; a two-seater version was silver with a red frame.

In all other respects however, the V11 Sport was a thoroughly modern motorcycle. The engine was the trusted two-valve 1,064cc fuel injected unit, now with a six-speed gearbox. Power was 90 horsepower at 7,800rpm and the chassis similar to that of the previous Sport 1100. With a dry weight of 221kg (487lb), the claimed top speed was in the region of 230km/h (143mph).

Following the V11 Sport came a GT version, with full touring fairing and bags, introduced at the Munich Intermot Show in September 1998. As with the Centauro, there was a variety of dedicated accessories such as a front fairing and carbon-fibre exhausts.

# THE QUOTA 1100 ES

Somewhat surprisingly, considering its rather poor sales figures, the Quota was resurrected in November 1997 at the Birmingham Show as the 1100 ES. However, the ES was a significant improvement over the earlier 1000, and was aimed at the top end of the enduro market. Whether it is more successful in the marketplace remains to be seen.

A re-tuned 1100 engine was now used, with new camshafts and Weber-Marelli fuel injection with 42mm throttles, a new-generation, and more compact 1.5 CPU was employed. Tuned for a broad spread of power, 70 horsepower was produced at 6,400rpm. More importantly for an enduro bike, 90 per cent of the maximum 8.7kgm of torque was available between 2,800rpm and 5,800rpm. Given the intended nature of the ES it was also surprising that

**BELOW** The V10 engine was very short, making it ideal for racing where both a short wheelbase and weight on the front wheel are desirable.

an increase in front brake disc diameter to 296mm and a fully adjustable Sachs-Boge rear shock absorber. Most of the dimensions were similar to its predecessor and with a claimed weight of 245kg (540lb) the Quota ES was still a huge motorcycle. Production began in July 1998.

As the expansion of the company continued following the increase in paid-up capital, this was reflected not only in improved quality, but also increased turnover. By 1997 turnover was 85 billion lire with production at 6,432 motorcycles. It was seen as the crucial year for the company in 1998, with many decisions taken as to the direction Moto Guzzi should take in the future. By raising capital to 35 billion lire in June 1998 and borrowing 20 billion on the market to create 55 billion lire, it was anticipated that production could increase to 20,000 units by the year 2001. The most exciting news was 30 billion lire in product development that would allow for a new engine and would hopefully see Moto Guzzi back racing on the world stage.

## THE VA 10

Designed by a new team of engineers led by Danilo Mojoli, this first all-new Moto Guzzi engine since Lino Tonti's small twin, followed the Guzzi tradition of being innovative and traditional. First discussed in September 1996, the idea came to fruition in January 1997 with the assistance of Ricardo in England.

Retaining the usual transversely mounted V-twin, the all-alloy water-cooled engine featured the cylinders angled at 75°. 'This was done to reduce frontal area,' said Mojoli. 'We also wanted to keep the engine as short as possible with as much weight on the front wheel so we initially rotated it 10° forward but have now increased that to 15°.'

While the 75° engine did not offer perfect primary balance, this was obtained by spacing the crankpins 30° apart, the short spacing maintaining crank stiffness. Secondary balance was achieved by using longer con-rods, longer than the usual two times the stroke. Bore and stroke for the 1,000cc engine were 100 x 63.3mm, but 850cc, 1,100cc, and 1,200cc versions were to follow. No longer were the valves operated by rockers, but twin overhead camshafts to both cylinder heads opened the two 39.6mm inlet and 33mm exhaust valves per cylinder. Included valve angle was a narrow 26½°, 14° for the inlet and 12½° for the

the entire gearbox and final drive was shared with the 1100 Sport.

Although the frame and swingarm were similar to the earlier Quota, the ES featured a number of improvements, not the least being a dramatic reduction in seat height to 820mm (32¼in). Other changes were

exhaust. Drive to the camshafts was by chain from a shaft above the crank turning in the opposite direction to cancel torque reaction. This shaft also drove the water pump. Lubrication was by dry sump, with an external oil tank. As expected, Weber-Marelli electronic fuel injection was used, with twin injectors for racing. Throttle bodies were 60mm for racing, reducing to 54mm on street bikes.

The biggest departure for Guzzi was the loss of shaft drive. A 90° gear from the crankshaft took the drive to a multi-plate clutch (dry for racing and wet for production) and to a usual separate six-speed gearbox but a chain final drive. With a total engine weight of 30kg (66lb), this was 30 per cent less than the then current Moto Guzzi 1100. Incredibly compact, the eventual street motorcycle had a 1,380mm (54⅓in) wheelbase and weighed only 190kg (419lb).

Equally revolutionary for Moto Guzzi was the all-alloy beam frame and swingarm, encased by full bodywork. 'This is not an engine that needs to be seen like the older one,' Mojoli says. With bench testing

beginning in May 1998, production was initially slated for the year 2000, with a return to the race track in 2001. However, this was an optimistic expectation.

Oscar Cecchinato had plans to expand production levels to those that Moto Guzzi had not seen during the 1950s. This called for a larger model range than what was currently on offer, and a move from Mandello to premises closer to a major industrial centre. The prosperity of the 1950s had been created by the sales of a large number of smaller motorcycles and with this in mind Moto Guzzi entered into an agreement with Piaggio in April 1998 to acquire a 600cc four-stroke single for an enduro, followed by a scooter in 125cc and 250cc. The enduro used the engine originally from the Gilera Saturno and was to be built to the Gilera design by Moto Guzzi. Production was scheduled for May 1999, followed by the scooter in November. The scooter endeavoured to emulate the earlier Galletto by successfully combining both motorcycle and scooter features in a unique vehicle.

BELOW The V11 Sport finally made it into production during 1999, and was similar to the prototype.
Moto Guzzi

RIGHT The V11 GT was also released during 1999, just prior to the Aprilia purchase of the company.
Moto Guzzi

With the planned expansion in production, Moto Guzzi signed an agreement in May 1998 with Philips Electronics to acquire their industrial site at Monza. However, this agreement caused considerable unease at Mandello where many of the workforce had been at Moto Guzzi for several generations. In September 1998, with the support of influential board member Gianni Bulgari, former financial director Dino Falciola replaced Cecchinato and the move to Monza was cancelled. This also put the future of new models in doubt, including the Piaggio scooter and enduro, and further delayed the V11 Sport. However, with a commitment to the company remaining at Mandello there was further investment in new machinery and equipment. This culminated in the merger of the Moto Guzzi Corporation with NACC on 10 March 1999. Shortly afterwards, on 24 March 1999, 57-year-old Mario Scandellari was appointed the managing director of the company.

# THE CALIFORNIA JACKAL AND SPECIAL

By the end of 1998 the Piaggio connection was abandoned, but life continued much as before at Mandello del Lario. With the delay of the V11 Sport and the success of the California EV, the company maintained its commitment to the large cruiser. An obvious lack of development capital was undoubtedly slowing production of the V11 Sport, but it was a relatively easy process to produce variations of the California EV11. The first of these was the Special, an unabashed American-style cruiser. While retaining the basic California engine and chassis, there were wider handlebars, more-forward footpegs, and a lower seat. Other styling considerations saw a

more enveloping rear mudguard, larger headlight, and individual rider's and pillion seats. While the engine specification was unchanged the rocker covers were more rounded.

Continuing the expansion of the California range during 1999 was the California Jackal, an entry-level cruiser sold as a base for customising. This was accompanied, in July 1999, by an official range of Moto Guzzi accessories. Inspired by the American 'bobber', a forerunner of post-war American cruisers, the Jackal was a no-frills cruiser. 'To bob' meant 'to cut' back in the immediate post-war years and that is what Moto Guzzi did to the California EV to create the Jackal. Everything about the Jackal was reduced to the minimum; there was widespread use of black-painted parts, simpler instruments, and a single front disc brake.

With over 40 accessories, customisation was incorporated as an integral part of the Jackal's concept. These included a windshield, luggage carrier, shock absorbers, second front disc, rev counter, pillion bars, and panniers. Moto Guzzi saw the Jackal as a way of expanding the appeal of their superb California beyond their traditional more mature customer base, targeting it at the more fashion-conscious younger market. Also during 1999, the V11 Sport finally made it into production, but generally the year was one of uncertainty for the company with no new models for the 2000 model year. Finally, after many rumours of potential buyouts, it was announced on 14 April 2000 that the Italian motorcycle manufacturer, Aprilia SpA was to purchase Moto Guzzi. As one of Europe's leading manufacturers with an extremely high racing profile, this heralded a new era for Moto Guzzi.

The V11 Le Mans was
introduced during 2001,
the first of the V11 series
with a fairing.
Moto Guzzi

# 14 THE EAGLE FLIES AGAIN: A NEW LIFE UNDER APRILIA AND PIAGGIO

Ivano Beggio, president of Aprilia, first signified an intent to buy Moto Guzzi in 1988, but at that stage Aprilia did not possess the capital of 15 billion lire that De Tomaso demanded. Twelve years later, the company was up for sale again, and Beggio was involved in a secret auction with Ducati and Piaggio. Although his bid of 82 billion lire was less than that of Ducati, Beggio's was accepted because he could finance it immediately.

The contract for the sale of Moto Guzzi was signed in September 2000 and Beggio immediately announced that Moto Guzzi would remain at Mandello. The company would be re-launched on the world stage, but their tradition would be maintained. As Aprilia was a relatively new marque, Beggio was proud to inherit Moto Guzzi's illustrious history, and his first objective was to improve reliability and production quality. Aprilia soon introduced new tooling into the ageing Mandello factory, and recruited a team of engineers to proceed with the development of a new-generation engine. The first fruit of the Aprilia purchase, the limited-edition V11 Sport Rosso Mandello, was displayed at the Munich Intermot towards the end of 2000.

## 2001

### THE V11 SPORT ROSSO MANDELLO

To celebrate Moto Guzzi's 80th birthday, 300 examples of the V11 Sport Rosso Mandello were produced for 2001. Although essentially identical to the V11 Sport, the Rosso Mandello featured a number of carbon-fibre components (silencers, front fender, and instrument panel), along with red-anodised frame plates and rocker covers. There was also a new hydraulic clutch and lighter front brake discs. The clutch was a single-sintered metal disc type, and many components were accentuated in black, including the engine, fork, wheels and rear drive housing. A numbered plaque on the side panels

**LEFT** The first new Moto Guzzi to appear following the Aprilia take-over was the V11 Sport Rosso Mandello, built to celebrate 80 years of Moto Guzzi.

**BELOW** Also built to celebrate the 80th anniversary was the California EV80. Moto Guzzi

system received a braking proportioning and delay valve. Aprilia wasted no time in making their mark at Mandello del Lario, and a new production line was in operation by March 2001.

# THE V11 LE MANS AND CALIFORNIA EV80

The impact of Aprilia's purchase on Moto Guzzi became more evident towards the end of 2001 and into 2002. New production lines and machinery allowed the range of cruisers and custom models to be expanded, and there were significant technical updates. The slow-selling Quota 1100ES was dropped and Aprilia continued to celebrate Moto Guzzi's 80th birthday. They introduced two new models and updated others during 2001; the V11 Le Mans, and the California EV80 special edition.

also differentiated each Rosso Mandello from the regular V11 Sport. Under the transition to Aprilia ownership the V11 Sport, California EV, California Special, California Jackal, 350 and 750 Nevada, and Quota 1100ES all remained as they had in 1999 and 2000, although the California EV integral braking

Just as the V11 Sport was styled to replicate the original V7 Sport Telaio Rosso, the V11 Le Mans was intentionally named to create an association with one of the most famous and enduring models in Moto Guzzi's history. Based on the V11 Sport, the V11 Le Mans established a sport touring model within the sporting line-up, and included an aerodynamic half fairing, and wider (5.50 x 17in) rear wheel to accommodate a larger, 180/55 tyre. The wheelbase was increased to 1,490mm (59in). The California EV80, like the V11 Sport Rosso, was built to celebrate 80 years of Moto Guzzi, and featured a Poltrona Frau leather seat, saddlebags, and handgrips. Poltrona Frau, from the Marche, was one of the most prestigious leather design houses in Italy. Also setting the EV80 apart was a new windshield and footboards, a larger and more powerful headlight, and chrome-plated valve covers. Under Aprilia, Moto Guzzi was more strongly split into two distinct co-existing families; sport and touring, with an expansion of models within each group.

**ABOVE** Introduced for 2002, the Le Mans Tenni was a limited-edition model celebrating the great Moto Guzzi racer Omobono Tenni. *Moto Guzzi*

**BELOW** Only small updates set the 2002 V11 Sport apart from the earlier versions. *Moto Guzzi*

# 2002

## SPORT AND SPORT TOURING MODELS

# THE V11 LE MANS TENNI, V11 SPORT AND V11 SPORT SCURA

The V11 Sport Rosso Mandello signalled a new era of limited-edition versions, and the special edition Le Mans for 2002 was the Le Mans Tenni. Aprilia was intent on utilising Moto Guzzi's illustrious racing history to maximum marketing effect. Omobono Tenni was a distant figure of the racing past, but he symbolised the greatness of Moto Guzzi. Tenni was passionate, brave, a great champion, and the Le Mans Tenni was a tribute to him. Painted in the traditional racing green of the 1950s racers, with a unique imitation leather seat, the Le Mans Tenni included a lighter, single-plate clutch, milled foot levers, and titanium nitride fork tubes on the 40mm Marzocchi fork for a smoother action.

The V11 Sport continued as the naked sporting model for 2002, with a new frame to allow for a wider 5.5in rear rim and 180/55 x 17in rear tyre. The frame and instrument support coverings were more durable and clip-on handlebars and rear seat unit were re-designed. Another variant of the V11 Sport became available during 2002, the V11 Scura. While the 1,064cc engine (without catalyst) was as before, the Scura featured the single-plate clutch of other limited-edition sporting twins, plus uprated suspension. The upside-down front fork was a 43mm Öhlins, and there was an Öhlins rear shock absorber. Also setting the Scura apart were the Öhlins steering damper, carbon-fibre front mudguard, tank protector, starter motor housing, instrument mounting and mufflers. The colour was black carbon, and the Scura came with a small cockpit fairing, much like the first Le Mans of 1976. Production was limited, and each example had a numbered plaque. With its high-quality suspension, and minimal sporting attire, the V11 Scura was undoubtedly the most impressive new-generation sporting Moto Guzzi. It also indicated that Aprilia was not content to continue the earlier tradition of minimal development.

## TOURING AND CUSTOM MODELS

# THE CALIFORNIA STONE, STONE METAL, SPECIAL SPORT, EV, EV TOURING AND NEVADA 750

There was some revision of the touring and custom line-up under Aprilia. The Jackal was discontinued, but the American cruiser style continued as the California Stone. This was even more Spartan, and essentially a back-to-basics cruiser without any unnecessary accruements. Like the Jackal, the front brake was only a single disc, and it was joined by the Stone Metal, with a chrome-plated fuel tank. Replacing the California Special was the California Special Sport, with additional custom trimmings, a restyled front fork, new springs, a new dashboard support, eagle's beak chromed profile mudguard, convex chromed side panels, and polished, rounded cylinder head covers.

The California EV also received some updates for 2002. The diameter of the handlebars was increased to 30mm, the gearbox revised to reduce shift throw and effort, and make neutral location easier. The front fork had revised damping and new springs, while the frame and swingarm were modified to allow a wider tyre. Also announced at the end of 2001 for 2002 was the California EV Touring, but this did not become available until 2003. The early announcement and subsequent delayed release of new models was typical of the early days of Aprilia control.

By the 2000s, all motorcycle companies were endeavouring to increase sales and the most cost-effective method for small-scale European manufacturers was to offer more variations on a theme. By utilising existing platforms and mixing and matching components the line-up could be expanded with minimal investment. One model that had remained virtually unchanged for over ten years was the Nevada 750. Always a steady seller in Italy, the custom Nevada was now only a 750, and retained the smaller V-twin engine that was brought out back in 1977. Small updates for 2002 included a new seat, but there was little to distinguish the 2002 version from earlier examples.

While Moto Guzzi at Mandello was in the throws of rejuvenation, the enthusiasm for the marque continued around the world. In March 2002, in Maxton North Carolina, USA, the Moto Guzzi 'Cooked Goose' Land Speed Record Team set three new world records, reaching speeds in excess of 254km/h (158mph) on a modified 1100 Sport. Moto Guzzi now held records in nine different classes for 2,000cc production pushrod engines.

# 2003

## THE GRISO AND MGS/01 PROTOTYPES

By the end of 2002 it became obvious that Aprilia's revitalisation of Moto Guzzi was extending beyond the simple expansion of existing model ranges. Two new exciting concept motorcycles were displayed at the Munich Intermot in September 2002

demonstrating Aprilia's commitment to the continuation of Moto Guzzi as a leading motorcycle marque. While adhering to the traditional air-cooled 90° V-twin engine with shaft drive these new models included significant technical advances and were designed to indicate the path of Moto Guzzi's future development. There was also considerable expansion of official accessories and merchandise, with a range of specific products available for each model. Among the future technical developments there was an innovative Formula One-style electro-assisted gearbox and continuing where the earlier Convert left off, clutch and gear changing would be controlled by an electronic control unit. Three model options would be available: Normal, Sport, and Automatic.

With the establishment of a 'Style Laboratory' at Mandello early in 2002, style was now an important consideration and was embodied in a radical new motorcycle, the Griso. This name came from the novel of Alessandro Manzoni, *Promessi Sposione*, set on the Lecco branch of Lake Como near Mandello del Lario.

Griso was a naked character, a bodyguard of the past, and the bike was a muscular and aggressive naked design. A unique combination of high-performance Superbike and naked street fighter, the Griso was powered by the earlier four-valves per cylinder engine. This was installed in an unusual, large-section tubular steel frame that swept down from the steering head to a massive single-sided aluminium swingarm with a single shock absorber with a parallelogram linkage and rising-rate rear suspension. The engine and swingarm were finished in matt black.

As a styling exercise the Griso was long and large, rolling on a 1,560mm (61.4in) wheelbase and weighing 199kg (439lb). The front suspension was a 43mm upside-down fork, and while the brakes and wheels were similar to those of the V11 Sport, the front brake calipers had differential pistons (36mm and 32mm). The rear wheel was a 6 x 17in with a huge, 200/50 x 17 tyre. Looking unlike any previous Moto Guzzi the Griso was initially a concept model built to gauge public reaction, but it would eventually go into production.

Sharing the Griso's four-valve engine was another radical concept bike, the MGS/01 (Moto Guzzi Sport No. 1). The resurrected Daytona and Centauro engine was mated to a six-speed gearbox for the first time and installed in an up-to-date chassis, with stunning styling. For those enthusiasts who bemoaned the departure of the true sporting Moto Guzzi, the MGS/01 was the successor to the V7 Sport, Le Mans, and Daytona. Moto Guzzi racing specialists Ghezzi & Brian were engaged to create the MGS/01 as a pure, no-frills, Superbike but had less than nine months to complete the project.

Giuseppe Ghezzi took the Daytona four-valve twin, boosting the power to 102 horsepower at 8,400rpm, and integrated the V11 six-speed gearbox in the timing case. With a new box-section single-spar ALS 450 steel backbone frame, and a 505mm box-section aluminium swingarm with rising rate suspension, the result was the shortest and lightest large-capacity Guzzi V-twin ever. The suspension was Öhlins, with 43mm forks and a vertical rear shock absorber allowing room for the 15-litre airbox. The wheels were Oz. Alberto Cappella's styling was also elemental and minimalist, accentuated by the single exhaust pipe exiting underneath the Monoposto seat. With a dry weight of 194kg (428lb) the MGS/01 was the most sporting interpretation of the Moto Guzzi V-twin ever and the

**LEFT** Styled like no previous Moto Guzzi, the Griso prototype was powered by the earlier four-valve engine.
Moto Guzzi

**BELOW LEFT** First displayed at the end of 2002, the MGS/01 continued a sporting lineage that began with the V7 Sport.
Moto Guzzi

**BELOW** Introduced for 2003, the Breva 750 was an impressive entry-level motorcycle.
Moto Guzzi

initial response was so enthusiastic that Moto Guzzi CEO Roberto Brovazzo engaged CSM International to conduct market research into its production feasibility. As a result, it was decided to make the MGS/01 available as soon as possible, and in June 2003 selected journalists were given an opportunity to test the first running prototype at the Adria circuit.

## THE BREVA 750 IE

Signifying the wind of change, or breath of fresh air, blowing through Mandello, the new compact lightweight Moto Guzzi motorcycle for 2003 was called the Breva, named after the light southerly wind that brings fine weather to Lake Como. Designed as an entry-level model to compete with motorcycles like the Ducati Monster 620 IE, the Breva V750 I.E.

emphasised balance and manoeuvrability. As heir to the earlier V35 and V50 it retained a classical minimalist look. The engine was the familiar smaller Nevada V-twin, with parallel valves and Heron cylinder heads, but now with Weber-Marelli electronic fuel injection with 36mm throttle bodies. The injectors directed fuel towards the inlet valve. Numerous internal modifications included graphite-coated pistons, a new camshaft, and an improved crankcase ventilation system. Power was increased marginally to 35.5kW (48.28 horsepower) at 6,800rpm. Shared with the Nevada was the five-speed gearbox, although there was a modified selector and neutral mechanism with new ratios.

There were no breakthroughs with the Breva chassis, and the front fork was a conventional 40mm Marzocchi, while twin Paioli shock absorbers controlled the rear end. The frame, with detachable lower frame rails, was

rear shock absorber, and a Bitubo steering damper. The standard Le Mans included a larger diameter (43mm) Marzocchi upside-down fork, with a 25mm diameter axle (up from 20mm), to improve front-end rigidity.

The frame was no longer constructed from chrome-molybdenum, but of high-strength steel. The fuel pump was now located inside the fuel tank, and there was a new instrument layout with revised instruments and warning lights. The generator warning light was replaced by a second direction indicator light. The V11 Scura and V11 remained unchanged for 2003, retaining the previous non-catalysed 1,064cc engine with lower, 9.5:1 compression ratio.

also similar to the Nevada, but the wheels were three-spoke 17in cast-alloy. The Breva may have been a revamp of a familiar theme, but Luciano Marabese's styling cleverly disguised this. The deeply scalloped seat provided a seat height of only 790mm (31in), and alloy footpeg support plates enveloped the swingarm pivot. The brakes (single front disc with a four-piston caliper) were similar to the Nevada, while the sporting character was emphasised with a small fairing. The Breva looked new, functioned effectively, and although only moderately powerful, its weight of only 182kg (401lb) made it extremely appealing to a wide variety of riders. As a result, it was extremely successful.

## SPORT TOURING AND SPORT MODELS

# THE V11 LE MANS ROSSO CORSA, LE MANS, SCURA, V11

To meet the new Euro 2 emission standard the Le Mans now featured a new injection control unit, exhaust Lambda sensor, and trivalent catalysers (platinum/palladium and rhodium) in the silencers. The compression ratio of the Le Mans engines was increased to 9.8:1 and a balance pipe linked the exhaust manifolds. Oil jets now cooled the pistons, and there were redesigned forged con-rods. The limited edition Le Mans for 2003 was the Rosso Corsa. Apart from the red valve covers, the engine and drivetrain (with dual-disc clutch) was shared with the standard Le Mans. Where the Rosso Corsa differed from the Le Mans was the chassis, which had an Öhlins 43mm front fork, Öhlins

## TOURING AND CUSTOM MODELS

# THE CALIFORNIA EV TOURING, EV, STONE TOURING, TITANIUM, ALUMINIUM, STONE AND NEVADA 750

For 2003 the California received a number of engine updates. The compression ratio was increased from 9.5:1 to 9.8:1, and low rpm power was improved through a new balance tube connecting the two exhaust manifolds. Oil jets through new forged con-rods cooled the piston crowns and the crankcase ventilation system in the timing case was modified. There was a Lambda sensor and two three-way catalytic converters in the exhaust, the sensor measuring the quantity of gas and transmitting the data to the electronic control unit. The clutch was now a lighter, single-disc steel plate. Other updates on the California included the replacement of the mechanical valve tappets of a quieter hydraulic type.

Also available for 2003 was the California EV Touring which had a wide range of accessories and a standard windshield, and was an attempt to re-create a US-style 1970s sport touring motorcycle. Standard equipment included a colour-coordinated windshield and 40-litre panniers. Joining the California EV and EV Touring in the touring line-up for that year was the more basic Stone Touring. This retained the Stone's single front disc brake, and included a Plexiglas windshield and Hepco-Becker panniers.

**BELOW** With its colour-matched fairing and standard luggage the California EV Touring was a luxury factory sport tourer.
Moto Guzzi

The California Custom range also grew for 2003. Alongside the basic Stone, were the California Titanium and Aluminium. Symbolising advanced technology, the Titanium included lower handlebars, forward-mounted footpegs, and a small cockpit fairing, it was marketed as a performance cruiser. The California Aluminium was similar, but for a bright aluminium finish on the fuel tank, side covers and engine cases, and no fairing. The Nevada 750 continued unchanged this year.

**ABOVE** The Stone Touring was a more basic touring machine than the EV Touring and featured a single-disc front brake and plain windshield.
Moto Guzzi

**BELOW** New for 2003 was the California Titanium performance cruiser.
Moto Guzzi

**LEFT** As an all-round touring machine the Breva 1100 continued the style of the original V7.
Moto Guzzi

# 2004

With motorcycle sales increasing 29 per cent in Italy, 50 per cent in the US, and 32 per cent in the UK during 2003, Aprilia's programme of development and range expansion was now vindicated. The promise of a production Griso and MGS-01 also raised Moto Guzzi's profile, but the most significant new model for 2004 was the Breva 1100.

## THE BREVA 1100

The Breva 1100 was essentially a larger-capacity version of the successful Breva 750. Whereas the 750 continued the style of the earlier small twins, the 1100 sustained the original V7 philosophy of an all-round large-capacity touring bike, absent since the demise of the Mille GT in 1993. Unlike the 750, the Breva 1100 engine and drive train design was considerably updated. While the same bore and stroke of 92 x

80mm was retained, the engine included a new sump, repositioned automotive-type 650-watt alternator, longer and 10 per cent lighter con-rods, and lighter pistons. The piston was shorter, the lighter rings are positioned differently, and the skirt included two oil jets to improve lubrication of the gudgeon pin. Metal cylinder head gaskets replaced the old Klingerite type for improved thermal conduction and stud grip. As the alternator was located between the cylinders rather than on the crankshaft the engine was 20mm shorter and could be mounted further forward. There were now two spark plugs per cylinder, the valve seats were sintered and no longer cast iron, while the valves were stainless steel.

Modifications to the lubrication system included the pressure relief valve moved from the end of the lubrication circuit to the middle, allowing excess oil to be released from the pump's suction line. This reduced power loss and eliminated oil foaming, while locating the oil filter outside the engine simplified maintenance. The Weber-Marelli electronic injection included an automotive 'stepper' motor valve to aid starting and idling and Pico injectors in the intake manifolds improved combustion. To meet the stricter Euro 3

**BELOW** The 1,100cc engine for the Breva 1100 was considerably updated, and included twin spark plugs per cylinder. Moto Guzzi

**RIGHT** The MGS-01 Corsa was offered for 2004, with Brembo radial front brakes. Moto Guzzi

emissions standard, the stainless steel two-into-one exhaust system included a 3-way catalytic converter. As the Breva was a touring model, the 84 horsepower at 7,800rpm was less than the V11, but the delivery was smoother and more linear.

Even more significant was the chassis development, with the drive shaft incorporated inside a new aluminium single-sided swingarm, similar to that displayed on the prototype Griso in 2002. Patented by Moto Guzzi as 'CARC' (*cardano reattivo compatto* – compact reactive shaft drive) this was designed to minimise shaft drive effect during acceleration and braking in the manner of BMW's Paralever. The pinion gear and the drive shaft oscillated inside the one-piece swingarm and the drive shaft was equipped with two universal joints with built-in torsional dampers. Unlike the Paralever however, the reaction shaft was not load-bearing. The swingarm also connected to the single shock absorber through a rising rate linkage.

A conventional 45mm fork controlled the front end, with the usual Brembo 320mm dual-disc front brake with four caliper pistons and a single 282mm disc with twin piston caliper on the rear. New for the Breva 1100 was a digital display, including an onboard computer operated by handlebar controls. Optional equipment included a windshield and ABS braking.

## THE MGS-01 CORSA

After its successful introduction at the end of 2002 it was announced that production of the MGS-01 would proceed in two phases: a limited series non-homologated racing MGS-01 Corsa appearing in the first quarter of 2004, followed by a homologated production MGS-01 Serie in October. Sixty Corsas were envisaged for initial manufacture in early 2004, but this was an optimistic forecast. The Corsa was displayed at the Milan EICMA in September 2003 and was created by Giuseppe Ghezzi for racing classes that allowed air-cooled twins up to 1,300cc. Displacing 1,256cc, the pistons were 100mm three-ring 11:1 Cosworth, with ceramic-coated cylinders, and many of the plain bearings in the four-valve engine were replaced by a roller type. The Nimonic valves went up to 36mm inlet and 31mm exhaust, and with 50mm throttle bodies the power was increased to 122 horsepower at 8,000rpm. The Con-rods were Carillo with a 144mm eye-to-eye length and the injection system a Marelli IAW 15M.

The Öhlins suspension, with radial Brembo front-brake calipers came from the 2003 Aprilia RSV-R, and the 17in wheels were extremely light forged five-spoke Oz. Excellent handling was assured by the long, 505mm swingarm (with parallelogram linkage) that provided near 50/50 weight distribution. The wheelbase was 1,428mm (58.3in)and the weight 192kg (423lb). The MGS-01 Corsa promised to provide Moto Guzzi with race glory that had been absent since Dr John Wittner's 'Battle of the Twins' racer and a prototype took part in the trials for the World Endurance Championships in Albacete in June 2004. It also managed third and fourth, at the Speed Week of Brno in July.

## SPORT TOURING MODELS

# THE V11 LE MANS NERO CORSA, LE MANS ROSSO CORSA AND LE MANS

As the Le Mans had been updated for 2003 there was little change for 2004. Joining the Le Mans Rosso Corsa was the similar Le Mans Nero Corsa, in black instead of red. The Öhlins upside-down fork had TIN-coated fork tubes to reduce friction and the engine was identical in specification to that of 2003.

## NAKED SPORT MODELS

# THE V11 COPPA ITALIA, CAFÉ SPORT, SPORT BALLABIO AND BREVA V 750 IE

For 2004, the V11 Sport was offered in three variants and now featured the higher compression ratio Le Mans engine with catalytic converter. All three versions included a small cockpit fairing, similar to that of the Scura but positioned slightly further forward, and raised handlebars instead of the previous

clip-on style. The base model was known as the V11 Sport Ballabio, named after the Ballabio–Resinelli race which is part of the Italian Hill Climb Championship. This model retained a 43mm Marzocchi fork and Sachs shock absorber, and was available as the traditional 'Rosso Race', or minimalist 'Grigio Resinelli.'

Replacing the Scura was the V11 Café Sport, with bronze wheels, valve covers, and frame plate and with carbon-fibre mudguards, starter motor cover and side panels. It retained the Öhlins suspension and steering damper. To celebrate participation in the 2003 Italian Naked Bike Championship, the V11 Coppia Italia was produced for 2004. Except for the colours, this was almost identical to the Café Sport, but a titanium racing exhaust system with modified footpeg mounts was available as an option. The front fork was an Öhlins 45mm, as was the rear shock absorber and steering damper, while the wheels were lightweight forged Oz similar to the MGS-01 Corsa. Only introduced a year earlier there was no change to the Breva V750 IE for 2004.

**ABOVE** The V11 Café Sport with higher handlebars replaced the V11 Scura for 2004.
Moto Guzzi

**BELOW** The V11 Coppia Italia was produced to celebrate participation in the Italian Naked Bike Championship.
Moto Guzzi

## TOURING AND CUSTOM MODELS

# THE CALIFORNIA EV TOURING, EV, STONE TOURING, TITANIUM, ALUMINIUM, STONE AND NEVADA 750 (CLUB)

As the Touring and Custom line-up received considerable attention for 2003 there was little change to this series for 2004. The range of colours was expanded for the EV Touring and EV, while the Titanium, Aluminium, and Stone remained unchanged. The long-running Nevada was updated, and there were now two versions, the 'Base' and 'Club'. As the Nevada was now seen as a city bike suited for female riders the style was less custom and the ergonomics designed for comfort. As with all

models there was a wide range of accessories available.

Although the presentation of the MGS-01 and Griso concept bikes had raised the awareness of Moto Guzzi as a serious motorcycle manufacturer, the parent company Aprilia was in deep financial trouble by 2004. Misreading the demand for larger-capacity scooters had hurt Aprilia deeply and during that year, the company had sought a prospective purchaser. After considering an offer from Ducati for Moto Guzzi only, it ultimately remained as part of the Aprilia Group which was acquired by Piaggio & C. SpA on 30 December 2004.

The Piaggio Group (Chairman Roberto Colaninno, Deputy Chairman Matteo Colaninno, Chief Executive Officer Rocco Sabelli and General Manager Gianclaudio Neri) now controlled 100 per cent of Aprilia-Moto Guzzi. Piaggio had a turnover of 1.5 billion euros, 24 per cent of the European and 35 per cent of the Italian two-wheel market, sales of over 600,000 units a year, 6,000 employees, eight manufacturing plants around the world, and a presence in over 50 countries.

# 2005

In less than 24 months Moto Guzzi's engineers had transformed the concept bikes into reality and the final versions of the MGS-01 Corsa, Griso, and Breva 1100 were displayed at the Munich Intermot Show in September 2004. This was prior to the sale of Aprilia to Piaggio and there was still a question mark over when production would commence. Daniele Bandiera was appointed chief executive officer of Moto Guzzi SpA on 3 March 2005, with the task of managing company recovery and turnaround. Almost immediately the Breva 1100 was launched, followed in September by the Griso 1100.

## THE MGS-01 CORSA AND GRISO

Development of the MGS-01 Corsa continued during 2004. Race testing saw redesigned crankcases and chrome liners for the aluminium cylinders, and slightly higher compression three-ring Cosworth

pistons (11.6:1). The power increased slightly to 128 horsepower at 8,000rpm, with maximum torque of 11.5kgm at 6,400rpm. Chassis development included a longer, 513mm (20in) box-section aluminium swingarm. This extended the wheelbase to 1,450mm (57in), with near-perfect weight distribution of only 200 grams difference between the front and rear. The front fork remained a 43mm Öhlins with radial Brembo brakes and 320mm front discs.

The final Griso prototype was also shown at Intermot in September 2004, retaining 90 per cent of its original design features. The engine was no longer a four-valve unit, but the new V1100 Evolution engine with the Breva 1100 reactive shaft drive system had the drive shaft incorporated in the aluminium swingarm with a rising-rate linkage. The Griso's 1,064cc two-valve engine produced 87 horsepower at 8,000rpm, slightly more than that of the Breva 1100.

## THE BREVA V 1100

After hundreds of hours of bench testing and around 15,000 hours of gruelling full-throttle rolling road testing, equivalent to about 200,000km (125,000 miles) of normal engine life, the V1100 Evolution engine gained the seal of approval from Moto Guzzi's

engineers. Further testing in chassis on the mountain
roads around Mandello resulted in small alterations to
the steering geometry and suspension, with the weight
distribution improved by repositioning the engine
higher and further forward. Production commenced
shortly after the Piaggio takeover, in March 2005.

## SPORT TOURING AND NAKED MODELS

# THE V11 LE MANS NERO CORSA, LE MANS ROSSO CORSA, LE MANS, SCURA R, COPPA ITALIA, CAFÉ SPORT, SPORT BALLABIO AND BREVA V750 IE

In the wake of the Piaggio acquisition the three-model
Le Mans range, V11 Le Mans Nero Corsa, V11 Le
Mans Rosso Corsa and V11 Le Mans, continued
unchanged. There was also no change to most of the
naked sport models, the V11 Coppa Italia, V11 Café
Sport, V11 Sport Ballabio and Breva V750, all
continuing as for 2004. New this year however, was
the V11 Scura R. The Scura had been absent for a year
but made a return as the Scura R with the higher

handlebar set-up of the other V11 naked models. The
Öhlins suspension was retained and there were a
number of carbon-fibre body components to provide a
distinctive racing appearance and to reduce weight.
The Scura R was to be the final sporting Moto Guzzi
built on the existing V11 platform.

## TOURING AND CUSTOM MODELS

# THE CALIFORNIA EV TOURING, EV, STONE TOURING, NEVADA CLASSIC 750 IE, CALIFORNIA TITANIUM, ALUMINIUM AND STONE

The line-up of touring and custom models was also
largely unchanged for 2005. Colours were again
changed for the California EV Touring and the only
new model was the Nevada Classic 750 IE. The
Nevada 750 had been in Moto Guzzi's line-up since
1990 and the Nevada Classic 750 IE was 87 per cent
new. Of 441 parts, 383 were redesigned or replaced,
the most significant update electronic fuel injection
with a Lambda probe catalyser. Other updated parts

included the side panels, shock absorber covers, the seat with a low, 760mm (30in) height, rear mudguard, taillight, rider's footrests, and a 40mm Marzocchi fork. The brakes included a 320mm front disc with four-piston Brembo caliper, and a 260mm disc on the rear. Instrumentation included an LCD display and there was a wide range of dedicated accessories available.

# 2006

The year 2006 marked Moto Guzzi's 85th anniversary and Piaggio commemorated this by celebrating the marque's touring tradition. This emphasis on touring saw the demise of the sport touring Le Mans, the naked sport V11 models, and a rationalisation of the custom range. Like other manufacturers, Piaggio's quest was increased sales and this was most easily achieved by offering more variations on a theme. But whereas this was previously custom and naked sport models, the emphasis was now on touring and naked for 2006. A range of dedicated accessories continued as an important component in the pursuit to maximise profitability.

Following the launch of the Griso 1100 in September 2005, several new models were announced at the EICMA in Milan in November. These included the touring Norge 1200, and two 850s, the Breva 850 and the Griso 850. Available from April 2006, the 850s marked a return to a traditional Moto Guzzi engine capacity. The Norge 1200 was released in May, and in July, 14 international journalists emulated the 4,429km (2,752-mile) journey to the Arctic Circle in Norway made by Giuseppe 'Naco' Guzzi in 1928 on his pioneering G.T. 500 'Norge.'

These new models ensured the passion for Moto Guzzi did not diminish, and 15,000 enthusiasts from 20 countries met at Mandello in September for the fourth GMG (Giornate Mondiali Guzzi) meeting.

# THE NORGE 1200 T, TL, GT AND GTL

After an absence of nearly 20 years, Moto Guzzi re-entered the market for long-distance touring motorcycles with the Norge 1200. Available in four versions, this was named in memory of Moto Guzzi's first GT of 1928 (with a then revolutionary swingarm and rear suspension). At the heart of the new Norge

1200 was a 1,151cc evolution of the Breva V 1100 engine. Both the bore and stroke were increased (95 x 81.2mm) and with dual spark plugs and a Magneti Marelli IAW5A engine management system (with 45mm throttle bodies and Weber IWP 162 injectors) the power was increased to 95 horsepower at 7,500rpm.

Other developments included sintered valve guides for reduced friction and wear resistance, a higher capacity oil pump, and oil jets directed to the exhaust valve through a small hole in the cylinder head. The crankcases, sump and cylinder heads were modified to improve oil flow and an oil cooler was mounted in front of the alternator. As on the Breva 1100, power was transmitted to the rear wheel through a six-speed gearbox and a single-sided aluminium swingarm with the CARC compact reactive shaft-drive system.

Integral to the Norge 1200's design was complete rider protection, including a fairing, front leg shields, and a rear splash guard. Incorporated in the fairing were four polyelliptical headlights. To improve balance and weight distribution the engine was mounted higher and further forward in the traditional steel frame. The suspension was similar to the Breva 1100, a 45mm front fork and the rear suspension was a monoshock with rising rate linkage. Braking was also similar to the Breva 1100, with twin 320mm front discs and four-piston calipers, and a 282mm disc on the rear; ABS was standard.

The four versions were designed to fulfil the needs of urban riding, short-range travel and luxury long-distance touring. City riding was catered for by the Norge 1200 T, with a manually adjustable windshield, more basic fairing, and without standard luggage. The Norge 1200 TL was derived from the T, but included an electrically adjustable windshield. For heavier touring duties there was the Norge 1200 GT, the fairing incorporating leg shields at the front and splash guards at the rear. The windshield was manually adjustable, the handgrips heated, and dedicated panniers were standard. The top-of-the-line touring model was the Norge 1200 GTL, with an electrically operated windshield, rear top box, and a satellite navigation system as standard.

**BELOW** The California
Vintage was styled to replicate
the earlier V7 Special.
Moto Guzzi

## TOURING MODELS

# THE NEVADA 750 TOURING, BREVA 750 TOURING, CALIFORNIA TOURING AND CALIFORNIA VINTAGE

Alongside the Norge 1200 was an expanded range of touring models for 2006. Based on the fuel-injected Nevada 750 Classic, the Nevada 750 Touring included panniers and windshield. The Breva 750 Touring was similarly specified, while the engine of the California Touring was now almost entirely shared with the Breva 1100 range. This included Breva cylinder heads, cylinders, con-rods, pistons, sintered valve seats and guides and Nimonic exhaust valves. Longer con-rods were introduced, altering the stroke to con-rod length ratio, and reducing vibration.

The alternator was uprated from 300 to 350 watts and the crankshaft and flywheel were new. Ignition was by two spark plugs per cylinder and there was a return to mechanical tappets. Styling upgrades extended to new graphics and new guards for the 40mm throttle bodies, while the touring features included an integrated front fairing and a 45-litre top box colour coordinated with the panniers.

In response to the increased demand for retro models, Moto Guzzi released the California Vintage for 2006. Thirty-five years earlier the 757cc V7 Special had been successfully launched in the USA and the California Vintage was a tribute to this ground-breaking model for Moto Guzzi. Based on the California, with the updated V1100 style engine, the California Vintage was largely a styling exercise. This included wire-spoked wheels, redesigned steel mudguards, black Brembo brake calipers, and police-style supplementary fog lights. Stainless-steel strips highlighted the windshield, chrome steel tubes protected the cylinder heads and there were dedicated panniers.

**BELOW** When it finally made it into the production, the Griso was powered by the Breva's two-valve engine but the style remained unchanged from the prototype.
Moto Guzzi

## NAKED MODELS

# THE BREVA 750, 850, 1100, GRISO 850 AND 1100

The naked model line-up was significantly rationalised for 2006, and now comprised only two types, the Breva and Griso. Apart from new colours and graphics, and an optional lower seat, the Breva 750 was like the 1100 but as before, was now available with an ABS option. The most significant new model was the Griso 1100 which appeared after a tantalising wait. When it finally made the production line this was much as it had appeared at the end of 2004. The Breva 1100-based two-valve engine (with the 540-watt alternator mounted between the cylinders) now produced 88.1

horsepower at 7,600rpm. Although sharing many components with the Breva 1100 the Griso featured an upside-down 43mm fork and presented a more radical image. With the large oil tank on the right-side of the engine and distinctive exhaust system on the left, the Griso 1100 was unlike any other motorcycle.

Two 850s also joined the naked line-up, and both were downsized 1100s. Powering the Breva 850 was an 877cc version of the V1100, the smaller capacity achieved through a shorter, 66mm stroke. The power was reduced to 71 horsepower at 7,600rpm and new valve covers and a grey engine, swingarm and engine support plates set it apart from the larger version. In other respects the six-speed 850 was identical to the 1100 and likewise the Griso 850 was ostensibly identical to the 1100, but the oil tank was absent on the right-side of the engine, the frame was painted black, and the transmission housing was grey.

## CUSTOM MODELS

# THE NEVADA CLASSIC 750 AND CALIFORNIA CLASSIC

Like the naked line-up, the custom range was reduced for 2006. All the California-based customs (Stone, Titanium, and Aluminium) were discontinued, with only the California Classic remaining. Apart from a new catalytic converter the Nevada Classic 750 was unchanged, while the California Classic included all the Breva V1100 engines updates shared with the two other Californias. In all other respects the California Classic continued an extremely successful custom cruiser style that had formed the backbone of Moto Guzzi's sales for several decades.

# THE MGS-01 CORSA

The MGS-01 Corsa finally became available in limited numbers during 2006 and was launched in a blaze of glory at Daytona. As an exclusive model, the MGS-01 Corsa was built to order only, supplied with a personalised booklet recording the rider's details and particular frame number, bike cover and stand, and personalised delivery packaging. On 6 and 7 March Gianfranco Guareschi won two 'Battle of the Twins' races as part of the AHRMA/Modern Roadrace series. The MGS-01 also gained two second places in the 'Sound of Thunder' category, a more competitive class as it was also open to Superbikes. With three wins and two second places Guareschi also won the 2006 Italian Supertwins title on the MGS01 while Daniele Veghini on another MGS01 finished third in the championship.

# 2007

The success of Piaggio's rationalisation of the Moto Guzzi line-up was immediately evident as production increased by 46.4 per cent over 2005 to more than 10,000 motorcycles. This was the first time production at Mandello del Lario had surpassed 10,000 since 1983. After 2004, when fewer than 4,000 motorcycles were built, production gradually

increased to over 7,000 in 2005 and passing the magic 10,000 mark in December 2006 with a new 1200 Sport rolling off the production line.

Several other models were also announced for 2007. The 1200 Sport was followed by the Griso 8V and Bellagio, while later in the year came the 850 Norge. A future concept motorcycle was unveiled in February during a Piaggio Group dealer convention. This was a road-going enduro called the Stelvio (after the famous Stelvio Pass in Northern Italy), and would go into production during 2008.

# THE 1200 SPORT

After a one-year hiatus the large-displacement sporting Moto Guzzi made a return in October 2006 with the 1200 Sport. This was more multi-purpose than earlier sporting incarnations of Moto Guzzi's V-twin, and was available with an optional racing kit at one end of the spectrum, or touring equipment at the other.

Powering the 1200 Sport was the same 95 horsepower, 1,151cc twin-spark engine of the Norge 1200, but with newly designed rocker covers and a left-side racing-style exhaust system. Along with a high performance air filter the intake and exhaust passages were modified, and the ECU mapping was programmed for sports use. The injectors were positioned directly over the inlet manifolds near the valves and the power was transmitted by the same six-speed gearbox and CARC shaft-drive system as the Norge.

A racing kit was also available to boost the power beyond 100 horsepower. This included high compression cylinder heads with hand-polished manifolds, the removal of the air filter box, a special racing two-into-two exhaust system, and a remapped ECU. Other racing kit features included a special screen and rear seat 'pod', both with racing number graphics, a sporting seat, rear-set footpegs, and forward-positioned aluminium handlebars.

The chassis included a steel frame, 45mm fork with TiN-coated tubes to reduce friction, and twin 320mm wave discs on the front with four-piston calipers. ABS

was also an option, with conventional front discs. The rear, 298mm disc brake included a caliper with parallel floating pistons, while optional accessories extended to 29-litre panniers, 28- or 45-litre top box, tank bag, and a 30mm lower seat.

# THE GRISO 8V AND BELLAGIO 940 CUSTOM

At EICMA (Milan), soon after the release of the 1200 Sport, Moto Guzzi displayed their 2007 line-up. This included a prototype Griso 8V (eight-valve) and the 940 Custom which would become the Bellagio after its release in February. Displayed as a prototype, the Griso 8V mirrored the initial Griso as it was powered by a new, eight-valve engine. The new 1,151cc engine featured a single overhead camshaft operating four-valves per cylinder through noiseless timing chains, the power being 110 horsepower at 9,500rpm. Also setting

the Griso 8V apart was a distinctive twin pipe exhaust system, new seat, streamlined side panels and Brembo P4/34 radial caliper brakes acting on 320mm wave floating discs. The Showa upside-down fork tubes had 43 layers of carbon nitride treatment. While the Griso 8V would become available for 2008, the release of the Bellagio 940 Custom was more imminent.

With the Bellagio 940 Custom, Moto Guzzi has created a new niche market segment alongside the California. Although drawing from the American 'power cruiser' style, detail touches were European and the name Bellagio chosen to symbolise the relationship between Moto Guzzi and beauty of the Lariano area. Very much a stylistic exercise, the Bellagio was considerably more sporting in its orientation than the California. The wheelbase was shorter, and the weight redistributed to the rear to create a lighter look.

Powering the Bellagio was a new 940cc engine. Based on the existing new-generation 1,151cc engine the 95mm pistons were retained, but the 66mm stroke of the 877 Breva and Griso provided 935.6cc. With a

**LEFT** The sporting Moto Guzzi
made a welcome return for 2007
with the new 1200 Sport.
Moto Guzzi

**BELOW** Creating a niche market
for a sporting style cruiser was the
Bellagio 940 Custom of 2007.
Moto Guzzi

slightly higher (10:1) compression ratio the power was 75 horsepower at 7,200rpm, with maximum torque of 8kgm at 6,700rpm. As 80 per cent of the torque was produced between 2,800rpm and 4,800rpm the power characteristics were perfectly suited for this sports cruiser application. Other features shared with the 877cc version were electronic fuel injection, twin spark plugs per cylinder, the injectors positioned directly over the inlet manifolds, and the alternator between the cylinders. Lightened con-rods, pistons and rings reduced weight and sintered valve guides provided increased wear resistance. Unique to the Bellagio was a dual muffler exhaust on the left.

Power was transmitted to the rear wheel via a six-speed gearbox and the now-familiar CARC, with a single-sided aluminium swingarm. Retro styling details extended to spoked wheels, chrome tank decorations, drag-style handlebars, forward-mounted footpegs, and instrumentation. Because the spoked wheels provided limited space the front Brembo brake calipers were a narrower twin-piston floating type acting on 320mm discs. The conventional front fork was a 45mm Marzocchi and the front wheel was 18in. Despite weighing a considerable 224kg (494lb) the Bellagio was a brilliant attempt by Moto Guzzi to break into the classic retro market as Ducati and Triumph had done with considerable success over the previous few years.

## THE MGS-01

The MGS-01 continued to be available, unchanged from 2006 and was built on request. This year, Gianfranco Guareschi repeated his victory in the Daytona 'Battle of the Twins' race, providing Moto Guzzi with victory number 3,332 in front of 40,000 spectators. He narrowly beat Valter Bartolini's NCR Millona, the lead being swapped 15 times during the race. Guareschi again finished second in the 'Sound of Thunder' category which also included Superbikes.

For its American appearance, Guareschi's MGS-01 had a special livery combining the Italian flag and the US Stars and Stripes. The Team Moto Guzzi-Guareschi MGS-01 Corsa was prepared by Gianfranco's father Claudio in Parma and produced 136 horsepower at 8,700rpm. While most of the engine was identical to the series Corsa the exhaust collector was increased from 50mm to 52mm, providing an increase of 6 horsepower.

## NAKED MODELS
# THE BREVA 750, 850 (ABS), 1100 (ABS), GRISO 850 AND 1100

With the introduction of the previously described 1200 Sport the 'naked' range grew to three families: touring (Breva), fashion (Griso) and sport (1200 Sport). The Breva and Griso were ostensibly unchanged from 2006 although new colours were specified for the Breva, along with new electrical switches, a new seat covering, and a special lower seat for the Breva 750 to suit female riders. Optional carbon-fibre components were available for the Griso, the 1100 now available in sanitised orange and the 850 in yellow.

## THE 850 AND 1200 NORGE

The 120 Norge range (1200 T, TL, GT and GTL) was
unchanged for 2007 but new this year was the 850cc
Norge. This was powered by the same 877cc unit as
the 850 Griso and Breva, and the equipment (including
manually operated screen) was shared with the 1200 T.
ABS was standard.

**CUSTOM MODELS**

## THE NEVADA CLASSIC 750, CALIFORNIA CLASSIC AND CALIFORNIA VINTAGE

As with the naked line-up the custom range was also
divided in to families for 2007; Custom Classic

(Nevada and Bellagio) and Cruiser/Custom (California
Classic and Vintage). The California Vintage was
re-categorised as a Custom instead of Touring, but
there were few updates to this range. Added to the
range though, was the previously described Bellagio,
while the Nevada Classic 750 had new upholstery and
new colours, and the 1,100cc engine for the California
Classic and Vintage included the heat exchange
components from the Breva 1100.

Moto Guzzi's former World Champion Bill Lomas
died on 15 August 2007, at the age of 79 years, and
17,000 attended the GMG 07 (*Giornate Mondiale
Guzzi*) at Mandello in September. The guest of honour
was Hollywood actor Ewan McGregor who collected a
new Guzzi California and rode it back to London.

# 2008

A change of management was announced in October
2007, Tommaso Giocoladelli replacing outgoing
director Leonardo Caputo. Giocoladelli was
subsequently named chief executive officer and general
manager of Moto Guzzi SpA, while Daniele Bandiera
remained Moto Guzzi's chairman.

Although most models continued virtually
unchanged for 2008, there were four significant new
introductions. After a brief and tantalising display at
the end of 2006, the Griso 8V finally went into
production towards the end of September 2007 for the
2008 model year. The two-valve range was also
expanded, with the 1200 Breva joining the 850 and
1100 versions, and the V7 Classic was introduced. The
Stelvio enduro was also unveiled at EICMA 2007,
completing Piaggio's revival of Moto Guzzi. Most of
the existing line-up continued unchanged for 2008,
including the MGS-01 Corsa, which was still available
to special order.

## THE GRISO 8V

The most exciting release for 2008 was the return of
the eight-valve V-twin in Moto Guzzi's regular
production line-up. The Griso was originally conceived
with an eight-valve engine and like the original, was
inspired by *I promessi sposi* by Alessandro Manzoni.
Griso was the head of a group known as the 'Bravi', to

**BELOW** Although the style of the
Griso 8V was similar to the earlier
Griso, the exhaust system was unique.
Moto Guzzi

whom the most dangerous jobs were entrusted, and the
Griso 8V embodied this character.

Although based on the existing Griso 1100, the
Griso 8V was a considerably updated motorcycle. The
new engine was an evolution of the 1,151cc overhead
valve unit of the 1200 Norge and 1200 Sport, but was
75 per cent new. With 563 new components it included
a single overhead camshaft per cylinder head, operating
four hydraulic valves per cylinder and driven by
noiseless Morse timing chains. These chains included
hydraulic tensioners. The valves were set at a very
shallow angle, the intake at 15.5° and the exhaust at
16.5°, while the valve stems were a thin, 5mm, and the
valve springs a conical section to eliminate resonance
and power loss at high revs. Each cylinder head was

independently oil-cooled, the oil ducts separated
between the cylinder heads and exhaust valve seats.
The cylinders were more compact, with reshaped
cooling fins, and the rocker covers were redesigned to
include 'Quattrovalvole' logos.

More-compact crankcases now included an
integral front support for the bearings, while the rear
support featured a new flange and more efficient oil
feed system. A new type of con-rod bearing was
specified and the three-segment forged Asso pistons
provided an 11:1 compression ratio. The pistons were
also cooled by oil jets and lubrication and cooling
were by two gear-driven coaxial pumps. Also new
was the distinctive exhaust system, with two-into-one
coiled pipes.

While retaining the Marelli injection system, the
throttle bodies were increased to 50mm, and there
were new Marelli IWP 189 injectors. Power was
transmitted by the usual six-speed gearbox, with a
single-plate clutch. All this development made the
Quattrovalvole the most powerful ever production
Moto Guzzi engine, with 110 horsepower at 7,500rpm
and maximum torque of 11kgm at 6,400rpm. A final
drive ratio of 12/44 allowed a top speed of over
230km/h (143mph).

A number of updates delineated the 8V from the
Griso 1100. New streamlined bodywork, a new dual
seat, black anodised aluminium handlebars and
footpegs provided a more sporting riding position,
while the front fork was an adjustable upside-down
Showa, the fork tubes with 43 layers of carbon nitride
treatment. A first for a production Moto Guzzi was the
inclusion of Brembo P4/34 radial caliper front brakes,
these acting on 320mm wave floating discs. An
adjustable Boge suspension unit was fitted to the rear.

The Griso 8V frame was a tubular steel twin-cradle
type connected to a single-sided aluminium rear
swingarm with Moto Guzzi's CARC system. Still a
large motorcycle, the steering geometry was carefully
calculated to provide stability with agility, with a 26.5°
steering rake and 108mm of trail. The wheelbase
measured 1,544mm (60¾in) and the Griso 8V weighed
in at 222kg (489lb). Three colours were initially
offered: Jet Black, Moon White, or Corsa Red.

## THE STELVIO

Also sharing the Griso's 8V engine was the dual-purpose
Stelvio, Moto Guzzi's answer to the popular BMW
R1200GS. The 110 horsepower 'Quattrovalvole' engine
received a modified exhaust, intake and injection set-up,
and was housed in a tubular steel twin-cradle frame.
The steering head received additional strengthening, and
while the engine was still an important stress-bearing
component it was mounted at four points.

The front fork was a 50mm upside-down unit and at
the rear was the usual Guzzi single-sided swingarm with
CARC final drive. Like the Griso 8V, the front brake
calipers were radial Brembo. The windscreen and seat
were adjustable, saddle bags standard and a small,
lockable storage compartment (controlled from the
handlebars) was placed between the screen and tank.
The colours were red or white set off by the 19in and
17in spoked wheels with anodised alloy rims and
tubeless tyres. Anticipated availability was the end of
2007, and with a dry weight of 214kg (472lb) and a seat
height of 840mm (33in) the Stelvio was an enduro for
larger riders.

## THE V7 CLASSIC

Contrasting the 110 horsepower, and over 210kg (463lb)
8V machines was the V7 Classic. Celebrating the 40th
anniversary of the V7 and based on the Breva 750, the
V7 Classic was aimed as an entry-level motorcycle for
less-experienced riders who appreciated the retro classic
image. It was also envisaged as a competitor in the
classic retro market for the popular Triumph Bonneville
and Ducati GT1000. The 50 horsepower two-valve
750cc engine was shared with the Breva 750, as was the
tubular steel cradle frame, conventional front fork and
twin rear shock absorbers. Front braking was by a single
Brembo caliper and disc, and the wheels were the classic
wire-spoked type with chrome-plated rims and tube
tyres. The V7 Classic was a hybrid of various V7
influences. While the general style drew on the original
V7 the shape of the fuel tank was influenced by V7
Sport and the chrome and decorative components were
inspired by the V7 Special. Also symbolising an earlier
era were the cigar-shaped silencers, flat quilted seat and
the side covers with similar stowage compartments to
the original V7.

## NAKED MODELS

# THE GRISO, 1100, 850, BREVA 1200, 1100 (ABS), 850 AND 1200 SPORT

Alongside the new Griso 8V, the two-valve Griso 1100 and 850 continued unchanged for 2008, but new was the 1200 Breva. Ostensibly combining the 1100 Breva chassis with the 1200 Norge engine, there were more than 60 changes over the 1,064cc model. The 1,151cc

engine also included a nitride-treated crankshaft, Nimonic exhaust valves, lobe pump oil lubrication and a modified oil passage that included a duct taking cool oil to the heads for the exhaust valves. The exhaust system now featured double chamber manifolds and a muffler with an integrated catalyser, eliminating the V1100's manifold compensator.

A Marelli Multipoint sequential ECU took care of the fuel injection and included a stepper motor and twin spark plugs to ensure emissions were within Euro 3 standards. As on the other 1200s, the power was 95 horsepower at 7,500rpm with maximum torque of 100Nm at 5,800rpm (85 per cent of torque between

updates for 2008. The 1,151cc engine was fitted with the 'Quattrovalvole' single-plate clutch and there were new instrument panel graphics, recalibrated suspension and a new stand which provided increased road clearance.

## CUSTOM MODELS

# THE NEVADA CLASSIC 750, BELLAGIO AND CALIFORNIA VINTAGE

Although the Nevada Classic 750 continued as before, rationalisation of the Custom line-up saw the California Classic dropped. The Bellagio had a new colour scheme of contrasting colours blending with a chromed frame and engine covers, and the only traditional large capacity Moto Guzzi cruiser was now the California Vintage which was available in classic black or pearlescent white, as favoured by Ewan McGregor.

Over the decade between 1998 and 2008 a lot had happened at Mandello del Lario. In 1998 Moto Guzzi was struggling and its future was unclear. Hope lay with a new water-cooled V-twin but it was a tenuous expectation as there were insufficient resources to develop this engine and put it into production. A decade, and two management changes later, saw Moto Guzzi in a very different position. No longer content to sell a small number of motorcycles each year to an existing sympathetic clientele, Moto Guzzi's range was constantly expanded and broadened to appeal to a wider variety of customers.

From a four-model line-up in 1998, the 2008 range encompassed 14 models in four distinct families. Under Piaggio quality had improved and the updated line-up was functionally superior. Although Moto Guzzi will never be a large-volume mainstream motorcycle manufacturer it remains committed to the trademark 90° V-twin with shaft-drive, and continues to produce quality motorcycles that retain their individuality. The future looks very bright for the motorcycles from Mandello as these successfully manage to embrace traditional concepts with modern technology.

2,300rpm and 4,800rpm). Apart from the electrical controls which were now shared with the Norge, the Breva 1100 ABS and 850 continued as before. The 1200 Sport was only a recent introduction and was unchanged but for new handlebars that slightly altered the riding position.

## TOURING MODELS

# THE 850 AND 1200 NORGE

In the space of two years the Norge had become Moto Guzzi's best-selling model and there were only a few

Introduced in 2015, one of the
new wave Moto Guzzi cruisers
was the retro-styed Eldorado.

# 15 BIGGER CRUISERS

While Piaggio already owned 100% of Moto Guzzi S.p.A. shares, until 2008 Moto Guzzi still operated as a separate company. This changed in December 2008, when Moto Guzzi S.p.A merged with Piaggio & C. S.p.A. The purpose was to create a single type of motorcyle to sell globally that shared industrial, commercial, and financial resources, while maintaining Moto Guzzi's unique brand features. After several years without an arrangement, in 2008 Guzzi won contracts to supply 35 Moto Guzzi Norge GTs to the Berlin Police force, and 20 Moto Guzzi California Vintage bikes to the Corazzieri, the Honor guard of the President of the Italian Republic. Late in 2009, the Piaggio Group announced a significant investment program, involimg the expansion of future Moto Guzzi models and renovation of the Mandello del Lario production facility. This included extensive upgrades and modernisation of the plant to improve quality and efficiency.

## 2009

The economic downturn and motorcycle sales slump experienced during 2008 resulted in only five new models being released in 2009; all variations on existing themes. The Griso 8V Special Edition (SE) joined the Griso 8V, the 1200 Sport received the four-valve engine, the V7 Classic evolved into the V7 Café Classic, and the Stelvio 1200 TT joined the Stelvio 1200. Despite economic difficulties, Moto Guzzi's range still comprised 15models. The revamped Nevada 750 was also introduced, and the MGS-01 was still available to order. The existing V7 Classic, Griso 8V, Breva V1200/850, Stelvio 1200 4V, Norge 1200/850, Bellagio, and California Vintage continued unchanged.

## GRISO 8V SE

Introduced as a collectors' model, the Griso 8V SE was ostensibly a cosmetic variation on the standard 2008 Griso 8V. Setting the SE apart was the satin green Tenni colour scheme, a stitched leather saddle, BER spoked wheels, and decorative colour-coordinated logos on the tank and tailpiece. The 110 horsepower transverse V-twin was unchanged, as was the frame, suspension, and

TOP In 2009, the Griso evolved
into the beautiful 8V SE.

BOTTOM The Stelvio 1200 4V
TT was a variation of an existing
model. This adventure enduro
included engine protection
guards and aluminium panniers.

braking system. Beautifully executed and appealing to the classic purist, the Griso 8V SE was an important model in sustaining Moto Guzzi's naked styling and performance image.

# STELVIO 1200 4V TT

A variation on an existing theme, the Stelvio 1200 4V TT was Moto Guzzi's attempt at the Maxi Enduro, and was styled similarly to the BMW R1200GS Adventure. Based on the Stelvio 1200 4V, the TT added a sump shield, engine protectors, aluminium panniers, cylinder protection bars, C.A.R.C. transmission protectors, integral hand guards, additional headlights, and an optional set of knobbly tyres; 150/70 R17 rear tyre fitted to a 4.25 x 17-inch rim. In addition to the regular Stelvio colours of red, black, or pearl white, the Stelvio TT was available in a magnesium colour scheme. All Stelvio models were available with Brembo ABS.

# 1200 SPORT 4V

In 2009, the 1200 Sport 4V replaced the 1200 Sport. This new model included the four-valve engine. While the engine was basically the same unit fitted to the Griso and Stelvio, a different intake and exhaust system saw the outright power reduced to 105 horsepower at 7,500rpm. The exhaust included an aluminium muffler with an over-and-under finned exhaust system. The engine also acted as a load-bearing component of the tubular steel double cradle frame.

The chassis was largely unchanged from the two-valve version, but now included a conventional 45mm Marzocchi front fork, Brembo gold series radially-mounted four-piston front brake calipers, twin 320mm front discs, and a single 298mm rear disc. Set apart with new graphics and rear taillight assembly, the 1200 Sport 4V rolled on a slightly longer (1,485mm) wheelbase; its dry weight increased to 240kg. The 1200 Sport 4V was available in black or elegant titanium grey. Both versions included a subtle green, white, and red stripe. Unfortunately, the added weight detracted further from the 1200 Sport 4V's sporting ability, and it was only offered for one year.

## V7 CAFÉ CLASSIC

Inspired by the 1972 V7 Sport, the V7 Café Classic was initially an Italian market model. Sharing the V7 Classic's 48.8 horsepower engine and twin-shock chassis, the Café Classic included clip-on handlebars, wire-spoked wheels, higher mufflers, an integrated tailpiece, digital instruments that replicated the vintage white-faced Veglia Borletti, and a new green colour scheme.

## NEVADA 750

The venerable Nevada was given a new lease of life with 383 of the 441 components redesigned or replaced. Still powered by the small block twin-cylinder engine first produced in 1977, with an 80mm bore and a 74mm stroke, the 744cc unit now featured aluminium alloy cylinders and pistons with a special wear-resistant graphite coating. Fed by a Weber Marelli electronic fuel injection system and breathing though 36mm diameter throttle bodies, remapping and a new catalytic converter helped to reduce emissions. The side panels, shock absorber covers, seat, rear mudguard, taillight, and rider footrests were also new. The exhaust system derived from the V7 Classic, as did the digital instruments that now included an LCD display. The seat height was adjusted to 760mm, which improved low-speed ergonomics. The suspension included a conventional 40mm Marzocchi front fork, a single 320mm disc, and a Brembo four-piston caliper. Styled to resemble the California, the Nevada 750 was available in a new Burgundy colour scheme with a silver pinstriped tank. As an entry-level motorcycle, it continued as one of Moto Guzzi's best selling models.

LEFT The Nevada 750 was
completely updated, and was
styled similarly to the California.

BELOW The three models in
the Aquila Nera custom range:
Bellagio, Nevada, and California.

# 2010

At the 2009 EICMA show in Milan, three 1200cc futuristic concept models were displayed: V12 LM, V12 Strada, and V12 X. All were the product of former Ducati designers Miguel Galluzzi and Pierre Terblanche; both now working with the Piaggio Group. Although these models received the Motorcycle Design Association award (a design association with 165 members in four continents) for Best Motorcycle Design, they were destined to remain as concepts. As the Piaggio Group was still restructuring Moto Guzzi and updating the Mandello factory, there were no new models released, and a few of the less popular two-valve versions were

discontinued. This included three 850s (Griso, Breva and Norge), Griso 1100, Breva V1100 and 1200, 1200 Sport, and the California Classic. The rest of the existing range remained unchanged. This year saw Aquilia Nera (Black Eagle) versions of the California, Bellagio, and Nevada introduced. The V7 range also increased with the introduction of the prototype V7 Clubman Racer. As the motorcycle industry remained in a slump, Moto Guzzi's sales only totalled 4,500 units.

## CALIFORNIA, BELLAGIO, NEVADA AQUILA NERA

The custom California 1100, Nevada 750, and Bellagio 940 were now available as Aquila Nera variants. While technically unchanged, the Aquila Nera included a matte Coal Black tank, side panels, mudguards, and engine block. This contrasted with the aluminium cylinders and chrome wheels and exhaust. The Moto Guzzi Golden Eagle tank badge also returned.

The California Aquila Nera featured lightened engine guards, leg shields, windshield, and panniers. This contributed to a dry weight of 251kg, compared to the 263kg of the California Vintage. The California was the only remaining Moto Guzzi that used the linked braking system that had once typified the marque.

# STELVIO 1200 ABS, 1200 NTX

The 1200 4-valve Stelvio engine was revised to improve torque. It included new camshafts, updated injection mapping, and a larger capacity airbox. The power was unchanged, but the maximum torque was now 113Nm at 5,800rpm, compared with the previous versions 108Nm at 6,400rpm. The 1200 TT became the 1200 NTX.

# 2011

Alongside the 150th anniversary of Italian unification, Moto Guzzi commemorated its 90th anniversary. This included the release of the Norge 1200 GT 8V, and an updated Stelvio 1200 and Stelvio NTX. After the V7 Clubman Racer appeared as a prototype in 2010, it was released in 2011 as the V7 Racer. The V7 became one of Moto Guzzi's best selling models, contributing to more than 5,800 sales worldwide during 2011, a 30% increase over 2010. The 1400cc cruiser and V7 Scrambler prototypes were also unveiled. To celebrate the 20th anniversary of the 750 Nevada, Moto Guzzi

introduced the Nevada Anniversario. The existing Griso 8V SE, V7 Classic, and Nevada 750 Classic continued unchanged. The California Aquila Nera continued as before, but the Bellagio and Nevada Aquila Nera were discontinued.

# NORGE GT 8V

The Norge was significantly updated in 2011. The engine was the same four-valve unit that powered the Griso and Stelvio, but incorporated electronic improvements, new cam timing, and updates to the cooling and exhaust systems. An oil radiator was fitted to the lower fairing lug, along with a thermostat-controlled electric fan, and the satin-finished aluminium muffler was larger and quieter than the previous version. Maximum torque exceeded 104Nm at 5,500rpm, with peak power over 102 horsepower at 7,000rpm; an increase of 20% when compared to the two-valve version. The new engine included a more compact crankcase and the cylinder fins tapered towards the front.

The chassis included a double cradle steel frame with single-sided swingarm, while the conventional 45mm adjustable front fork and a single adjustable rear shock received new springs. The braking system consisted of electronic ABS, a pair of 320mm front discs, Brembo opposed four-piston calipers, and a rear 282mm disc. The one-piece fairing was all-new, the only component carried over being the headlight. Other new features included an electrically-operated windscreen, side panels integrated with the fuel tank, a widened seat, and a lower handlebar pulled back. Standard equipment was extended to include ABS, satellite navigation and an on-board computer. Practical features included a 12-volt external power socket, below-seat compartment, heated handgrips, integrated passenger handles, and newly designed panniers. Colours were initially Metallic Black and Diamond White. As the Norge GT 8V was such a complete package, it continued mostly unchanged for several years.

## STELVIO, STELVIO NTX

In 2011, the Stelvio and Stelvio NTX were updated. The four-valve engine, electronics, camshaft timing, and cooling system received updates similar to the Norge GT 8V. With a new integrated ignition and injection system, an ECU with two lambda probes, and 105 horsepower at 7,250rpm. No changes were made to the steel upper dual beam frame. It was still connected to the engine in six points, had a rake of 27°, a 125mm trail, and a 1,535mm wheelbase. The front suspension utilised a 50mm upside-down Marzocchi fork, and the rear a Sachs monoshock. The Brembo braking system, with Continental ABS, included front radial-mounted calipers, and new 320mm discs, incorporating lighter flanges and improved heat dissipation. New alloy wheels came as standard with the NTX, the rear 4.25 x 17-inch now with a 150/70 x 17-inch tyre. NTX BER rims with Alpina spokes were optional.

The styling was updated by integrating the fuel tank and indicators into the double headlight half fairing. As with the Norge GT 8V, the headlight was the only component shared with the previous model. The new fairing significantly improved rider protection, and the fuel tank capacity increased to 32 litres. As before, the NTX was the adventure version, which included an oil sump guard, engine guard, cylinder guard, and hand guards. Aluminium panniers and additional halogen lights were also added. The new Stelvio, particularly as the NTX, would continue for several years with minimal updates.

## V7 RACER

After first making an appearance as the prototype V7 Clubman Racer, the V7 Racer went into production during 2011. Another model paying homage to the classic V7 Sport, it acknowledged the 850 Le Mans, and earlier Gambalunga, with its small fairing and single seat.

Produced as a numbered edition, with a commemorative plaque on the top triple clamp. The V7 Racer included a chrome-plated fuel tank (created using innovative metal particle deposition technology) and was embellished with a leather strap. This was reference to the past, as were the metal accents in the Moto Guzzi badge. Inspired by the first 150 examples of the V7 Sport, the Telaio Rosso, the V7 Racer's red frame had a special gloss finish. A suede solo seat with aerodynamic tailpiece incorporated lateral race number panels that carried the number seven in honour of 1952 250cc world champion, Enrico Lorenzetti, who favoured this number. A minimalist front mudguard accentuated the sporting style.

The widespread use of bespoke components in brushed and drilled aluminium distinguished this special edition. These included the side panels, throttle body guards, and silencer mounting brackets. The rear-set footpegs were machined from solid billets, while the upper triple clamp guard, valve covers, and exhaust heat shields were chrome plated. The chrome

instrument cluster featured 1970s dials and graphics.

Technically, the V7 Racer was identical to the V7 Café. The double cradle ALS steel frame featured a detachable bolted lower section. The suspension included a 40mm Marzocchi front fork fitted with dust gaiters and a pair of fully adjustable Bitubo rear shock absorbers. Braking was operated by a single 320mm floating front disc with a four-piston Brembo 30/34 caliper, and a 260mm rear disc with a 32mm Brembo caliper. The wire wheels, 2.50 x 18 and 3.50 x 17, had silver spokes and nipples mounted on a matte black rim, and remained unchanged from the V7 Café.

While the V7 Racer was beautifully executed, it was still powered by the venerable two-valve, five-speed, 48.8 horsepower, Heron head engine that it shared with the other V7s. Even with the optional Arrow exhaust system, the V7 Racer was seriously underpowered, but this didn't stop sales exceeding 1,000 units during 2011.

# NEVADA ANNIVERSARIO (ANNIVERSARY EDITION)

Celebrating 20 years of the custom Nevada, the Anniversario was a more sporting rendition and sat alongside the recently updated (2009) Classic. While it shared the Classic's engine and chassis, the side covers were redesigned, chrome-plated taillight and grab handles were added, while a new dual seat sat over the wheel-hugging rear mudguard and wide rear tyre. Lower and narrower handlebars accentuated the sporting style, as did the two-tone black and white colour scheme.

**TOP** Celebrating twenty years of the Nevada, the Nevada Anniversario was a sportier version of the Nevada Classic.

# 2012

As a replacement California was in the pipeline, a final special edition California 1100 was produced. A new V7 engine now powered the Nevada and V7 range. While the 8-valve Norge and Stelvio had remained unchanged since 2009, the Griso 8V SE was cosmetically updated with new silver graphics and red wheel logos. Nicknamed the Black Devil, it was designed to be more aggressive in style. Annual motorcycle sales totalled 6,600 units and the Piaggio Group allocated 42 million euros for the investment of new models, on top of the investment already allocated for the refurbishment of the Mandello plant. This included reclassifying and cleaning up industrial land inside the site, and establishing the production line for the new California 1400. Engine development for all Piaggio Group models was now undertaken at the Polo Meccanica Site in Pontedera (near Pisa). During 2012, industrial action increased in Italy and strikes caused production delays at Mandello.

## CALIFORNIA 90

With more than 50,000 examples built since 1993, the California 1100 was Guzzi's most successful model in its long history, but this would be its final year.

As it had now been 40 years since the release of the 1971 California, and to continue Guzzi's precedent of releasing anniversary models, the final California 1100 was offered as a commemorative edition in celebration of Moto Guzzi's 90th anniversary. Built as a limited edition, the California 90 was based on the Vintage, but featured a special orange and white colour scheme. The tank logo replicated that of the early 1930s racing models, and the seat was hand-stitched cowhide. Each example carried a numbered identification plate.

The 1064cc V-twin engine remained unchanged. It still included aluminium cylinders, graphite-coated

**LEFT** In 2012, the Griso 1200 8V SE received new colours, but was otherwise unchanged.

pistons, and a Weber Marelli IAW electronic injection system with 40mm diameter throttle bodies. Maximum power was 73.4 horsepower at 6,400rpm. The steel double cradle frame, 45mm Marzocchi fork, 320mm disc front disc, and Brembo front braking system with four-piston calipers were unchanged; the integral braking system also remained. Standard features included supplementary fog lights, 18- and 17-inch wire-spoked wheels, a windshield with a stainless steel support, velvet lined hard saddlebags, and a chrome-plated luggage carrier.

# V7 STONE, V7 SPECIAL, V7 RACER, NEVADA, NEVADA ANNIVERSARIO

Since the introduction of the V7 Classic in 2008, followed by the Café Classic and Racer, the V7 range had cemented itself as one of the most important in Guzzi's line-up. While the V7 was designed to be compact and lightweight, compared to other 750cc twins, it was still underpowered. To address this, in 2012 the V7 was redesigned. It became more powerful, refined, comfortable, and had better fuel economy than the previous version. The range was revised to include three distinct models. Initially launched as the V7, the basic model was soon renamed the V7 Stone. Replacing the V7 Classic, the V7 Special appealed to the classic aficionado. The V7 Racer continued in the same style

as the previous model. The Nevada and Nevada Anniversario also received the updated engine. Both remained otherwise unchanged, but for new colours: Verde Giada and Aquila Nera. The Nevada had been a Mandello mainstay for twenty-two years, but this year would be its last.

First appearing in 1977, Lino Tonti's small block V-twin had been continuously updated over the years. Displacement increased to 750cc and electronic fuel injection replaced the carburettors. Rounded cylinder fins that were reminiscent of the first V7 replaced the square cylinder fins; a legacy of the 1970s and 1980s. The shape of the aluminium valve covers paid homage to those of the original V7. A single intake manifold with a single throttle body replaced the two intake manifolds with twin throttles. The first V-twin Moto Guzzi with a single throttle body, it had a single ribbed and straight rubber Y-shaped manifold, 36mm in diameter from the injector groups and 39mm in diameter to the throttle body. It was linked to a single 38mm diameter Magneti Marelli MIU3G throttle, which included two oxygen sensors. The redesigned cylinder head featured larger diameter intakes with a smaller and centrally located (10mm) sparkplug. New pistons saw the compression ratio increase to 10.2:1. The cylinder fins were also larger and spread further apart, while the new air filter box was moved under the seat, leaving the V shape of the engine more visible. The power increased by 12%, now 50 horsepower at 6,200rpm. Improved efficiency reduced fuel consumption and emissions by 10%. The transmission remained five-speed, but received a new pre-selector.

**BELOW** The 2012 V7 range consisted of three models: V7 Stone, V7 Special, and V7 Racer.

**RIGHT** Apart from the black valve covers, the 2013 limited edition V7 Racer was indistinguishable from the 2012 version.

The double cradle frame, with bolted and removable lower elements, was unchanged, while the 40mm fork was recalibrated. As before, the V7 Racer fork received rubber gaiters. The rear shock absorbers were also recalibrated, the V7 Racer retaining a pair of Bitubo WMT remote reservoir gas shock absorbers. The braking system remained unchanged, consisting of a 320mm floating front disc and a 260mm rear disc. The entire range was now equipped with one of two different types of new wheels: the V7 Stone had cast alloy wheels with six split spokes, the Special had wire-spoked wheels with new polished aluminium rims, and V7 Racer had anodised black wheels with red hubs to match the frame. The V7 Stone's alloy wheels provide a weight reduction of 1440g at the front and 860g at the rear, with a consequential drop in

gyroscopic inertia of about 30 per cent. The earlier V7 Sport influenced the shape of the 22-litre fuel tank, now in steel rather than polyethylene. The dry weight of the new V7 was 179kg, down slightly on the previous version.

The three V7s each fulfilled a particular market segment. As an entry-level model, the V7 Stone was finished in plain colours, while the two-tone V7 Special replaced the earlier V7 Classic. The sporting V7 Racer retained the chrome-plated fuel tank, numbered plaque, and the racing number panel that was now white on black. A wide range of accessories were available for the V7 series, including a specific V7 Record Kit. Evoking the 1969 world record V7s, this kit comprised a fibreglass rounded top fairing and single seat. Production of the new V7 commenced at Mandello in March 2012.

# 2013

With European motorcycle sales still in decline and down 4 per cent from the previous year, the Piaggio Group struggled. Despite this scenario, for the third consecutive year Moto Guzzi bucked this downward trend and increased motorcycle sales by 2.4 per cent, selling 6,800 units. In 2013, after seven generations, four engine capacities, and more than 100,000 units manufactured, Moto Guzzi's iconic California evolved into the new

**LEFT** The updated 2012 V7 engine featured a Y-shaped intake manifold and rounder cylinder finning.

1400 model; undoubtedly the most significant new Moto Guzzi since the Aprilia/Piaggio takeover. The 1400 was the largest twin-cylinder motorcycle engine to emanate from Europe, and was a product of Argentinian designer Miguel Galluzzi, head of the new Piaggio Group Advanced Design Center (PADC) Pasadena, California. The Griso, Stelvio, and Norge continued unchanged, while the V7 Stone, V7 Special, and V7 Racer received minor cosmetic updates. The engine valve covers on all three models were all black, and the V7 Stone and Special were available in a wider range of colours.

While the reclassification of industrial land within the Mandello del Lario plant continued, the 1400 California production line was completed. V7 and 1400 engines were now assembled at the Piaggio facility in Pontedera, and a new photographic system was installed on the vehicle packaging line to ensure the quality of dispatched vehicles.

# CALIFORNIA 1400 TOURING/CUSTOM

After seven generations, four engine capacities, and over 100,000 units produced, the new flagship California 1400 was finally introduced. Initially in two guises, Touring and Custom, it pioneered several innovations. It was the largest ever European twin-cylinder, the first custom motorcycle equipped with electronic traction control and multimap ride-by-wire technology, and the first custom motorcycle to be equipped with LED daytime running lights.

Eclipsing the 1225cc MGS01 as Moto Guzzi's largest ever twin, the new California engine was an evolution of the existing 1151cc Quattrovalvole (Four Valve). It also shared the same stroke, a 104mm bore that gave 1380cc. The cylinder heads retained four valves per cylinder, and were driven by an overhead camshaft in each bank through a roller rockers system, which reduced friction losses. The ignition was provided by a twin sparkplug per cylinder. The cylinders received larger fins, and cooling was enhanced with an oil radiator that was equipped with a thermostat-controlled electric fan. The fuel economy improved by 15-20 per cent over the smaller four-valve.

As with the new V7, the size of the single Magneti Marelli throttle body increased to 52mm, while a single Y-shaped manifold with long intakes and IWP 243 Marelli injectors fed the engine. For the first time, Moto Guzzi included a Magneti Marelli IAW7SM ride-by-wire electronic engine management system, which allowed the choice of three engine management mappings: Turismo (touring), Veloce(fast), and Bagnato

**BELOW** The 1400 California Touring provided a mixture of modern technology with traditional styling features. The black with white stripes were reminiscent of the earlier V7 and V850.

(wet). Three levels of electronic traction control, Moto Guzzi Controllo Trazione (MGCT), were also offered. With a 10.5:1 compression ratio, the 90-degree V-twin produced 96 horsepower at 6,500rpm. The transmission was now six-speed instead of five. A new dry single-disc clutch with a built-in flexible coupling replaced the twin-disc type. The shaft final drive was also redesigned.

Continuing a tradition of engineering innovation, the 1400 California introduced a new elastic engine mounting system. The powertrain was mounted in the frame with an elastic-kinematic supports system. It consisted of a front rocker, two side rockers, and a series of rubber dampeners that allowed the engine to shake around its own centre of gravity. This filtered the vibrations transmitted to the rider and passenger. The closed double cradle steel frame was also strengthened with a larger steering head and larger diameter swingarm. As normally found on a cruiser, the steering head was raked out to 32° with 155mm of trail. The

wheelbase was lengthened considerably over the California 1100 to 1,685mm.

Retro features included a new 46mm front fork and black covered stanchions that replicated the first V7 and V850. A traditional solution was also chosen for the rear suspension with a pair of shock absorbers. More than 30 years after the T4, lightweight alloy wheels reappeared on the California 1400, now with an original ribbed design. The choice of wheel sizes went against the trend, with an 18-inch front and a 16 x 6-inch rear. Tyre sizes were 130/70 x 18 and a massive 200/60 x 16. After thirty years, Moto Guzzi's legendary integral braking system made way for a modern dual channel ABS system, this included four-piston Brembo radial calipers with a pair of 320mm floating discs at the front, and a twin-piston Brembo caliper with a 282mm disc at the rear.

Styling cues continued in the tradition of earlier models, with the seat profile, chrome grab handle, and side panels inspired by the T3. The size ratio between

**BELOW** In 2013, alongside the 1400 California Touring was the sportier 1400 California Custom.

the 21-litre fuel tank and engine followed the style of the V7 and V850. The poly elliptical headlight was equipped with DRL daylight running lights, while the 150mm circular instrument panel was inspired by the earlier V7. Cruise control was available for the first time on a Moto Guzzi, as was iGuzzi. This allowed a smartphone connection to the multimedia platform, providing vehicle and travel information.

The Touring version came equipped with a windscreen, supplementary chrome-plated headlights, 35-litre panniers, and an engine and pannier guard kit. Colours were California Highway Patrol inspired white, or classic V7 black. The Custom was a more sporty, aggressive, and muscular interpretation. Unadorned with shiny accessories, it was equipped with a drag handlebar and a pair of remote reservoir shock absorbers. Apart from the grey or black colours, styling differences extended to black wheels with a red Moto Guzzi logo and black rear view mirrors.

Balancing tradition and the future, the new 1400 was intended to evoke the traditional California, in a more modern and sumptuous way. With the lines of the tank and seat converging to form an imaginary cross, typical of previous models, the centre of the bike strongly recalled this tradition. The wide rear tyre and modern front headlight assembly provided modern style and innovation. An important design feature was to keep the 90-degree V-twin engine as visible as possible, thus maintaining Moto Guzzi's uniqueness.

While the new California 1400 was significantly larger and heavier than its predecessor, it also represented a technological leap forward and winning several awards: *Cycle World's* 10 Best Bikes of the Year, Cruiser category; *Motorcyclist's* Motorcycle of the Year, Cruiser category. Already enjoying a long association with Moto Guzzi and owning ten examples, including a 1972 V7 Sport and 2001 V11 Tenni, Ewan McGregor continued his involvement with the California 1400 advertising campaign 'My Bike, My Pride.'

BELOW LEFT Although technically unchanged, in 2014 the Norge GT 8V was available in this new colour scheme.

BELOW RIGHT The V7 Special was the classic model in the V7 line-up. New in 2014, the colours replicating the earlier 750S3. All V7s this year had a new alternator and restyled front engine cover.

# 2014

The continued renovation and reorganisation of the Moto Guzzi plant at Mandello del Lario resulted in a pause in the introduction of new models. Known as the Arrocco project, Politecnica Srl oversaw the design. This included new buildings as well as renovations to the existing plant. Completed in July 2014, the project included a new museum, services, and canteen block. Updates this year focused on the V7, while the Norge GT 8V received a new colour scheme.

The V7 Stone, V7 Special, and V7 Racer were still offered as a three-model line-up. The minimalist V7 Stone was now all black, the V7 Special featured the Essetre (S3) graphics of the earlier 750S3, while the V7 Racer was much as before. All V7s received a new wet flywheel, this replacing the previous dry alternator. The front of the engine was modified with a more compact and sleeker alternator cover. With the exception of the engine and exhaust, which retained the standard aluminium and chrome finish, the V7 Stone was now mostly finished in black. This included the rear view mirrors, shock absorbers, mudguards, and side panels. The tank colours were: red, Rosso Corposo; green, Verde Agata; black, Nero Ruvido.

The V7 Special continued as the more classic model, now in two colour versions: silver with black stripes, or as its ancestor, black with orange stripes. On both versions, the tank logo had historic embossed type, while the wheel rims were black instead of chrome. Unlike the Stone and Racer, the V7 Special had a fork stanchion guard instead of dust gaiters. The third edition of the V7 Racer also featured black components. These included side panels, mirrors, silencer support brackets and footrest guards. The number 7 on the front and rear plates was now chrome plated. The rear suspension was by a pair of WMY01 Bitubo shock absorbers with 12-click damping adjustment.

# 2015

With the renovations and additions at Mandello completed, more new models and model updates appeared. This year, the V7 became the six-speed V7 II, while the California range grew to include the Eldorado, Audace, and 1400 Touring SE. The Stelvio, Griso, and Norge continued unchanged. While in some markets superseded models such as the 1200 Sport 8V (ABS) were still available, existing stock was also converted into a Corsa Special Edition. The introduction of a range of custom accessory kits for the V7 II was a significant development. 7,880 motorcycles left the Mandello factory during 2015, a 24% increase over 2014. Compared with 2014, sales of the V7 range increased by 44% and the California 1400 by 36%. Revenue from the sale of Moto Guzzi motorcycles was up 27.4%.

TOP In 2015, the six-speed V7 II replaced the V7. The V7 II Stone was available in this new colour scheme.

MIDDLE The V7 II Special was also available in new colours. The engine was repositioned to improve ergonomics and aesthetics.

BOTTOM Some of the accessory kits available for the V7 II. From the left: the Scrambler, Dark Rider, Legend, Dapper and accessorised Stone.

# V7 II STONE, V7 II SPECIAL, V7 II RACER, V7 II RACER LIMITED EDITION, LEGEND KIT, DARK RIDER KIT, SCRAMBLER KIT, DAPPER KIT

In 2015, the continual evolution of the V7 series resulted in an updated V7 II. While still offered in three versions (Stone, Special and Racer), the gearbox was now six-speed. The lower first, fifth, and sixth ratios decreased the drop in rpm between one gear and the next. The primary drive ratio was lowered from 16:21 to 18:23. The clutch action improved with modifications to the lever, linkage, and cable. Engine specifications were otherwise unchanged.

The chassis and dynamics were improved, and the engine lowered by 10mm and rotated 4° forward in the frame. This lowered the centre of gravity, allowing the footpegs to be 25mm lower, which provided more legroom for the rider. A by-product of this was improved side-on aesthetics with a less nose-up look, and a lower 790mm seat height. The rear axle and shock absorber mounts were also relocated, lowering the shaft final drive by 50mm. ABS and MGCT systems were introduced on the V7 II. A simpler system than on the California 1400, the ABS was two-channel. The MGCT was a sophisticated electronic setup that prevented the rear wheel from sliding during acceleration. In response to the growing demand for individualisation, a wide range of accessories were produced for the V7 II. These ranged from fairings and seats, to an exhaust and centre stand.

The V7 II Stone featured new colours: black, red, grey and yellow, and a satin finish. Black extended to the restyled taillight, clutch, and brake levers. The V7 Special continued with the previous Essetre (S3) black and orange graphics, and were available in two new colour schemes, metallic red or light blue; both with a silver stripe. As with the Stone, the Special included redesigned black brake and clutch levers, and a new rear light cluster.

The V7 II Racer continued with the chrome-plated tank and similar graphics, but alongside it this year was a V7 II Racer Limited Edition. Exclusive to the

**BELOW** With its 16-inch wire
wheels and retro styling, the
Eldorado celebrated the earlier
850 version.

North American market, only 50 examples were
produced in classic Verde Legnano colours, paying
homage to the legendary 1971 Telaio Rosso V7 Sport.
Quality components included footpegs machined from
solid billets, a lightened steering stem, and chromed
triple clamp guard ring. As on the standard V7 II
Racer, the rear shock absorbers were adjustable
WMY01 Bitubo.

A significant option for the V7 II range was a series
of factory custom bolt-on kits. These came in four
variations: Legend, Dark Rider, Dapper, and
Scrambler. The Legend kit found inspiration from
Moto Guzzi's history, the military Alce era of the
1940s. It had a dark satin finish, high two-in-one
silencer, knobbly tyres, olive green fuel tank, side
fairings and fender, high handlebar, and leather bags.
The Dark Rider kit was designed to create a gothic
look. The inspiration coming from Omobono Tenni,
whose nickname was the Black Devil. The dedicated
accessories included black aluminium upper and side

fairings, aluminium fenders, and a black fuel tank with
the traditional red Moto Guzzi eagle. The Scrambler kit
included 18 accessories to give the V7 II an off-road
look; a satin finish replacing the chrome. The Dapper kit
transformed the bike into a seventies-style Café Racer:
polished aluminium fenders, injector covers, number
plates, low handlebar, and solo seat. The earlier Record
kit celebrating the 1969 world records was still available.

# ELDORADO, AUDACE AND 1400 TOURING SE

Another product of Miguel Galluzzi (PADC), the
Eldorado celebrated Moto Guzzi's American heritage
with styling cues from the 1972 850 Eldorado. Although
based on the California 1400 platform, setting the
Eldorado apart were wire-spoked wheels, a larger seat, a
wraparound rear fender, gem-shaped taillight, and cow

horn handlebar. The twin exhausts were styled to match the taillight, while the earlier Eldorado inspired the two-tone colours (Nero Classico and Rosso Pregiato), and incorporated white pinstripes and chrome tank panels. Classic whitewall tyres were mounted on polished aluminium 16-inch wheels, a 3.5-inch on the front and 5.5-inch on the rear. Retro features extended to full-cover shock absorbers and rounded turn signals, while a low seat height and footboards emphasised cruising comfort. Modern electronics allowed the wireless connection of an innovative multimedia platform via a smartphone. As with other models in the Moto Guzzi line-up, a wide range of dedicated accessories were also available.

Complementing the retro Eldorado was the more brutal all black Audace. A modern and urban take on the California 1400 Custom, the Audace was more muscular and aggressive. A low drag handlebar, footpegs moved forward, and an abbreviated seat helped to create a stretched riding position. The narrower 45mm front fork with exposed stanchions, carbon-fibre front fender and round headlight also provided a cleaner looking front-end. Other unique styling cues included a front engine spoiler, aluminium radiator grille, and short megaphone exhausts. A pair of remote reservoir shock absorbers handled the rear end, and the cast aluminium wheels gained personalised Moto Guzzi logos. The engine and electronic specification were shared with the California 1400 Custom.

The California 1400 Touring was also available as an SE this year. This featured new two-tone colours, built-in passenger backrest with grab handle, with a seat and side panels reminiscent of the earlier T3. The 46mm telescopic fork included chrome-plated tubes, but the general specification was shared with the California 1400 Touring.

## 2016

Moto Guzzi celebrated its 95th anniversary this year and announced several new models. After releasing the concept MGX-21 Flying Fortress in 2015, the eventual production version was presented in the heartland of the American cruiser at Sturgis, South Dakota, in August 2016. Other new models included the V9 Bobber and Roamer, and the V7 II Stornello. A soft off-roader, the Stornello was another retro-themed model, initially available as a limited edition. Completing the 16-model range was the V7 II Stone, Special and Racer, eight-valve Griso SE, Norge, Stelvio, and California 1400. This year 20 special California Touring 1400 were provided to the Corazzieri. Moto Guzzi sales increased by more than 13 per cent. This was mainly due to the success of the V9 Roamer and Bobber, the introduction of the MGX-21, and Moto Guzzi entering the Thai market for the first time.

BELOW A radical addition to the
2016 Moto Guzzi line-up was the
MGX-21 Flying Fortress Bagger.

# MGX-21 FLYING FORTRESS

Another product of Galluzzi and the PADC, the MGX-21 Flying Fortress provided Moto Guzzi an entry into the world of the factory Bagger; it would become the flagship of the California-based line-up. Characterised by a large 21-inch front wheel, this unique design also featured built-in rigid 58-litre side panniers, numerous carbon-fibre components, luxurious instrumentation, and an entertainment system. This was capped off by the usual electronic assists: ABS, traction control, and ride-by-wire throttle and cruise control. MGX signified Moto Guzzi eXperimental, 21 referring either to the year of Moto Guzzi's first motorcycle or the size of the front wheel.

Designed for the American market as an Italian take on the long distance cruiser, the MGX-21 Bagger emphasised design and build quality, as well as attention to detail. This included black billet aluminium machined levers, mirrors, and master cylinder covers. The futuristic looking large Batwing-styled fairing was inspired by Bertone's Alfa Romeo BAT concept car designs of the 1950s. CFD (Computational Fluid Dynamics) simulations combined with wind tunnel testing resulted in the design achieving optimum air protection.

The front wheel included carbon-fibre covers with small openings where the spokes intersect with the channel. This design improved airflow across the hub, while increasing stability and ease of handling. Other carbon-fibre parts included the front fender, tank panels, and engine covers; these contrasting with the bright red four-piston brake calipers and valve covers. The California 1400 frame was modified to accommodate the 3.50x21-inch front wheel, while retaining the elastic-kinematic engine supports. The suspension consisted of a 45mm front fork and the rear wheel was a narrower 16x5.5-inch. This allowed a smaller 180/60R16 tyre to complement the extreme 120/70R21 front tyre. The wheelbase was stretched out to 1,700mm and the kerb weight an intimidating 341kg. As a factory Bagger custom, the MGX-21 Flying Fortress was a brave, daring, and strikingly unconventional design.

**TOP** With its 19-inch front wheel, the V9 Roamer was more conservative in style.

**BOTTOM** The V9 Bobber rolled on a pair of 16-inch wheels with a wide front tyre.

# V9 ROAMER, V9 BOBBER

Marking ninety-five years as Italy's oldest motorcycle manufacturer, Moto Guzzi introduced a pair of new models under the V9 designation. Sitting in the middle of the range, an intermediate step between the four-strong entry-level V7 II and 1200cc Stelvio and Griso, this new duo of cruiser-inspired twins targeted different customers. Developed by the Centro Stile Piaggio Group, with input from PADC, the V9 Roamer served as an everyday roadster/rider, while the V9 Bobber was a custom lifestyle model, both offered with a complete array of aftermarket accessories.

Powering the two new V9 variants was a new small block 90-degree V-twin engine. With air/oil cooling, a pair of pushrod-operated overhead valves, with new cylinders, heads, and strengthened crankcases. The bore and stroke was 84x77mm and provided 853cc. The engine included a lighter single pin crankshaft, updated wet sump, a lubrication system that included cooling oil jets underneath the piston crowns, and a low-flow oil pump with revised crankcase ventilation system. Whereas all previous small block engines retained the Heron cylinder head design intoduced in 1977, the V9 moved to a conventional hemispherical combustion chamber with a pair of opposed valves and a central sparkplug. The compression ratio was 10.5:1, a single camshaft was located at the cylinder base, with rocker arms operating the inclined valves via threaded adjusters. The alternator cover was also new and included a blow-by gas output. With a new MIU single-body Marelli electronic injection system and an auxiliary air system, the V9 complied with Euro 4 emission standards. Despite the improved cylinder head design, the maximum power was a very moderate 55 horsepower at 6,250rpm.

The new single plate clutch was a larger diameter (170mm) and was matched to a wider ratio six-speed transmission. The shaft drive now had a second universal joint to allow for a wider rear wheel and 150mm tyre. The V9 chassis included a new steel twin tube cradle frame, with additional steering head gussets, a cast aluminium double-sided swingarm, traditional 40mm telescopic fork, and a pair of new spring preload-only adjustable shock absorbers. The braking system consisted of a Brembo opposed four-piston caliper with a single 320mm front disc, and a twin-piston floating caliper with 260mm disc on the rear.

While the V9 Roamer and Bobber shared the same basic engine, chassis, and electronic aids, such as switchable traction control; the front wheel and tyre sizes differed. To emphasise the classic cruiser style, the Roamer was fitted with a 2.50x19-inch front wheel, low seat, and raised chrome handlebar. Both versions had matte black painted diamond-cut wheels, and had a 4.00x16-inch rear wheel with a 150/80x16-inch tyre. The 1,465mm wheelbase had a relatively steep steering head angle of 26.4° and a 125.1mm of trail (116.1mm for the Bobber), ensuring the steering was light. The kerb weight was 199kg.

**TOP LEFT** Unlike the V7 II, the V9 engine featured a hemispherical combustion chamber.

**BOTTOM** Initially offered as a limited edition, the V7 II Stornello was styled to replicate the 1971 125 Scrambler.

**TOP RIGHT** To allow for a wider rear tyre, the V9 driveshaft included two universal joints.

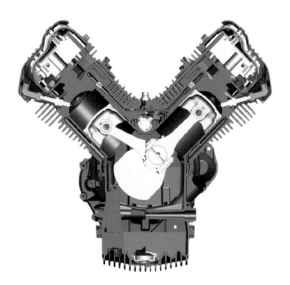

The V9 Bobber was a styling effort designed to recall the early cut-down bob-job customs that returning GIs created out of surplus post-Second World War military motorcycles. To run on fast dirt tracks, these bobbers were invariably fitted with oversized tyres, providing a wide footprint. Following this style, the V9 Bobber eschewed chrome and a gloss finish, and a 130/90x16-inch tyre was mounted on the wide 3.50x16-inch front wheel. A low drag bar and lowered seat provided a crouched and sporting riding position. Both the Roamer and Bobber accentuated a non-plastic custom style with metal mudguards, with aluminium side panels, fuel cap, levers, switch blocks, and forged footrests.

As with other recent Moto Guzzis, the V9 offered a set of advanced electronic systems, including two-channel ABS and two-level MGCT (Moto Guzzi Traction Control). The electronic instrumentation consisted of a single analogue speedometer. Accessories included the MG-MP (Moto Guzzi multimedia platform) that connected a smartphone and provided information including: a rev counter, instantaneous power, instantaneous torque, instantaneous and average fuel consumption, and average speed. While a wide range of accessories were available for both versions, a specific range for the V9 Bobber included a new seat, fairing, polished aluminium fenders, and a sportier exhaust system.

## V7 II STORNELLO

With a history of building successful off-road models, it wasn't surprising to see Moto Guzzi enter the world of the retro-styled Scramblers. Moto Guzzi's off-road history began with the Lodola Regolarità in 1960, continued in 1965 with the Stornello Fuori Strada and Regolarità, and also the Stornello Scrambler USA in 1966. These were serious off-road machines, but when an updated Stornello Scrambler became available in 1968, it morphed into a soft off-road model. This became the 125 Scrambler in 1971, and the inspiration for the V7 II Stornello. Both motorcycles have a high exhaust system, knobbly tyres, white fuel tank, and red frame.

BOTTOM One of the factory customs available in 2016 was this Project Guzzi Alce.

BELOW The V7II Racer received new graphics and a matte finish in 2016.

A product of Marco Lambri and the Piaggio Group Style Centre, the V7 II Stornello was initially offered as a factory custom Scrambler in a limited edition of 1,000 units; each unit had an individually numbered plaque. The basic architecture was a V7 II with a six-speed Heron head 750cc V-twin, but with a unique two-in-one Arrow high-rise exhaust system on the right. The frame, brakes, and suspension were basically the same as the V7 II, but with a pair of Spanish Ollé shock absorbers to complement the Guzzi-made 40mm front fork. The extended seat included special foam and electro-welded upholstery. Many components were made from aluminium, this included the side panels, injector covers, footpeg extensions, and number plates. The mudguards were also hand-beaten brushed aluminium. While the V7 II Stornello already had many optional extras, an extended range of accessories were available for further customisation.

BOTTOM One of the factory customs available in 2016 was this Project Guzzi Alce.

# V7 II STONE, SPECIAL, RACER, SCRAMBLER, PROJECT CLUBBER, PROJECT ALCE, PROJECT LADY GUZZI, DARK RIDER STYLE, SCRAMBLER STYLE, LEGEND STYLE, DAPPER STYLE

The V7 II Stone and Special were unchanged this year, but the Racer received new graphics with a matte finish; replacing the previously glossy finish. The fuel tank was no longer chrome plated, but finished in satin black and grey. The number plate holders were also grey, without the number 7, and the solo seat with a rear seat unit made a return. The Plexiglas top fairing was reminiscent of the earlier racing Gambalunga. Other new features included a redesigned clutch, brake levers, and a black taillight assembly. In the US the V7 II Special was no longer offered, with the V7 II Scrambler available instead.

The range of accessories for the V7 II was increased, with the addition of three more factory projects under the nomenclature Moto Guzzi Garage. Project Guzzi Clubber presented a full on café racer style. It had a satin aluminium fairing, smoked

TOP In September 2017, Gianfranco and Vittoriano Guareschi rode a Le Mans to victory in the Italian and European Vintage Endurance Championship at Imola.

Plexiglas screen, sporting handlebars and rear-set footpegs. Project Guzzi Alce continued the off-road heritage style of the Legend Alce. While Project Lady Guzzi, with elegant colours and a lower seat, was designed for the female rider. The earlier four heritage styles (Dark Rider, Scrambler, Legend and Dapper) continued as before.

# 2017

Towards the end of 2016, two new models were introduced at Intermot in Cologne: the Audace Carbon and luxurious California Touring. The release of the V7 III and updated V9 followed shortly afterwards. Racing success also returned to Moto Guzzi in September, with Gianfranco and Vittoriano Guareschi dominating the 4-Hour Italian and European Vintage Endurance Championship race at Imola, riding a Le Mans V-based racer. Leading home a field of Japanese Superbikes, the Guareschi brothers proved there was still life in the venerable two-valve Le Mans as a competitive racer.

# AUDACE CARBON AND CALIFORNIA TOURING

Designated Moto Guzzi's Muscle Bike, the Audace Carbon featured improved ergonomics and a more comfortable riding position. Matte red valve covers and Brembo front brake calipers contrasted with the general black finish, the footboards were removed to provide for more rearward foot controls, the drag handlebar lowered and extended, and the leather seat lowered. New handlebar switches allowed for the inclusion of cruise control, and the electronic throttle was an updated ride-by-wire system. The Audace Carbon was also offered with a wide range of dedicated accessories.

The California Touring was offered with increased luxury and refinement, now with cruise control and the new ride-by-wire throttle. Along with new two-tone colours, Nero Gentleman and Rosso Charme, the specification remained similar to previous SE version, with a built-in passenger backrest and grab handle, and style inspired by the earlier T3 and V7.

TOP LEFT Along with red
brake calipers and valve
covers, improved ergonomics
distinguished the Audace Carbon.

TOP LEFT Along with red
brake calipers and valve
covers, improved ergonomics
distinguished the Audace Carbon.

TOP RIGHT A more luxurious
California Touring was available
in 2017.

# V7 III AND V9

To celebrate the V7's 15th anniversary, Moto Guzzi
introduced the V7 III. Replacing the V7 II, an
Anniversario joined the existing three-model range.
This third generation 750 was slightly more powerful.
With new cylinder heads and inclined valves, as on the
V9, it finally replacing the outdated Heron design.
Along with the new cylinder head were new pistons,
piston-cooling oil jets, cylinders, and a stiffer
crankcase. With single throttle body Marelli injection
system, and a 9.6:1 compression ratio, the power was a
very moderate 52 horsepower at 6,200rpm, while
maximum torque was 60Nm at 4,900 rpm, with a flat
torque curve. Other V7 III updates included a new oil
sump, crankcase ventilation system, and alternator
cover. The drivetrain included a 6-speed transmission,
with new first and sixth gear ratios, and 170mm dry
single plate clutch. Standard equipment included a
two-level switchable traction control and dual-channel
ABS.

As on the V7 II, the V7 III featured an ALS steel
double cradle frame, but the front section was
redesigned and reinforced with new steering geometry
(steeper rake of 26.4° and less trail at 106mm) and a
slightly longer wheelbase (1,463mm). The steel frame
retained the double cradle layout with removable tubes
and the same weight distribution: 46% at the front,
54% at the rear. Along with new dual preload-
adjustable Kayaba shock absorbers, the seat height was
lowered to 770mm. New lower and further forward
aluminium footpegs were also added. Rear wheel
travel was reduced (on the Stone, Special, and
Anniversario) from 111mm to 93mm. were A new

locking screw-on gas cap, new injector covers, sleeker
side panels, new seat, and updated instrumentation were
also included.

Continuing the previous style, the base-model V7 III
Stone included matte black bodywork and blacked-out
components, cast wheels, a single instrument gauge,
dedicated seat graphics, a passenger grab strap, fork
gaiters, and a shorter front fender. As on the earlier
Special, the V7 III Special had chrome exhausts, mirrors,
and passenger grab rail. It also had blue bodywork with
special stripes on the side panels and tank, dual
instruments, vintage seat stitching, fork protectors, and
spoked wheels with polished rims and black hubs. The
numbered edition V7 III Racer was also much the same
as before, with a red frame, satin-finish chrome fuel
tank, lower handlebars, a hump seat with removable
passenger seat cowl, removable passenger footpegs (for
the first time), a brushed aluminium front number plate/
flyscreen, billet aluminium rear-set footpegs, black
anodised components, Öhlins shocks, fork gaiters and
spoked wheels with black rims. The fourth version,
the V7 III Anniversario, was based on the Special, but
included a chrome gas tank with historic eagle emblem, a
leather seat, billet aluminium locking fuel cap, brushed
aluminium fenders, and spoked wheels with polished
rims and grey hubs. Production was limited to 750
worldwide. A smartphone app was an option on all V7
IIIs, the media platform allowing a smartphone to
display speed, rpm, horsepower output, torque output,
instant and average fuel consumption, average speed,
battery voltage, longitudinal acceleration, and included a
comprehensive trip computer. Both the V9 Bobber and
Roamer received a new riding position, higher and
further rearward footpegs, a longer and thicker seat, and
matte black wheels.

**TOP LEFT** The cylinder heads on the V7III now featured inclined valves, similar to the V9. This is the basic black V7III Stone.

**BOTTOM LEFT** The 2017 V7III Racer had a satin-finish chrome fuel tank

**TOP RIGHT** In the V7 range, the V7III Special continued as the classic model.

**BOTTOM RIGHT** The V7III Anniversario celebrated fifty years of the V7. This is the V7III Anniversario and the original V7.

# 2018

In 2018, The V7 III family grew with three new variants: the Carbon, Rough, and Milano. Also updated were the V9 Bobber and Roamer, these now with two distinct personalities; one sportier and the other more touring focused. The rest of the range continued unchanged, this included the MGX-21, Eldorado, Audace, and California Touring. The Norge 1200GT, Stelvio NTX, and Griso 1200 SE continued to be available in the US, but not in Europe. The previous V7 II range was still available in the US, the only V7 II offered in Europe being the limited and numbered edition Stornello. The most significant introduction was the concept V85, destined to spawn a new range in the lead up to Moto Guzzi's centenary in 2021.

# V7 III CARBON, MILANO, ROUGH

As the best selling model in Moto Guzzi's line-up since 2009, it wasn't surprising to see three new variants offered alongside the existing V7 III Stone, Special, and Racer. The V7 featured in the Italian Sky television show 'Lord of the Bikes', the first TV series dedicated to motorcycle customization, and the V7 proved an excellent customisation base. As a homage to customisation, the three new versions; V7 III Rough, V7 III Milano, and V7 III Carbon were distinguished by different packages of special parts. These provided each with a unique character.

With its knobbly tyres, the V7 III
Rough provided an urban/country
crossover style.

Limited to in 1921 examples,
the V7 III Carbon featured
carbon-fibre mudguards and side
covers, and an Alcantara seat.

While the existing black-finished Stone, chrome
Special, and sporting Racer were basically unchanged,
each version had a dedicated seat with new graphics
and a cover. More minimalist, the V7 III Stone,
Rough, and Carbon featured only a round
speedometer. The Special, Racer, and Milano also
included a tachometer. The V7 III Carbon was the
only numbered and limited edition model in the V7
III range, celebrating the year of Moto Guzzi's birth
with only 1921 units available. Set off by carbon fibre
mudguards and side covers, the V7 III Carbon had a
completely matte black look that was enhanced by red
Brembo front brake caliper, logos and cylinder head
covers. The dedicated seat was of water repellent
Alcantara.

Emphasising an urban/country style, the V7 III
Rough included knobbly tyres mounted on wire-spoked
wheels, aluminium side covers and mudguards, and fork
gaiters. Black features extended to the headlight and
exhaust system. The final new V7 was the V7 III
Milano. Based on the V7 Special, this continued with a
chrome exhaust and glossy paint, but included cast alloy
wheels, with aluminium mudguards and side covers.
The Moto Guzzi Garage customisation philosophy
continued and a wider range of dedicated accessories
were available for all V7 IIIs. These include replacement
shock absorber springs, windscreens, luggage, and seats.

## V9 BOBBER AND ROAMER

Although only introduced two years earlier, in 2018
the V9 Bobber and Roamer received mild updates.
Still emphasising a custom culture, the V9 Roamer
now included a small fairing and new shock
absorbers, while the V9 Bobber highlighted a total
black style. The V9 continued with a predominance
of steel and aluminium parts, while plastic was
reduced to a minimum. The 55 horsepower 853cc
V-twin was unchanged, as was the chassis with
double-jointed driveshaft.

LEFT The V7 III Milano was based
on the V7 III Special, but included
alloy wheels to provide a
more modern look.

Designed to continue the legacy of the long-running Nevada, the V9 Roamer featured new shock absorbers, these with a 99mm stroke, up slightly from the previous 97mm. The seat height increased to 818mm, up from 785mm. To provide a profile more suited to touring, the standard small Plexiglas fairing sat above the round headlight. A larger windscreen, luggage rack with removable backrest, and dedicated panniers were optional. The Bobber received a new dual seat, the passenger section now removable to convert to a single seat. The V9 Roamer was available in two new gloss colours, Verde Nobile and Grigio Eleganza, while the V9 Bobber available in three matte colours; Blue Impeto, Nero Notte, and Grigio Tempesta.

# V85

Just as the non-conformist and innovative MGX-21 Flying Fortress represented a step into the future, so did the concept V85. Filling in the chasm between the classic V7/V9 families and the 1400 cruisers, the V85 was initially displayed as an adventure model with a 1980s retro feel. From the 1939 ISDT in Austria, when the GT 20s won four gold medals, to the 1957 Lodola Regolarità, 1962 Stornello Regolarità, and Paris-Dakar in 1985 and 1986 with the V65 and V75 Baja, Moto Guzzi had a long tradition of producing off-road-style motorcycles based on production models. And as increasing traffic and speed restrictions encroached on the enjoyment of a traditional street motorcycle, the adventure market was expanding. While the initial V85 would be an adventure-style model, it was envisaged it would form the technical platform for a new family of mid-range motorcycles.

Moving away from the physical enormity of some earlier adventure Moto Guzzis, notably the Quota and now-defunct Stelvio, the V85 featured more modest proportions, enabling it to be accessible to riders with a wider range of experience. The narrow fuel tank was inspired by earlier off-road rally versions, and the high front mudguard and double headlamp from the NTX650 and Quota 1000. The yellow and white colours also paid tribute to the mid-1980s rally bikes. Modern features included fully digital instrumentation and an LED DRL light for the front headlight.

A new engine powered the concept V85. Although still a two-cylinder 90° transverse air-cooled 850cc,

BELOW The adventure concept V85 would form the basis of a new range of mid-range motorcycles to be released in the lead up to Moto Guzzi's centenary in 2021.

it was completely redesigned, and maximum power increased significantly to 80 horsepower. The tubular steel frame was also new, no longer a full cradle, but incorporating the engine as a stressed member. The asymmetric aluminium swingarm was curved on the left to allow for a single high rise muffler, the right arm housing a new shaft drive. A single Öhlins remote reservoir shock absorber connected the chassis directly to the right side of the swingarm. The front suspension on the concept V85 included a stout upside down front fork with dual front Brembo four-piston radial brake calipers, while the rear brake was a disc with a twin-piston caliper. As on the V7 III Rough, the wire spoked wheels were shod with knobbly tyres.

Although one of the greatest names in motorcycling, by the end of the 1990s Moto Guzzi was struggling and their future was uncertain. But with ownership changes involving firstly Aprilia, and later Piaggio,

Moto Guzzi has evolved from a company struggling to survive into one proud of its name and tradition. While maintaining their existing sympathetic clientele, Moto Guzzi's range has been constantly expanded and broadened to appeal to a wider variety of customers, particularly with more American-style cruisers. Moto Guzzi have also remained committed to the trademark 90-degree air-cooled V-twin with shaft-drive, and continued to produce individualistic motorcycles. As they prepare to celebrate their centenary, Moto Guzzi's goal is to implement an expanded range, largely centred on the mid-range concept V85 platform. It will be interesting to see how Moto Guzzi manages to adapt their traditional air-cooled models to comply with ever increasing noise and emission requirements. But a centenary of history has shown that Moto Guzzi will continue to thrive and preserve their heritage as a legendary marque.

# APPENDIX 1:
## MOTO GUZZI PRODUCTION FIGURES 1921–97*

The total production from 1921 until 1939 – 50,586 units

| Model | Year | Number | Model | Year | Number |
|-------|------|--------|-------|------|--------|
| P. 175 | 1932-37 | 1,503 | Zigolo | 1953-65 | 129,771 |
| P. 250 | 1934-37 | 1,886 | Lodola | 1956-65 | 26,757 |
| P.L. 250 | 1937-39 | 1,474 | Galletto | 1950-65 | 71,055 |
| P.L.S. 250 | 1937-39 | 744 | Ercolino | 1956-70 | 29,974 |
| Ardetta 250 | 1939-40 | 599 | Dingo | 1964-5 | 25,450 |
| Egretta 250 | 1939-40 | 784 | Stornello | 1960-74 | 58,444 |
| P.E. 250 | 1934-39 | 1,568 | 3x3 | 1961 | 204 |
| P.E.S. | 1938-39 | 75 | Aiace | 1961-3 | 2,180 |
| Airone (Tube frame) | 1939-41 | 1,139 | MZ2, MZ0 | 1961-5 | 10,103 |
| Airone (Pressed-steel frame) | 1940-61 | 26,926 | Motocotivat | 1964-5 | 1,777 |
| 250 TT/SS | 1926-33 | 377 | Nuovo Falcone | 1969-76 | 14,955 |
| Normale 500 | 1921-27 | 2,065 | V7 | 1966-76 | 6,189 |
| Sport 500 | 1923-28 | 4,107 | V7 Special/Ambassador | 1968-74 | 11,806 |
| Sport 14 | 1929-30 | 4,285 | 850 GT/Eldorado | 1971-75 | 13,061 |
| Sport 15 | 1931-39 | 5,979 | V7 Sport/750 S | 1971-75 | 3,791 |
| S (500) | 1934-40 | 4,004 | 850 T | 1974 | 5,301 |
| S (Pressed-steel frame) | 1940 | 67 | 850 T3/T3 California | 1975-87 | 11,940 |
| C 2 V | 1923-30 | 683 | 750 S3 | 1975 | 950 |
| 2 V.T. | 1931-34 | 917 | 850 Le Mans | 1975-8 | 7,036 |
| V (500) | 1934-40 | 2,119 | V 1000 Convert | 1975-6 | 2,468 |
| W (500) | 1935-40 | 160 | 850 Le Mans II | 1978-81 | 7,335 |
| G.T. (500) | 1928-29 | 78 | 850 Le Mans III | 1980-85 | 10,056 |
| G.T. 16 | 1931-34 | 754 | CX 100 | 1979-81 | 353 |
| G.T. 2 VT | 1931-34 | 167 | Le Mans IV | 1984-88 | 4,230 |
| G.T.S. | 1934-41 | 2,952 | California II | 1981-87 | 9,604 |
| G.T.V. | 1934-49 | 6,555 | V35 C | 1982-87 | 9,950 |
| G.T.W. | 1935-49 | 1,106 | V50C | 1982-86 | 1,417 |
| G.T.E. (Pressed-steel frame) | 1942 | 2 | V65C | 1983-87 | 4,280 |
| 250 TT,SS | 1926-33 | 377 | V35 Florida | 1986-91 | 2,426 |
| C4V, 4V TT,SS | 1924-33 | 486 | V65 Florida | 1986-94 | 4,134 |
| G.T.C. | 1937-39 | 161 | California III/Classic (carb) | 1987-93 | 6,819 |
| Condor/Dondolino | 1939-49 | 123 | California C.I. (carb) | 1988-92 | 570 |
| Albatros | 1939-49 | 59 | California C.I. I.E. | 1989-93 | 157 |
| G.T. Militaire | 1928-30 | 245 | Le Mans V | 1988-93 | 2,113 |
| G.T. 17 | 1932-39 | 4,810 | 1000 S | 1989-93 | 1,360 |
| G.T. 20 | 1938-39 | 248 | California III/Classic I.E. | 1990-93 | 658 |
| Alce and Super Alce | 1938-58 | 12,325 | 350 Nevada | 1991-97 | 1,450 |
| Trialce | 1940-43 | 1,762 | 750 Nevada | 1989-97 | 3,841 |
| 500 U | 1942-45 | 2,981 | California 1100 (carb) | 1993-97 | 1,601 |
| Mototelaio | 1928-30 | 225 | California 1100 I.E. | 1993-97 | 4,346 |
| Mototriciolo 32 | 1933-36 | 1,058 | California 1000 (carb) | 1994-95 | 1,317 |
| Mototelaio S | 1936-39 | 830 | California 1000 I.E. | 1994 | 50 |
| ER | 1938-42 | 5,143 | California 1100 P.A. (Police) | 1994-97 | 319 |
| 500E, 555, 556, 559 Motocarri | 1940-42 | 59 | Daytona | 1991-97 | 1,433 |
| 125 | 1946 | 2 | Quota | 1992-97 | 176 |
| Gambalunga | 1946-49 | 13 | 1100 Sport (carb) | 1994-96 | 1,771 |
| Edile | 1946 | 150 | 1100 Sport I.E. | 1996-97 | 1,341 |
| Astore | 1950-52 | 2,712 | Centauro | 1996-97 | 1,532 |
| Ercole | 1945-75 | 38,597 | California EV | 1997 | 1,438 |
| Falcone | 1950-68 | 8,405 | Centauro GT | 1997 | 72 |
| Cardellino | 1946-63 | 214,497 | Centauro Sport | 1997 | 116 |

*Official production figures have not been published since 1997

# APPENDIX 2:
## SPECIFICATIONS OF PRODUCTION MOTO GUZZIS 1921-2018

| Model | Years | Engine | Bore (mm) | Stroke (mm) | Displ (cc) | Comp ratio | Carburettor | Transmission | Front suspension | Rear suspension | Front tyre | Rear tyre | Wheel base | Weight (kg) |
|-------|-------|--------|-----------|-------------|------------|------------|-------------|--------------|------------------|-----------------|------------|-----------|------------|-------------|
| Normale | 1921-24 | 1 Cyl OHV /SV | 88 | 82 | 499 | 04:01:00 | Amac 15 PSY | 3 speeds | Girder fork | Rigid | 3x26 | 3x26 | 1380 | 130 |
| C2V | 1923-27 | 1 Cyl OHV | 88 | 82 | 499 | 5.25:1 | Amac 25 PSY | 3 speeds | Girder fork | Rigid | 3x26 | 3x26 | 1410 | 130 |
| Sport | 1923-28 | 1 Cyl OHV /SV | 88 | 82 | 499 | 4.5:1 | Amac 15 PSY | 3 speeds | Girder fork | Rigid | 3x26 | 3x26 | 1430 | 130 |
| C4V 4VTT 4VSS | 1924-33 | 1 Cyl 4 OHV | 88 | 82 | 499 | 06:01:00 | Amac 28.5mm | 3 speeds | Girder fork | Rigid | 2.75x27 | 2.75x27 (3x27) | 1380 | 130 |
| 250TT SS | 1926-33 | 1 Cyl OHV | 68 | 68 | 249 | 08:01:00 | Binks 25mm | 3 speeds | Girder fork | Rigid | 2.75x27 | 2.75x27 | 1360 | 105 |
| G.T. G.T.16 | 1928-34 | 1 Cyl OHV /SV | 88 | 82 | 499 | 4.5:1 | Amal | 3 speeds | Girder fork | Swingarm | 3.50x19 | 3.50x19 | 1430 | 150 |
| Sport 14 | 1929-30 | 1 Cyl OHV /SV | 88 | 82 | 499 | 4.5:1 | Amac | 3 speeds | Girder fork | Rigid | 3.50x26 | 3.50x26 | 1430 | 130 |
| 2VT GT 2VT | 1931-34 | 1 Cyl OHV | 88 | 82 | 499 | 5.25:1 | Amac | 3 speeds | Girder fork | Rigid/ swingarm | 3.50x26 | 3.50x26 | 1430 | 130/ 150 |
| Sport 15 | 1931-39 | 1 Cyl OHV /SV | 88 | 82 | 499 | 4.5:1 | Amal/ Dell'Orto | 3 speeds | Girder fork | Rigid | 3.50x19 | 3.50x19 | 1430 | 150 |
| Four Cylinder 500 | 1930 | 4 Cyl OHV | 56 | 65 | 492 | 05:01:00 | Cozette | 3 speeds | Girder fork | Rigid | - | - | - | 165 |
| Three Cylinder | 1932-33 | 3 Cyl OHV | 56 | 67 | 495 | 4.9:1 | Amal | 3 speeds | Girder fork | Swingarm | 3.25x19 | 3.25x19 | 1440 | 160 |
| P 175 (250) (P.E.) | 1932-37 | 1 Cyl OHV | 59 (68) | 63.7 (64) | 174 (232) | 06:01:00 | Amal, Dell'Orto 20 (22) mm | 3 speeds | Girder fork | Rigid (Swingarm) | 3.00x19 | 3.00x19 | 1320 | 115 |
| G.T. 17 | 1932-39 | 1 Cyl OHV /SV | 88 | 82 | 499 | 4.7:1 | Dell'Orto MC26F | 3 speeds | Girder fork | Swingarm | 3.50x19 | 3.50x19 | 1500 | 196 |
| 500 Bicilindrica | 1933-51 | 2 Cyl OHV | 68 | 68 | 494 | 8.5:1 | Dell'Orto | 4 speeds | Girder, Leading link | Rigid, Swingarm | 3.00x21 | 3.25x20 | 1390 | 151 |
| S G.T.S. | 1934-40 | 1 Cyl OHV /SV | 88 | 82 | 499 | 4.6:1 | Amal/ Dell'Orto | 4 speeds | Girder fork | Rigid, Swingarm | 3.25x19 | 3.50x19 | 1400 | 147 |
| V, W G.T.V. G.T.W. | 1934-49 | 1 Cyl OHV | 88 | 82 | 499 | 5.5:1 | Amal/ Dell'Orto | 4 speeds | Girder fork | Rigid, Swingarm | 3.25x19 | 3.50x19 | 1400 | 160 |

| Model | Years | Engine | Bore (mm) | Stroke (mm) | Displ (cc) | Comp ratio | Carburetor | Transmission | Front suspension | Rear suspension | Front tyre | Rear tyre | Wheel base | Weight (kg) |
|---|---|---|---|---|---|---|---|---|---|---|---|---|---|---|
| G.T.C | 1937-39 | 1 Cyl OHV | 88 | 82 | 499 | | Dell'Orto | 4 speeds | Girder fork | Swingarm | 3.00x20 | 3.50x19 | 1400 | 160 |
| P.L., P.L.S. P.E.S. Ardetta Egretta | 1937-39 | 1 Cyl OHV | 70 | 64 | 247 | 06:01:00 | Dell'Orto | 3 speeds | Girder fork | Rigid, Swingarm | 3.00x19 | 3.00x19 | 1320 | 105, 135 |
| G.T 20 Alce | 1938-45 | 1 Cyl OHV /SV | 88 | 82 | 498 | 4.7:1 | Dell'Orto MC 26F | 4 speeds | Girder fork | Swingarm | 3.50x19 | 3.50x19 | 1440 | 179.5 |
| Condor | 1939-40 | 1 Cyl OHV | 88 | 82 | 499 | 07:01:00 | Dell'Orto SS 32 M | 4 speeds | Girder fork | Swingarm | 2.75x21 | 3.00x21 | 1470 | 140 |
| Albatros | 1939-49 | 1 Cyl OHC | 68 | 68 | 249 | 8.5:1 | Dell'Orto SS 30 M | 4 speeds | Girder fork | Swingarm | 2.75x21 | 3.00x21 | 1430 | 135 |
| Airone | 1939-61 | 1 Cyl OHV | 70 | 64 | 246 | 06:01:00 | Dell'Orto SBF 22 | 4 speeds | Girder fork | Swingarm | 3.00x19 | 3.00x19 | 1370 | 135 |
| Tre Cilindri | 1940 | 3 Cyl DOHC | 59 | 60 | 492 | 08:01:00 | Cozette | 5 speeds | Girder fork | Swingarm | 2.75x21 | 3.00x21 | 1470 | 175 |
| 500 U | 1942-45 | 1 Cyl OHV /SV | 88 | 82 | 498 | 5.7:1 | Dell'Orto MC 26F | 3 speeds + rev | Girder fork | Swingarm | 3.00x19 | 6x16 (2) | 2300 | 405 |
| Dondolino | 1946-51 | 1 Cyl OHV | 88 | 82 | 498 | 8.5:1 | Dell'Orto SS 35 M | 4 speeds | Girder fork | Swingarm | 2.75x21 | 3.00x21 | 1470 | 128 |
| Gambalunga | 1946-51 | 1 Cyl OHV | 84 (88) | 90 (82) | 498 | 08:01:00 | Dell'Orto SS 35 M | 4 speeds | Leading link fork | Swingarm | 2.75x21 (20) | 3.00x21 (20) | 1470 | 125 |
| Edile | 1946-47 | 1 Cyl OHV | 88 | 82 | 499 | 5.5:1 | Dell'Orto MC 26 F | 5 speeds + rev | Girder fork | Rigid | 7.00x17 | 9.75x18 | 3065 | 1350 |
| Ercole | 1946-80 | 1 Cyl OHV | 88 | 82 | 499 | 5.5:1 | Dell'Orto MC 26 F | 5 speeds + rev | Girder fork | Swingarms | 4.00x19 | 6.50x16 | 2300 | 670 (1500) |
| Guzzino Motoleggera Cardellino | 1946-63 | 1 Cyl 2 stroke | 42 (45) (48) | 46 | 64 (73) (83) | 5.5:1 (6.4:1) (7:1) | Dell'Orto | 3 speeds | Blade forks (telescopic) | Swingarm | 1.75x26 2.25x20 | 1.75x26 2.25x20 | 1200 | 45 (58) |
| Superalce | 1946-58 | 1 Cyl OHV | 88 | 82 | 499 | 5.5:1 | Dell'Orto MD 27 F | 4 speeds | Girder fork | Swingarm | 3.50x19 | 3.50x19 | 1455 | 187 |
| 250 Parallel Twin | 1947-48 | 2 Cyl DOHC | 54 | 54 | 247 | 10:01:00 | Dell'Orto | 4 speeds | Telescopic fork | Swingarm | 2.75x21 | 3.00x21 | 1420 | 125 |
| Galletto | 1950-65 | 1 Cyl OHV | 62 (65) | 53 (58) | 160 (175) (192) | 5.6:1 (6:1) (6.4:1) (7:1) | Dell'Orto | 3 speeds (4 speeds) | Leading link forks | Swingarm | 2.75x17 | 3.00x17 | 1310 | 107 (134) |
| Astore | 1950-52 | 1 Cyl OHV | 88 | 82 | 499 | 5.5:1 | Dell'Orto MD 27 F | 4 speeds | Telescopic fork | Swingarm | 3.50x19 | 3.50x19 | 1475 | 180 |
| Falcone Sport Turismo | 1950-68 | 1 Cyl OHV | 88 | 82 | 499 | 6.5:1 (5.5:1) | Dell'Orto SS 29A | 4 speeds | Telescopic fork | Swingarm | 3.25x19 (3.50x19) | 3.50x19 | 1500 | 176 |
| Zigolo | 1953-65 | 1 Cyl 2 stroke | 50 (52) | 50 (52) | 98 (110) | 6:1 (7.5:1) | Dell'Orto | 3 speeds | Telescopic fork | Swingarm | 2.50x19 (17) | 2.50x19 (2.75x17) | 1240 (1250) | 75 (78) |

| Model | Years | Engine | Bore (mm) | Stroke (mm) | Displ (cc) | Comp ratio | Carburettor | Transmission | Front suspension | Rear suspension | Front tyre | Rear tyre | Wheel base | Weight (kg) |
|---|---|---|---|---|---|---|---|---|---|---|---|---|---|---|
| Lodola | 1956-65 | 1 Cyl OHC (OHV) | 62 (64) | 57.8 (68) | 175 (235) | 7.5:1 | Dell'Orto UB 22 BS | 4 speeds | Telescopic fork | Swingarm | 2.50x18 | 3.00x17 | 1314 | 109 (115) |
| Ercolino | 1956-70 | 1 Cyl OHV | 65 | 58 | 192 | 6.4:1 | Dell'Orto MA 19 B | 4 speeds + rev | Telescopic fork | Leaf spring | 3.25x14 | 4.25x15 | 1850 | 265 |
| Stornello Turismo Sport | 1960-74 | 1 Cyl OHV | 52 | 58 | 123 | 8:1 (9.8:1) (9.6:1) | Dell'Orto | 4 speeds (5 speeds) | Telescopic fork | Swingarm | 2.50x17 | 2.75x17 (3.00x17) | 1250 | 92 (113) |
| Motozappa | 1961-66 | 1 Cyl 2 stroke | 52 | 52 | 110 | 7.5:1 | Dell'Orto OVC 21/17/3 | 3 speeds | Rigid | Rigid | 3.00x8 | 3.00x8 | - | 135 |
| 3x3 | 1961 | 2 Cyl OHV | 80 | 75 | 750 | 6.5:1 | Weber 26 IMB | 6 speeds + rev | Telescopic fork | Swingarms | 6.00x15 | 6.00x15 | 2030 | 570 |
| Aiace | 1962-63 | 1 Cyl 2 stroke | 52 | 52 | 110 | 7.5:1 | Dell'Orto MAF 18 B | 3 speeds | Leading link fork | Hydraulic dampers | 4.00x8 | 4.00x8 | 1640 | 250 |
| Stornello Scrambler | 1962-74 | 1 Cyl OHV | 52 | 58 | 123 | 11.4:1 (9.6:1) | Dell'Orto UB 22 BS2 | 4 speed (5 speeds) | Telescopic fork | Swingarm | 2.50x19 (2.75x19) | 3.00x19 (3.00x17) | 1250 | 95 (117) |
| Dingo Super, GT Cross, MM Sport | 1964-76 | 1 Cyl 2 stroke | 38.5 | 42 | 49 | 08:01:00 | Dell'Orto | 3 speeds (4 speeds) (Auto) | Telescopic fork | Swingarm | 2.00x18 | 2.00x18 (2.15x28) | 1115 (1130) | 48 (50) (57) |
| Dingotre | 1965-68 | 1 Cyl 2 stroke | 38.5 | 42 | 49 | 7.5:1 | Dell'Orto SHA 14 | 3 speeds | Telescopic fork | Leaf springs | 3.00x12 | 3.00x12 | 1680 | 130 |
| V7 | 1966-76 | 2 Cyl OHV | 80 | 70 | 704 | 09:01:00 | Dell'Orto SS1 29D VHB 29C | 4 speeds | Telescopic fork | Swingarm | 4.00x18 | 4.00x18 | 1445 | 243 |
| Trotter (Special M) | 1966-73 | 1 Cyl 2 stroke | 37 (38.5) | 38 42) | 41 (49) | 7.5:1 (9.7:1) | Dell'Orto SHA 14 | 2 speeds 1 speed (Auto) | Rigid (Leading link) | Rigid (Swingarm) | 2.00x16 (2.15x16) | 2.00x16 (2.15x16) | 1035 (1058) | 35 (43) (48.5) |
| Furghino | 1968-70 | 1 Cyl 2 stroke | 38.5 | 42 | 49 | 09:01:00 | Dell'Orto MB 18 BS | 3 speeds | Telescopic fork | Leaf springs | 3.50x8 | 3.50x8 | 1590 | 200 |
| V7 Special Ambassador | 1969-74 | 2 Cyl OHV | 83 | 70 | 757 | 09:01:00 | Dell'Orto VHB 29C | 4 speeds | Telescopic fork | Swingarm | 4.00x18 | 4.00x18 | 1470 | 228 |
| Stornello 160 | 1969-74 | 1 Cyl OHV | 58 | 58 | 153 | 9.5:1 | Dell'Orto UB 20B | 4 speeds (5 speeds) | Telescopic fork | Swingarm | 2.50x17 | 2.75x17 (3.00x17) | 1250 | 107 (113) |
| V7 Sport 750 S 750 S3 | 1971-75 | 2 Cyl OHV | 82.5 | 70 | 748 | 9.8:1 | Dell'Orto VHB 30C | 5 speeds | Telescopic fork | Swingarm | 3.25x18 | 3.50x18 | 1470 | 206 208 |
| 850 GT Eldorado California | 1971-74 | 2 Cyl OHV | 83 | 78 | 844 | 9.2:1 | Dell'Orto VHB 29C | 5 speeds | Telescopic fork | Swingarm | 4.00x18 | 4.00x18 | 1470 | 235 255 |
| Nuovo Falcone | 1971-76 | 1 Cyl OHV | 88 | 82 | 499 | 6.8:1 | Dell'Orto VHB 29A | 4 speeds | Telescopic fork | Swingarm | 3.50x18 | 3.50x18 | 1450 | 214 |
| 850 T | 1973-75 | 2 Cyl OHV | 83 | 78 | 844 | 9.5:1 | Dell'Orto VHB 30C | 5 speeds | Telescopic fork | Swingarm | 3.50x18 | 4.1 0x18 | 1470 | 202 |
| Chiù | 1974-76 | 1 Cyl 2 stroke | 40 | 39 | 49 | 8.5:1 | Dell'Orto SHA 14.9 | 1 speed | Telescopic fork | Swingarm | 2.25x16 | 2.25x16 | 1130 | 48 |

| Model | Years | Engine | Bore (mm) | Stroke (mm) | Displ (cc) | Comp ratio | Carburettor | Transmission | Front suspension | Rear suspension | Front tyre | Rear tyre | Wheel base | Weight (kg) |
|---|---|---|---|---|---|---|---|---|---|---|---|---|---|---|
| 250 TS | 1974-82 | 2 Cyl 2 stroke | 56 | 47 | 231 | 9.7:1 | Dell'Orto VHB 25B | 5 speeds | Telescopic fork | Swingarm | 3.00x18 | 3.25x18 | 1330 | 137 |
| 125 Tuttoterreno Turismo | 1974-81 | 1 Cyl 2 stroke | 56 | 49 | 121 | 9.9:1 | Dell'Orto VHB 22 BS | 5 speeds | Telescopic fork | Swingarm | 2.50x21 | 3.50x18 | 1300 | 105 |
| Cross 50 Nibbio (Magnum) | 1974-82 | 1 Cyl 2 stroke | 40 | 39 | 49 | 8:1 (8.2:1) | Dell'Orto SHA 14 | 5 speeds | Telescopic fork | Swingarm | 2.50x19 (4.00x10) | 3.00x17 (4.00x10) | 1210 (1040) | 81 (58) |
| 350 GTS (400) | 1974-79 | 4 Cyl OHC | 50 | 44 (50.6) | 346 (397) | 10.2:1 | Dell'Orto VHB 20 D | 5 speeds | Telescopic fork | Swingarm | 3.00x18 | 3.50x18 | 1370 | 175 |
| Le Mans | 1975-78 | 2 Cyl OHV | 83 | 78 | 844 | 10:02:01 | Dell'Orto PHF 36B | 5 speeds | Telescopic fork | Swingarm | 100/90x18 | 110/90x18 | 1470 | 198 |
| 850 T3 California | 1975-82 | 2 Cyl OHV | 83 | 78 | 844 | 9.5:1 | Dell'Orto VHB 30C | 5 speeds | Telescopic fork | Swingarm | 3.50x18 | 4.10x18 | 1470 | 205 225 |
| V 1000 I Convert | 1975-84 | 2 Cyl OHV | 88 | 78 | 949 | 9.2:1 | Dell'Orto VHB 30C | 2 speeds | Telescopic fork | Swingarm | 100/90x18 | 110/90x18 | 1470 | 229 |
| V35, II (V50, V50 II, III) | 1977-86 | 2 Cyl OHV | 66 (74) | 50.6 (57) | 346 (490) | 10.5:1 (10.4:1) | Dell'Orto VHB 24 F | 5 speeds | Telescopic fork | Swingarm | 3.00x18 | 3.25x18 (3.50x18) | 1420 | 154 (158) |
| 254 | 1977-81 | 4 Cyl OHC | 44 | 38 | 231 | 11.5:1 | Dell'Orto PHBG 18 B | 5 speeds | Telescopic fork | Swingarm | 2.75x18 | 3.00x18 | 1270 | 117 |
| Le Mans II | 1978-81 | 2 Cyl OHV | 83 | 78 | 844 | 10:02:01 | Dell'Orto PHF 36B | 5 speeds | Telescopic fork | Swingarm | 100/90x18 | 110/90x18 | 1485 | 196 |
| 1000 SP NT | 1978-83 | 2 Cyl OHV | 88 | 78 | 949 | 9.2:1 | Dell'Orto VHB 30C | 5 speeds | Telescopic fork | Swingarm | 100/90x18 | 110/90x18 | 1480 | 210 |
| 1000 G5 | 1978-83 | 2 Cyl OHV | 88 | 78 | 949 | 9.2:1 | Dell'Orto VHB 30C | 5 speeds | Telescopic fork | Swingarm | 100/90x18 | 110/90x18 | 1470 | 220 |
| CX100 | 1979-81 | 2 Cyl OHV | 88 | 78 | 949 | 9.2:1 | Dell'Orto VHB 30C | 5 speeds | Telescopic fork | Swingarm | 3.50x18 | 4.10x18 | 1485 | 198 |
| V35 Imola V50 Monza | 1979-84 | 2 Cyl OHV | 66 (74) | 50.6 (57) | 346 (490) | 10.5:1 (10.4:1) | Dell'Orto VHB 26 F (PHBH 28B) | 5 speeds | Telescopic fork | Swingarm | 3.00x18 | 3.50x18 | 1420 | 158 (160) |
| 125 2C 4T | 1979-81 | 2 Cyl OHC | 45.5 | 38 | 124 | 10.65:1 | Dell'Orto PHBG 20 B | 5 speeds | Telescopic fork | Swingarm | 2.75x18 | 3.00x18 | 1290 | 110 |
| Le Mans III | 1980-85 | 2 Cyl OHV | 83 | 78 | 844 | 9.8:1 | Dell'Orto PHF 36B | 5 speeds | Telescopic fork | Swingarm | 100/90x18 | 110/90x18 | 1505 | 206 |
| 850 T4 | 1980-83 | 2 Cyl OHV | 83 | 78 | 844 | 9.5:1 | Dell'Orto VHB 30C | 5 speeds | Telescopic fork | Swingarm | 100/90x18 | 110/90x18 | 1470 | 215 |
| California II | 1981-87 | 2 Cyl OHV | 88 | 78 | 949 | 9.2:1 | Dell'Orto VHB 30C | 5 speeds | Telescopic fork | Swingarm | 120/90x18 | 120/90x18 | 1565 | 250 |
| V65 V65SP | 1982-87 | 2 Cyl OHV | 80 | 64 | 643 | 10:01:00 | Dell'Orto PHBH 30B | 5 speeds | Telescopic fork | Swingarm | 100/90x18 | 110/90x18 | 1440 | 165 (170) |

| Model | Years | Engine | Bore (mm) | Stroke (mm) | Displ (cc) | Comp ratio | Carburettor | Transmission | Front suspension | Rear suspension | Front tyre | Rear tyre | Wheel base | Weight (kg) |
|---|---|---|---|---|---|---|---|---|---|---|---|---|---|---|
| V35/50/65 Custom (Florida) | 1982-94 | 2 Cyl OHV | 66 (74) (80) | 50.6 (40.6) (57) (64) | 346 (349) (490) (490) | 10.5:1 (10.4:1) (10.3:1) | Dell'Orto VHB 26F (PHBH 28B) | 5 speeds | Telescopic fork | Swingarm | 100/90x18 (90/90x18) | 130/90x16 (120/90x16) | 1460 | 165 (170) |
| 850 T5 | 1983-85 | 2 Cyl OHV | 83 | 78 | 949 | 9.5:1 | Dell'Orto VHB 30C | 5 speeds | Telescopic fork | Swingarm | 110/90x16 | 130/90x16 (18) | 1505 | 220 |
| Le Mans IV | 1984-88 | 2 Cyl OHV | 88 | 78 | 949 | 10:01:00 | Dell'Orto PHM 40N | 5 speeds | Telescopic fork | Swingarm | 120/80X16 | 130/80X18 | 1514 | 215 |
| 1000 SP II | 1984-88 | 2 Cyl OHV | 88 | 78 | 949 | 9.2:1 | Dell'Orto VHB 30C | 5 speeds | Telescopic fork | Swingarm | 110/90x16 | 120/90x18 | 1514 | 250 |
| V35 Imola II V50 Monza II V65 Lario | 1984-89 | 2 Cyl 4 OHV | 66 (74) (80) | 50.6 (57) (64) | 346 (490) (643) | 10.5:1 (10.4:1) (10.3:1) | Dell'Orto PHBH 28 (PHBH 30) | 5 speeds | Telescopic fork | Swingarm | 100/90x16 | 120/90x16 | 1455 | 168 (170) (172) |
| V35/65 TT | 1984-87 | 2 Cyl OHV | 66 (80) | 50.6 (64) | 346 (643) | 10.5:1 (10:1) | Dell'Orto VHB 26 F (PHBH 30B) | 5 speeds | Telescopic fork | Swingarm | 3.00x21 | 4.00x18 | 1460 | 160 (165) |
| V35 III V75 | 1985-90 | 2 Cyl OHV (4 OHV) | 66 (80) | 50.6 (74) | 346 (744) | 10.5:1 (10:1) | Dell'Orto VHB 26 (PHBH 30 D) | 5 speeds | Telescopic fork | Swingarm | 100/90x16 | 110/80x18 (120/80x18) | 1470 | 160 (187) |
| 125 C (TT) | 1985-88 | 1 Cyl 2 stroke | 56 | 50 | 123 | 11.5:1 | Dell'Orto PHBL 25BS | 6 speeds | Telescopic fork | Swingarm | 80/100x16 (2.75x21) | 3.50x18 (4.10x18) | 1380 | 110 |
| V35,65,75 NTX | 1986-90 | 2 Cyl OHV | 74 (80) | 40.6 (64) (74) | 349 (643) (744) | 10.3:1 (10:1) (9.7:1) | Dell'Orto PHBH 30B | 5 speeds | Telescopic fork | Swingarm | 3.00x21 | 4.00x18 | 1480 | 170 (180) |
| 350/650 GT | 1987-95 | 2 Cyl OHV | 66 (80) | 50.6 (64) | 346 (643) | 10.5:1 (10:1) | Dell'Orto VHB 26 (PHBH 30 D) | 5 speeds | Telescopic fork | Swingarm | 100/90x16 (100/90x18) | 110/80x18 (110/90x18) | 1470 | 160 (165) |
| Mille GT | 1987-93 | 2 Cyl OHV | 88 | 78 | 949 | 9.2:1 | Dell'Orto PHF 30C | 5 speeds | Telescopic fork | Swingarm | 100/90x18 | 120/90x18 | 1530 | 246 |
| California III C.I. | 1987-94 | 2 Cyl OHV | 88 | 78 | 949 | 9.2:1 | Dell'Orto VHB 30C (Fuel injection) | 5 speeds | Telescopic fork | Swingarm | 110/90x18 | 120/90x18 | 1560 | 250 (270) |
| SP III | 1988-92 | 2 Cyl OHV | 88 | 78 | 949 | 9.5:1 | Dell'Orto PHF 36C | 5 speeds | Telescopic fork | Swingarm | 110/90x18 | 120/90x18 | 1514 | 230 |
| Le Mans V | 1988-93 | 2 Cyl OHV | 88 | 78 | 949 | 10:01:00 | Dell'Orto PHM 40N | 5 speeds | Telescopic fork | Swingarm | 100/90x18 | 120/90x18 | 1485 | 215 |
| 1000 S | 1989-93 | 2 Cyl OHV | 88 | 78 | 949 | 10:01:00 | Dell'Orto PHM 40N | 5 speeds | Telescopic fork | Swingarm | 100/90x18 | 120/90x18 | 1485 | 215 |
| 750 Targa SP Strada | 1989-93 | 2 Cyl OHV | 80 | 74 | 744 | 9.7:1 | Dell'Orto PHBH 30B | 5 speeds | Telescopic fork | Swingarm | 100/90x18 | 120/80x18 | 1480 | 180 (185) |
| 350/750 Nevada | 1990-04 | 2 Cyl OHV | 66 (80) | 50.6 (74) | 346 (744) | 10.6:1 (9.6:1) | Dell'Orto PHBH 28 (PHBH 30) | 5 speeds | Telescopic fork | Swingarm | 100/90x18 | 130/90x16 | 1505 (1482) | 182 |
| Daytona Racing RS | 1991-98 | 2 Cyl 4 OHV | 90 | 78 | 992 | 10:1 (10.5:1) | Electronic fuel injection | 5 speeds | Telescopic fork (upside down) | Cantilever swingarm | 120/70x17 | 160/60x18 (160/60x17) | 1475 | 205 (223) |
| Quota | 1992-97 | 2 Cyl OHV | 88 | 78 | 949 | 9.5:1 | Fuel injection | 5 speeds | Telescopic fork | Swingarm Monoshock | 90/90x21 | 130/80x17 | 1620 | 210 |

| Model | Years | Engine | Bore (mm) | Stroke (mm) | Displ (cc) | Comp ratio | Carburettor | Transmission | Front suspension | Rear suspension | Front tyre | Rear tyre | Wheel base | Weight (kg) |
|---|---|---|---|---|---|---|---|---|---|---|---|---|---|---|
| Strada 1000 | 1993 | 2 Cyl OHV | 88 | 78 | 949 | 9.5:1 | Dell'Orto PHF 36C | 5 speeds | Telescopic fork | Swingarm | 110/90x18 | 120/90x18 | 1514 | 210 |
| California 1100 (EV) (Classic, Vintage) | 1993-12 | 2 Cyl OHV | 92 | 80 | 1064 | 9.5:1 | Dell'Orto PHF 36 (Fuel injection) | 5 speeds | Telescopic fork | Swingarm | 110/90x18 | 140/80x17 (150/80x17) | 1575 (1560) | 240 (251, 263) |
| 1100 Sport (IE) | 1994-98 | 2 Cyl OHV | 92 | 80 | 1064 | 10.5:1 (9.5:1) | Dell'Orto PHM 40 (Fuel injection) | 5 speeds | Telescopic fork (upside down) | Cantilever swingarm | 120/70x17 | 160/60x18 (160/60x17) | 1465 | 221 |
| Centauro Sport GT | 1996-00 | 2 Cyl 4 OHV | 90 | 78 | 992 | 10.5:1 | Electronic fuel injection | 5 speeds | Upside down fork | Cantilever swingarm | 120/70x17 | 160/60x17 | 1475 | 224 |
| Quota ES | 1998-01 | 2 Cyl OHV | 92 | 80 | 1064 | 9.5:1 | Electronic fuel injection | 5 speeds | Telescopic fork | Cantilever swingarm | 90/90x21 | 130/80x17 | 1600 | 245 |
| V11 Sport (GT) | 1999-05 | 2 Cyl OHV | 92 | 80 | 1064 | 9.5:1 (9.8:1) | Electronic fuel injection | 6 speeds | Upside down fork | Cantilever swingarm | 120/70x17 | 170/60x17 (180/55x17) | 1471 (1490) | 221 (219) |
| V11 Le Mans | 2001-05 | 2 Cyl OHV | 92 | 80 | 1064 | 9.5:1 (9.8:1) | Electronic fuel injection | 6 speeds | Upside down fork | Cantilever swingarm | 120/70x17 | 180/55x17 | 1490 | 221 (226) |
| Breva V 750 IE | 2003-08 | 2 Cyl OHV | 80 | 74 | 744 | 9.6:1 | Electronic fuel injection | 5 speeds | Telescopic fork | Swingarm | 110/70x17 | 130/80x17 | 1449 | 182 |
| Breva V1100 | 2005-08 | 2 Cyl OHV | 92 | 80 | 1064 | 9.8:1 | Electronic fuel injection | 6 speeds | Telescopic fork | Single-sided swingarm | 120/70x17 | 180/55x17 | 1495 | 231 |
| MGS-01 Corsa | 2005- | 2 Cyl 4-OHV | 100 | 80 | 1225 | 11.6:1 | Electronic fuel injection | 6 speeds | Upside down fork | Monoshock swingarm | 120/70x17 | 180/55x17 | 1450 | 192 |
| Nevada Classic 750 ie | 2005-08 | 2 Cyl OHV | 80 | 74 | 744 | 9.6:1 | Electronic fuel injection | 5 speeds | Telescopic fork | Swingarm | 100/90x18 | 130/90x16 | 1467 | 184 |
| Griso 1100 | 2006-08 | 2 Cyl OHV | 92 | 80 | 1064 | 9.8:1 | Electronic fuel injection | 6 speeds | Upside down fork | Single-sided swingarm | 120/70x17 | 180/55x17 | 1554 | 227 |
| Norge 1200 | 2006-09 | 2 Cyl OHV | 95 | 81.2 | 1151 | 9.8:1 | Electronic fuel injection | 6 speeds | Telescopic fork | Single-sided swingarm | 120/70x17 | 180/55x17 | 1495 | 246 |
| Griso 850 | 2006-09 | 2 Cyl OHV | 92 | 66 | 877 | 9.8:1 | Electronic fuel injection | 6 speeds | Upside down fork | Single-sided swingarm | 120/70x17 | 180/55x17 | 1554 | 227 |
| Breva 850 | 2006-09 | 2 Cyl OHV | 92 | 66 | 877 | 9.8:1 | Electronic fuel injection | 6 speeds | Telescopic fork | Single-sided swingarm | 120/70x17 | 180/55x17 | 1495 | 231 |
| 1200 Sport | 2007-08 | 2 Cyl OHV | 95 | 81.2 | 1151 | 9.8:1 | Electronic fuel injection | 6 speeds | Telescopic fork | Single-sided swingarm | 120/70x17 | 180/55x17 | 1485 | 229 |
| Bellagio | 2007-10 | 2 Cyl OHV | 95 | 66 | 936 | 10:01:00 | Electronic fuel injection | 6 speeds | Telescopic fork | Single-sided swingarm | 120/70x18 | 180/55x17 | 1570 | 224 |
| Norge 850 | 2007-09 | 2 Cyl OHV | 92 | 66 | 877 | 9.8:1 | Electronic fuel injection | 6 speeds | Telescopic fork | Single-sided swingarm | 120/70x17 | 180/55x17 | 1495 | 242 |
| Griso 8V (SE) | 2008- | 2 Cyl 4 OHV | 95 | 81.2 | 1151 | 11:01:00 | Electronic fuel injection | 6 speeds | Upside down fork | Single-sided swingarm | 120/70x17 | 180/55x17 | 1554 | 222 |

| Model | Years | Engine | Bore (mm) | Stroke (mm) | Displ (cc) | Comp ratio | Carburettor | Transmission | Front suspension | Rear suspension | Front tyre | Rear tyre | Wheel base | Weight (kg) |
|---|---|---|---|---|---|---|---|---|---|---|---|---|---|---|
| Breva 1200 | 2008-09 | 2 Cyl OHV | 95 | 81.2 | 1151 | 9.8:1 | Electronic fuel injection | 6 speeds | Telescopic fork | Single-sided swingarm | 120/70x17 | 180/55x17 | 1495 | 236 |
| Stelvio (TT, NTX) | 2008-10 | 2 Cyl 4 OHV | 95 | 81.2 | 1151 | 11:01:00 | Electronic fuel injection | 6 speeds | Upside down fork | Single-sided swingarm | 110/80x19 | 180/55x17 (150/70x17) | 1535 | 214 |
| V7 Classic (Café Classic Racer) | 2008-11 | 2 Cyl OHV | 80 | 74 | 744 | 9.6:1 | Electronic fuel injection | 5 speeds | Telescopic fork | Swingarm | 100/90x18 | 130/80x17 | 1449 | 182 |
| 1200 Sport 4V | 2009 | 2 Cyl 4 OHV | 95 | 81.2 | 1151 | 11:01:00 | Electronic fuel injection | 6 speeds | Telescopic fork | Single-sided swingarm | 120/70x17 | 180/55x17 | 1495 | 240 |
| Nevada 750 | 2009-12 | 2 Cyl OHV | 80 | 74 | 744 | 9.6:1 | Electronic fuel injection | 5 speeds | Telescopic fork | Swingarm | 100/90x18 | 130/90x16 | 1467 | 184 |
| Norge GT 8V | 2011-17 | 2 Cyl 4 OHV | 95 | 81.2 | 1151 | 11:01:00 | Electronic fuel injection | 6 speeds | Telescopic fork | Single-sided swingarm | 120/70x17 | 180/55x17 | 1495 | 257 |
| Stelvio (NTX) | 2011-17 | 2 Cyl 4 OHV | 95 | 81.2 | 1151 | 11:01:00 | Electronic fuel injection | 6 speeds | Upside down fork | Single-sided swingarm | 110/80x19 | 150/70x17 | 1535 | 251 (259) |
| V7 Stone, Special, Racer | 2012-14 | 2 Cyl OHV | 80 | 74 | 744 | 10.2:1 | Electronic fuel injection | 5 speeds | Telescopic fork | Swingarm | 100/90x18 | 130/80x17 | 1449 | 179 |
| California 1400 Custom (Touring) | 2013- | 2 Cyl 4 OHV | 104 | 81.2 | 1380 | 10.5:1 | Electronic fuel injection | 6 speeds | Telescopic fork | Swingarm | 130/70x18 | 200/60x16 | 1685 | 318 (322) |
| V7II Stone, Special, Racer, Stornello | 2015-18 | 2 Cyl OHV | 80 | 74 | 744 | 10.2:1 | Electronic fuel injection | 6 speeds | Telescopic fork | Swingarm | 100/90x18 | 130/80x17 | 1449 (1450 Stornello) | 179 (177 Special, 186 Stornello) |
| Eldorado | 2015- | 2 Cyl 4 OHV | 104 | 81.2 | 1380 | 10.5:1 | Electronic fuel injection | 6 speeds | Telescopic fork | Swingarm | 130/90x16 | 180/65x16 | 1695 | 314 |
| Audace | 2015- | 2 Cyl 4 OHV | 104 | 81.2 | 1380 | 10.5:1 | Electronic fuel injection | 6 speeds | Telescopic fork | Swingarm | 130/70x18 | 200/60x16 | 1695 | 299 |
| MGX-21 | 2016- | 2 Cyl 4 OHV | 104 | 81.2 | 1380 | 10.5:1 | Electronic fuel injection | 6 speeds | Telescopic fork | Swingarm | 120/70x21 | 180/60x16 | 1700 | 341 |
| V9 Roamer, Bobber | 2016- | 2 Cyl 2 OHV | 84 | 77 | 853 | 10.5:1 | Electronic fuel injection | 6 speeds | Telescopic fork | Swingarm | 100/90x19 (130/90x16) | 150/80x16 | 1465 | 199 |
| V7III Stone, Special, Racer, Anniversario, Carbon, Rough, Milano | 2017- | 2 Cyl OHV | 80 | 74 | 744 | 9.6:1 | Electronic fuel injection | 6 speeds | Telescopic fork | Swingarm | 100/90x18 (110/80x18) | 130/80x17 | 1463 (1445) | 189 (193 Special, Anniver-sario, Milano) |

# THE DUCATI STORY

Ian Falloon's authoritative history of the marque – expanded for this 6th edition – tells the inside story of Ducati's chequered path to glory, and describes every model, from the original 48cc Cucciolo to today's exotic Superbikes.

Hardback • 27x21cm • 368 pages • 349 pictures
ISBN: 978-1-787110-85-4

# THE DUCATI STORY

SIXTH EDITION

RACING AND PRODUCTION MOTORCYCLES FROM 1945

IAN FALLOON

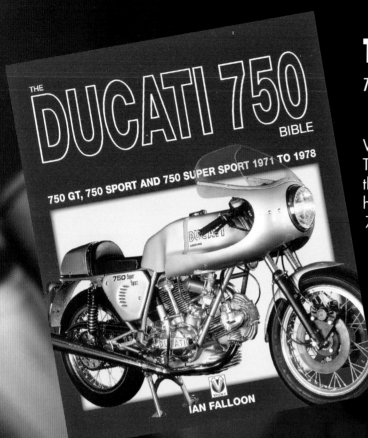

# The Ducati 750 Bible
## 750 GT, 750 Sport and 750 Super Sport 1971 to 1978

When the great Ducati engineer Fabio Taglioni designed the 750 Ducati in 1970 there was no way he could comprehend how important this model would be. The 750, the Formula 750 racer and the Super Sport became legends, and this book celebrates these machines in year-by-year, model-by-model, change-by-change detail. An absolute must-have for any Ducati aficionado.

Hardback • 25x20.7cm • 163 colour and b&w pictures • 160 pages • ISBN: 978-1-845840-12-9

# The Ducati Monster Bible
## New Updated & Revised Edition

When Ducati unleashed Galluzzi's Monster at the Cologne Show at the end of 1992, few expected it to become Ducati's most successful model. Dramatically styled, minimalist in stature, yet bristling with innovative engineering, the 900 Monster created a new niche market. Here is the ultimate guide to the Monster maze.

Paperback • 25x20.7cm • 197 colour and b&w pictures • 176 pages • ISBN: 978-1-845846-16-9

# The Moto Guzzi
# Sport & Le Mans Bible

A Veloce Classic Reprint.

Lino Tonti managed to take the large V7 Moto Guzzi touring engine and create a spectacular sporting motorcycle, the V7 Sport, in 1971. This remarkable machine evolved into the stylish 850 Le Mans. This book is a year-by-year account of development and specification changes of a great series of motorcycles.

Paperback • 25x20.7cm • 160 colour and b&w pictures
• 160 pages • ISBN: 978-1-787110-95-3

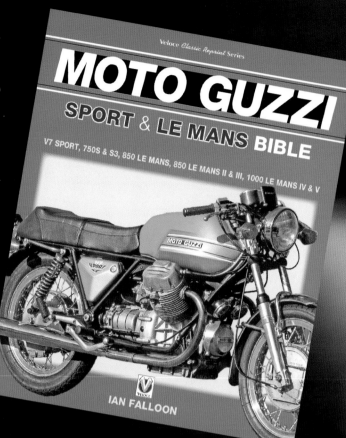

# Laverda Twins &
# Triples Bible

Reprinted after a long absence! A successful racing programme led to the release of the legendary 750SFC, the 1000cc triple, and then the spectacular Jota and new generation RGS during the 1980s. Containing year-by-year, model-by-model detail, this book is essential reading for both owners and enthusiasts.

Paperback • 25x20.7cm • 222 colour and b&w pictures
• 160 pages • ISBN: 978-1-787110-48-9

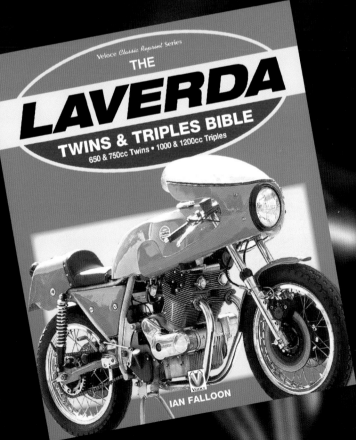

# INDEX